**IN PRINT
THEY CALLED HER
THE WORLD'S GREATEST BEAUTY.**

**IN PRIVATE
THEY HAD A LOT MORE TO SAY.**

In the golden age of movie-making, when legendary lovelies reigned, screen goddesses whose every desire was fulfilled, it took a lot to fill Hollywood with awe, and even more to shock it.

Her name was Ava Gardner.

———————————————

"A REVEALING BIOGRAPHY!"
—*Palm Springs Desert Sun*

# AVA
## ROLAND FLAMINI

### A Biography

BERKLEY BOOKS, NEW YORK

The author gratefully acknowledges permission from A. E. Hotchner to quote from *Papa Hemingway* by A. E. Hotchner, copyright © 1966 by A. E. Hotchner.

This Berkley book contains the complete
text of the original hardcover edition.

AVA

A Berkley Book / published by arrangement with
Coward, McCann & Geoghegan, Inc.

PRINTING HISTORY
Coward, McCann & Geoghegan edition / February 1983
Berkley edition / January 1984
Second printing / April 1984

ISBN: 0-425-07510-9

A BERKLEY BOOK ® TM 757,375
Berkley Books are published by The Berkley Publishing Group,
200 Madison Avenue, New York, New York 10016.
The name "BERKLEY" and the stylized "B" with design
are trademarks belonging to Berkley Publishing Corporation.
PRINTED IN THE UNITED STATES OF AMERICA

**For Diane with love**

# CONTENTS

# AVA

# 1

# The Train
# from the East

She arrived very early on the morning of August 23, 1941,
which was warm and cloudless. The San Bernardino Mountains, with their soft brown tones, rose slowly, tier upon tier,
in the distance, and an infinity of pink and fawn light soft-
ened every outline. Even the run-down buildings around the
Central Station in downtown Los Angeles looked tolerable.
Crumpled and train-weary, she stood unknown and unnoticed taking in the busy scene as doors were flung open
and the train from the East emptied its passengers onto the
platform.

There was a general ripple of recognition when Hedy
Lamarr stepped out, richly tanned after a vacation on the
French Riviera and flashing a large cabochon diamond
bracelet on her right wrist. Then David O. Selznick and his
wife, Irene, emerged. The mountainous maker of *Gone With*

*the Wind* chomped on an unlighted cigar. Assistants, maids and porters formed up behind the couple, and the procession moved importantly toward waiting limousines.

A platoon of reporters and photographers sought out, and eventually found, Eunice Squires, a twenty-one-year-old stenographer from Arkansas, who had given up her job in order to dedicate her life to her avocation, which was watching movies: 633 of them in the preceding twelve months, more than the combined annual output of all the Hollywood film studios. Between movies, she kept house for her mother and sister.

Historian Arthur Schlesinger, Jr., talks about the movies in the 1930s and '40s being "Near the operative center of the nation's consciousness. They played an indispensable role in sustaining and stimulating the nation's imagination." Eunice Squires had taken the process one step further. The movies *were* her consciousness. Her pretty, round face bore the occupational pallor that came from spending over a thousand waking hours in dark movie houses. She appeared to have no knowledge of herself outside her knowledge of herself as a moviegoer. She replied to reporters' questions with snatches of screen dialogue. Asked to name her favorite movie, she told them that she had seen *Rebecca* twenty-one times so far *(so far!)* and then proceeded to recite important scenes from it, doing different voices for Joan Fontaine and Laurence Olivier.

Yet when Warner Bros., apprised of her remarkable devotion, invited her to visit Hollywood, she was hesitant to accept at first. She had no desire to become a movie star herself, and she was afraid that personal contact with the movie world might destroy the fantasy. She was, in short, the apotheosis of the film fan.

But a desire to become a movie star was the motive that had brought to Los Angeles the screen-struck men and women who now drifted uncertainly toward the exit in search of cheap lodgings, watched idly by a yellow-eyed pimp on the lookout for possible new recruits. The pimp knew that few if any of them would make it past the guards at the studio gates. Meanwhile, a line had formed in front of the Travelers' Aid Society's booth in the station ticket hall—parents seeking the help of this voluntary organization in tracking down missing sons and daughters. There was an unmistakable small-town flavor about their appearance and their reactions to the bustle around them. This was 1941: the search for runaway teenagers began not in Haight-Ashbury but in Hollywood.

Ava Gardner, the new arrival, was in an enviable position. Her journey was buttressed by a contract from Metro-Goldwyn-Mayer Studios, the biggest and most glamorous of them all. She had even been given an official escort for the trip in the person of Milton Weiss. This young man from Metro's Publicity Department in New York spent much of his working life shuttling back and forth between the two coasts delivering young beauties who had been hired by the New York head office on behalf of the MGM Studios in Hollywood. Male newcomers were expected to get to Hollywood under their own steam, but females—the young actresses discovered in summer stock, the beauty-contest winners, the fashion models—got, among others, Milton Weiss.

He made sure they boarded the right train at Grand Central—the *Twentieth Century Limited*—and made the switch to the *Super Chief* in Chicago. Immediately on arrival in Los Angeles, he accompanied them to the studio in Culver City and then caught the next train home. It was an assignment full of tempting possibilities. On this occasion, however, Weiss had to contend with the inhibiting presence of Ava's eldest sister, Bappie, whose real name was Beatrice and who was nineteen years her senior. The three of them played endless rounds of pinochle, and Weiss delivered his standard lecture about movie stars being the American aristocracy.

Accustomed to displays of intense nervous expectation from the women he accompanied to Hollywood, Weiss was struck by the coolness of this stunning, green-eyed Southern country girl in the cheap cotton dress and white wedge sandals. The face, framed by a mass of auburn hair, was fine-boned, ending in a dimpled chin. The mouth was wide and full-lipped, and when she smiled she had a way of raising her right eyebrow which gave her a sardonic, worldly look, though she was neither.

Together, they traveled by taxi to MGM Studios, a vast, impregnable, sprawling, fortresslike compound enclosed by orange-colored walls amid the prosaic surroundings of Culver City, itself a town of small bars, tacky dime stores and washed-out apartment buildings. Metro had its own uniformed police, school, barbershop, funeral parlor, and—as its motto proclaimed—MORE STARS THAN THERE ARE IN HEAVEN. Near the main gate was the Thalberg Building, nerve center of the filmmaking enterprise because it contained the office of Louis B. Mayer, undisputed head of Metro and arguably the most powerful man in Hollywood. On the lot, the authority of this alarming autocrat was awesomely pervasive. In small matters as well as in major issues: for nearly twenty years, a horse was kept saddled every morning in the studio stables because L.B. (as he was known) had once made some vague reference to enjoying riding. But Mayer never once called for his horse. Nor did he drink the Chicken Soup à la L. B. Mayer which the studio commissary served daily and which was said to be based on his own mother's recipe. Mayer himself rarely ate in the studio commissary. He had a private dining room and a personal chef.

Clustered around the Thalberg Building was a jumble of semiclassical structures housing the offices and dressing rooms. And in the rear of the studio, not visible from busy Culver Boulevard, were the ten sound stages—huge, windowless, hangarlike buildings running north–south with heavy sliding doors. The largest, Stage 15, was the biggest sound stage in the world and was usually reserved for Metro's most important productions. In an era when Hollywood believed that any setting could be reproduced better in the studio than the original and considered location shooting a last resort, the sound stages were in constant use.

Stage 15, for example, had done duty as the elaborate, extensive garden of the Capulets in Irving Thalberg's ambitious production of *Romeo and Juliet*, starring his wife, Norma Shearer, as Juliet; the garden contained so much vegetation that moisture from it sometimes formed a cloud that hung over the set. Then Stage 15 swarmed with Munchkins for the filming of *The Wizard of Oz*. More recently, it became the beaches of Dunkirk for *Mrs. Miniver* as the war in Europe began to cast its shadow on Hollywood. Still farther south, beyond the sound stages, was the back lot, a sixty-acre spread of trees and brush sufficiently nondescript in botanical terms to be disguised as the African jungle and the English countryside. It was crisscrossed by dirt roads and culminated in a sizable knoll covered with thick brown undergrowth.

Ava Gardner was immediately whisked off to a small studio, made up, squeezed into a long black strapless evening dress supplied by the Wardrobe Department, and given a screen test. She had come to Metro on the strength of an earlier silent test which she had made in New York. Now she was required to speak. Aside from walking along a chalk line on the ground, sitting and standing, she answered off-camera questions about her family and her childhood in North Carolina. So thick was her Tarheel accent that she could have been speaking a foreign language. But she was lucky in one important respect: Lee Garmes, the brilliant cameraman who had brought eternal youth to several Metro goddesses— at any rate on the screen—happened to have been assigned to film the test, a rare occurrence for a man of his caliber, and he made the most of her dark beauty.

A few hours later, Garmes's black-and-white test was being shown in the executive screening room for L. B. Mayer himself. Mayer had the final word on prospective new additions to Metro's "talent" list. In the case of new males this authority was sometimes delegated to one of his lieutenants; in the case of women, never. It was Mayer who determined, on the basis of his famous intuition, how much time and effort Metro should invest in advancing the career of a starlet. This procedure also gave him automatic first refusal of every new arrival—a kind of *droit de seigneur* in reverse—before the studio executives, the producers, the stars, the pimps, the hangers-on or "gofers" began to swarm like bees around a hive.

Trying to determine who carried off the prize was often useful survival lore. Life at the studios—and especially at Metro—was often an unsavory stew, but no one dared lift the lid on it and rap those responsible over the knuckles with the ladle. Metro writers called the starlets "Moos" when they became the bosses' sacred cows. Often they would tip each other off: "Might be smart to write in a juicy part for So-and-so, she's L.B.'s latest Moo." Once, a male scenario writer deep in his cups swayed up to a luscious blonde wearing a diamond ring and asked, "Whose Moo is oo?" She snapped back, "Don't get fresh with me or I'll tell Sam Katz on you."

Mayer was not personally attracted to the new girl on the screen. His own taste ran to either Dresden Dolls or Refined Ladies: he preferred a more obvious kind of femininity. This beauty was made of sterner stuff. Though she moved awkwardly, and he could not understand her—he at first thought she was Hungarian—he was quick to note her lazy feline grace and her physical magnetism. No, Mayer was not stirred, but he knew a sexual screen presence when he saw one.

"She can't act, she can't talk, but she's terrific," he told George Sidney, later a noted producer and director, who then had the job of selecting new talent for the studio. "Give her to Gertrude [Vogeler, the studio voice coach] and Lillian [Burns, the dramatic coach] and let her have a year's training. Then test her again." On the screen, she had pronounced her name "Ahvuh Gahdnah," stretching each vowel like chewing gum. "What kind of a name is that?" Mayer exclaimed. "Well, we'll change it."

They didn't change it. When Mayer saw it written down he was persuaded it had possibilities. But little more besides the name was to remain of the girl whom fortune had catapulted from the tobacco fields to a unique kind of stardom in the movies. On her second day at Metro, Ava Gardner went to the Legal Department, where she signed an agreement accepting a form of voluntary bondage prevalent in Hollywood at the time—generally referred to as being under contract. In return for fifty dollars a week and the inferred commitment on the part of the studio to further her career, she surrendered herself exclusively to Metro for a period of seven years which was to run until August 1948. But additional weeks and months could be tacked on to compensate for suspensions incurred by breaking one of the contract rules buried in the minefield of small print.

Ava had to accept all roles assigned to her, and to agree to all promotional appearances requested by the studio, as well as any travel arising out of her work. She could not leave Los Angeles without permission, even when not filming. There was also a standard morals clause which read: "The artist agrees to conduct herself with due regard to public conventions and morals and agrees that she will not do or commit any act or thing that will degrade her in society, or bring her into public hatred, contempt, scorn, or ridicule, that will tend to shock, insult, or offend the community or ridicule public morals or decency, or prejudice the producer [i.e. Metro] or the motion picture industry in general." In addition, like all MGM contract holders, she was barred from making television appearances. Though television was still in its infancy, Metro was already on the defensive.

Having signed a contract, Ava was considered one of Metro's assets. A visit to the dentist followed to put caps on two front teeth. The studio also found her a one-room apartment in the run-down but respectable Wilcox Apartments off Sunset Boulevard, where many other starlets lived. The Publicity Department procured her an official identity. A release was written declaring her to have been a Powers model in New York (untrue), and her born name was given as "Lucy Ann Johnson" so that people would think Ava Gardner was a studio invention. The Business Department opened a checking account for her at the Culver City branch of the Security Pacific Bank. Anne Strauss, the fashion coordinator in the Publicity Department, prevailed upon I. Magnin, the Beverly Hills department store, to hire Ava's sister Bappie as a clerk.

Word spread on the lot that the new starlet was not an asset to be trifled with. Soon after her arrival, she had her first interview with Benny Thau, the executive with overall charge of Metro talent. Thau was a small man who spoke so softly that you had to lean close to his mouth to understand what he was saying. He was also one of the studio's most persistent girl chasers, with a button on his desk which automatically locked the door of his office. Unlike Mayer, he was stirred by Ava and, when she was on the point of terminating their interview, lunged forward to embrace her. She pushed him away sharply, but it was the string of colorful language she spat out that sent him reeling. It was not unusual to hear Metro girls swearing like drill sergeants, but from the start Ava Gardner used profanity with singular gusto.

The routine for a Metro starlet's first week would have done justice to boot camp. Together with Donna Reed and Kathryn Grayson, the studio's new singing find, Ava was expected to arrive at 6:30 A.M. and report to Makeup. Under the supervision of Jack Dawn, the beauty wizard, her eyebrows were shaped, her cheekbones accentuated and the dimple in her cleft chin toned down. A hair-wave set was used to turn up her lashes.

Then Sydney Guilaroff took over. The best-known hairdresser in the industry, he set her hair off her face to show off the good bone structure and the high sweep of her forehead, topping it with a wave. The whole coiffure was lacquered firmly into place. A small, gossipy man, Guilaroff instantly took to the new girl. Her salty language and precocious sardonic detachment amused him, and he soon became one of her few friends on the Metro lot.

The point of the beautification process was that starlets were on constant call as walk-ons and bit-part players in current productions. Indeed, these appearances were regarded as useful experience and good exposure. After Makeup, however, Ava was sent directly to Gertrude Vogeler's office to work on eradicating her North Carolina accent. If the system had been more flexible she might have been excused the elaborate cosmetic metamorphosis, but Metro was obsessive about glamor and vigilantly insisted on a high standard of personal appearance at all times. Consequently Ava continued to look terrific and sound terrible. She seemed to be constitutionally incapable of getting her tongue around the final *r*, as in the sentence "Ah cain't affohd a foah-doah Foahd." She dropped her *g*'s like magnolia blossoms. One morning, close to despair, Gertrude Vogeler discovered that Ava liked to sing and seemed to have a better grip on her diction when imitating her favorite vocalist, Judy Garland, than when she spoke. Thereafter, Ava concentrated on singing exercises.

She was taught to purr in the regulation Hollywood siren's voice: low, throaty and subdued. But the effort of losing her native accent had left her very insecure about her speaking voice, and that lack of confidence was to beset her throughout her career. Even before she began acting lessons, Ava was taking a grueling series of dance lessons—classical and modern—under the dynamic Kay Thompson, later the creator of *Eloise*. The dancing removed the awkwardness and gave her poise. She began to carry her full height, chin up, pencil straight.

Ava ate her meals in the studio commissary where the hierarchical structure of the Metro "family," as L. B. Mayer liked to call it, found its fullest expression. Producers sat at the big round table in the center of the room. There was a cage dice on it so that they could play each other for the bill. The other round tables were reserved for the top stars and their entourages—mostly male stars, for the women stars tended to eat in their dressing rooms. Clark Gable sat with his cronies, including actor Ward Bond, a close friend who worked on many Gable movies, director Victor Fleming, and Howard Strickling, head of the Publicity Department. Spencer Tracy ate with Katharine Hepburn, George Stevens and other members of their circle. The writers, unappreciated and overworked (in their own view), self-conscious and superior (in everybody else's), huddled together for comfort. Technicians sat at the rectangular tables closer to the door. Starlets and lesser folk found places where they could along the walls. The sense of exclusion was strong and deliberate: you had to earn your acceptance in the commissary.

A strict diet of cottage cheese and fruit was prescribed for contract girls, but this was one Metro rule Ava broke from the outset. She thrived on a full diet, beginning with an early morning Southern breakfast of her favorites, cooked by Bappie—fried chicken, hominy grits, hot biscuits. At lunch she was again ravenously hungry and would put away chicken soup, a meat course, a salad, two glasses of milk, and a large slice of apple pie. At the afternoon tea break she dug into a huge banana split. She also snacked with alarming frequency. One of her favorites was to drink the juice of cooked vegetables, or to dunk hunks of cornbread in it, Southern style. Her remarkable appetite did not escape the studio's notice, but since, by some blessed quirk in her metabolism, her measurements—taken weekly by Wardrobe—never varied, she got away with it.

Meanwhile, the only cameras she faced in those early days were the ones in the "Shooting Gallery," the dingy studio where she posed, in various stages of undress, for top-class still photographers such as Clarence Bull and Edward Hurrell. "Cheesecake" stills (more discreetly known as "leg art") were a Hollywood institution, and soon Metro was sending out half a dozen Ava Gardner pictures to the rotogravure press every week.

The theory behind the stills was simple: If a girl was destined for stardom the pictures would not hurt. If she was not, they would serve to publicize the studio. Each print was sent out with an identifying caption which carried a puff for one of the pictures under release. Ava's first still was captioned: "Ava Gardner, Metro starlet, poses on the prow of the steamship *Mexico*. MGM's *Mrs. Miniver* is currently showing at the —— Theatre." The newspaper had only to insert the name of the local theater.

Ava took these long photo sessions in her stride. She could not strike a wrong pose, especially when "cheesecake" was required. Clarence Bull would say, "C'mon, Ava, let's steam up the lens," and she'd slip naturally into a series of sexy poses—lips slightly parted, body arched against a prop fence or steamer rail, breasts straining under the fabric of her bathing suit. Despite her model's figure and erect posture, her fashion pictures were less successful. Loretta Young was held up to other starlets as the girl to emulate in fashion layouts. Loretta had made it her business to learn about fashion and modeling, and, as a result, her fashion stills were first-rate. Ava wore clothes well, but was not especially fashion conscious, and the number of costume changes that went into a photo session bored and tired her.

Working in the Shooting Gallery brought out the earliest signs of Ava's independent nature. After hours of posing she would complain to Anne Strauss, "Do I have to do this?"

"You know you do, Ava," Anne Strauss would reply.

"But what does it have to do with movies?"

"Well, it's good publicity."

Publicity was the fuel that propelled the Hollywood band-wagon. Publicity created the theatrical setting in which the star system was able to flourish, and it flourished best at MGM. The efficiency and thoroughness of Metro's Publicity Department were legendary. It had a staff of over sixty people and its own three-floor building on the studio lot, and it was run by Howard Strickling. Strickling was tough, quick-tempered, and stuttered nervously. But he was also skillful, loyal and could be compassionate. His devotion to L. B. Mayer was total. He boasted that he rose at 5:30 A.M. because Mayer was usually on his feet by 6 A.M. and might need him.

Under Strickling, Metro's publicity concentrated on the stars—and especially the women stars—rather than on the movies. As for directors, producers and writers, they were left to fend for themselves. The strategy was to build up a public following that would flock to the movie theaters to see its favorite star almost regardless of the movie. Metro distributors used to talk of releasing "one Garbo," "two Gables" and "three Crawfords."

It was a seller's market. The demand for "news" from Hollywood was at an all-time peak; the newspapers, with their large rotogravure Sunday sections, were hungry for material, and their readers lapped it up. The wire services considered the Hollywood dateline second only to Washington as a source of personality news. With a wordage of twenty thousand rattling over the wires every day, the Hollywood dateline was third in volume of copy after the nation's capital and the European war front.

Strickling's publicity staff perpetuated the notion that Metro girls were virginal. Scandal was kept out of the press by an effective combination of protection, persuasion and coercion. In 1941, Hollywood spent nearly $80 million in press and radio advertising. This gave the studios considerable leverage with the media, and they did not hesitate to use it to kill an unfavorable story about a star.

The stars' contact with the press and the public was carefully controlled. A member of Strickling's staff was present whenever a star was interviewed or made a personal appearance. Young stars like Ava were in constant demand at college hops and harvest balls, and a publicity staffer always went along as chaperone. The older ones were invited to conventions and big baseball games, and the ever-vigilant Strickling man (or woman) was never far away. The publicist was supposed to see that the star did not discuss politics, religion or sex either in interviews or in conversation. Children were considered unglamorous, were rarely mentioned and were even more rarely seen. Liquor glasses and cigarettes were carefully removed from sight before pictures were taken.

From the start, Ava found the ministrations of Strickling's

staff intrusive and oppressive, even though Anne Strauss became another of her few friends on the lot. The Publicity Department, for its part, found her rebellious and a trouble-maker. This early animosity would come home to roost in later years when the problems surrounding her personal life could have benefited from expert handling.

After a long, dizzying day at the studio, she would return, exhausted and bemused, to her one-room apartment with its pull-down bed, its stove with two burners—and Bappie's ministrations. Sometimes she would write long letters to her mother and her sisters in North Carolina. One theme persisted: being a budding movie star was a hard, lonely life.

# 2

# Hometown

You would have to look hard to find a map that would include Boon Hill, North Carolina. This community of scat-
tered farms sprawls six miles along a brutally dusty and
bumpy road from the town of Smithfield. Raleigh, the state
capital, was an hour's drive north, on Route 70. It was in
Boon Hill that Mary Elizabeth Gardner gave birth on Christmas Eve 1922 to her seventh child, a daughter, by cesarean
section because she was ten days overdue and getting larger
by the minute.

Having seven children was not considered unusual in
Mary Elizabeth's family. Her father, Henry Baker, who was
redheaded and hot-tempered, had had nineteen. Her
mother, Ava, had died giving birth to the last one, Lavinia.
Hence Mary Elizabeth's name for her newborn daughter,
Ava Lavinia.

Mary Elizabeth, known as Mollie, was forty when Ava Lavinia was born. She was a solidly built woman, handsome if

not actually pretty, brown-haired and five foot two. Her nature was rather joyless, burdened by money worries and by her austere Scottish Baptist background. Her husband of twenty years, Jonas Bailey Gardner, was her physical opposite but her temperamental double. He was a tall, angular, green-eyed Irishman who rarely smiled. He lived in unrelieved tension between passionate appetites and puritan inhibitions, personal diffidence and compensating physical bravado—conflicts which were to emerge in his youngest daughter. Despite his own healthy sexual appetite, he was strict to the point of oppression with his teenage daughters.

His grandfather had emigrated to the United States to escape the Irish famine and put down roots in Boon Hill. A blacksmith by trade, in time he married a local belle. Six of their children survived the difficult years of the post-Civil War Reconstruction in the defeated South. One of them was Jonas' father, who became a tenant farmer and began to grow the delicate plant that was then beginning to cover every square inch of the rolling green hills of eastern North Carolina—tobacco. In 1902 Jonas married Mollie Baker, whose family, also tobacco growers, had recently moved down from Virginia in search of work because North Carolina had begun to gain ascendancy as the tobacco-growing state.

Although Jonas was a Roman Catholic, the Baker family would not permit Mollie to sign the agreement to raise the children in the Catholic faith as required by the Church in mixed marriages. The Gardner children grew up attending Baptist services, while Jonas lapsed into indifference. The same year that Jonas married Mollie his father died, and Jonas took over his three-hundred-acre holding. The couple moved into the white clapboard four-bedroom house that went with it. It was to this house that the Gardners brought

Ava when Mollie was discharged from the hospital on January 2, 1923.

Bappie was then nineteen, sturdy, cheerful and just married—a second mother to the younger children. Elsie May was only eleven months younger than Bappie, but prettier, and sixteen-year-old Inez was the quiet one. Then came Melvin, fourteen, who was always called Jack. Another son, Raymond, was killed at sixteen months when a rifle shell, carelessly left by the fire, exploded. Had he lived, he would have been fifteen at the time of Ava's birth. Finally there was Myra, aged seven and her father's favorite.

Life on the Gardner tobacco farm was harsh American Gothic. True, tobacco was booming. But in the year of Ava's birth there were over 250,000 tenant farmers in North Carolina, all producing the bright-leaf tobacco needed by the huge new factories for mass-producing cigarettes. Overproduction had made it a buyer's market, depressing prices. With eight mouths to feed, the going was tough for Jonas Gardner, particularly since, with grown-up daughters instead of sons, he was forced to hire help—white itinerant workers. Negro labor was cheaper, but Jonas was an unrepentant racist and refused to employ blacks.

"My girlhood was full of insecurities," Ava once recalled. "What a generation! No wonder we're all neurotic and crazy. Her earliest memories have to do with tobacco. A rich and heavy aroma often hung over Boon Hill, so heady that it seemed visible in a golden light washed across the buildings: the exotic smell of tobacco, aging, blending, rolling forth in rows of cigarettes at the nearby factories. The dominant colors in her world were yellow and red—the yellow of the bright-leaf tobacco her father grew, and the deep red of the soil. But when the young Ava played barefoot in the tobacco fields a black, gummy, tarlike substance oozed from the earth between her toes. Her first trips out of Boon Hill were in her father's battered pickup truck to Wilson, where he sold his crop at rapid-fire auctions to manufacturers such as the Reynolds Tobacco Company, which had recently launched Camel brand cigarettes. When she was five, she smoked her first tobacco—it would be inaccurate to describe the rolled tobacco leaf wrapped in newspaper as a cigarette. She was, of course, thoroughly sick. But the experience did not deter her, and she was a cigarette smoker by the time she was eight. She earned her first pennies picking suckers, worms and other parasites off the tobacco leaves—and getting in the way of the men hauling the leaves away to be hung and cured in the barns.

By her own admission, Ava was a tomboy, climbing trees and fences, fighting the boys in the neighborhood and beating them at marbles. Boon Hill's water tower, which stood close to the Gardner farm, was an irresistible attraction. One hot July afternoon, Ava, aged six, climbed to the top because, like Everest, it was there. Climbing down from that great height was another matter, however. Her young nerve failed her, and she had to be rescued by her father. Another high-spirited adventure left its mark: in the course of a game of hide-and-seek she tried to crawl through a broken window into a locked shed; the glass tore a gaping hole in her upper right thigh, just below the buttock, and she carried the scar for the rest of her life.

Fortunately for Ava, her early childhood was not affected by the domestic tensions arising out of her parents' exigent propriety in dealing with her elder sisters. The Gardners' strictness—and especially Mollie's—verged on the Victorian. A daughter had only to return home from work or school half an hour later than usual without an explanation which satisfied her parents to be denied supper for two days.

When Ava was a year old, Elsie May married Charles

Creech, owner of a country store in Smithfield, and went to live in the house where Charles Creech's uncle had killed his wife and her lover. The Creech murders were a famous *crime passionnel* in eastern North Carolina. Two years later, Inez also extricated herself from her mother's grip, by marrying a local tobacco farmer named Grimes. Jack, now seventeen, went to live with his uncle in Winston-Salem to attend high school. This left Myra and Ava at home with Jonas and Mollie.

In 1929, the Depression descended on Smithfield. Tobacco prices plunged to nothing, and Jonas Gardner's already modest livelihood was snuffed out. Mollie Gardner took a job as housekeeper and cook at the local teacherage, the residence for teachers in the Smithfield school system. This included the consolidated grammar school in the neighboring community of Brogden, which Ava, then aged seven, attended with noticeable lack of enthusiasm and distinction. As their financial crisis worsened, the Gardners were forced to give up their holding and to quit the white house that had been their home for nearly thirty years.

Their plight produced a split in the marriage. Jonas found work as a supervisor in a sawmill near Smithfield and favored remaining in the area. Mollie, who had lost her job at the teacherage, was advised by members of her family to move to Newport News, Virginia, where the shipyards were less hard hit. Though the Gardners loved each other, they now drifted separate ways. Mollie took little Ava, whose suitcase consisted mostly of Myra's hand-me-downs and who clutched as a going-away present (and for years later a treasured possession) a blond doll given to her by her father, but Myra joined her brother in Winston-Salem.

With the help of her relatives, Mollie rented what Ava has called "a big, miserable old house on West End Street," near the Newport News shipyards, and began to take in boarders.

It was back-breaking work. The brick structure had a total capacity of twenty boarders and rarely had a vacancy for very long. With only Ava to help, Mollie had to clean the rooms daily and provide two meals a day: a good breakfast on which her boarders, mostly men, could face a heavy day in the shipyards, and an evening meal. A year later—December 1930—she had the added burden of a sick husband. Jonas fell ill with a streptococcus infection of the chest and was bedridden in his wife's boardinghouse. From all accounts, he was far from being a model patient. An electric buzzer had been rigged up from his bedside in his room at the top of the house to the kitchen on the ground floor. It was in constant use, but Mollie's stoic resignation never faltered. Jonas' illness also meant more work for Ava, mostly in the kitchen, and by the time she was nine years old she could cook and serve a meal for twenty hungry boarders with the proficiency of a girl twice her age.

In other respects, the move was full of small humiliations. Even in a small town like Newport News, Ava's country awkwardness stuck out. Her speech was rough and lumpy as the hard sod of Boon Hill, her clothes ill-fitting. Her tendency to kick off her unaccustomed shoes and run barefoot brought derision from her urban classmates. She was also afraid that her peers were going to discover that she knew next to nothing about the movies. Attending Sunday matinees at the Bijou or the Roxy was a way of life in Newport News, where the kids were movie crazy. Mondays were reserved for writing fan letters and requesting autographed portraits from the stars of Sunday's picture. Swapping them as duplicates came in, or as favorites changed, was a major occupation—a Gable for a Crawford, a Harlow for a Garland.

In Boon Hill, visits to the movies had been rare concessions because Mollie Gardner did not entirely approve of them. Thus Ava was totally unprepared to cope with the full

force of the Hollywood cult. Her ignorance compounded
her insecurity, but she began to slip away to the movies without her mother's knowledge. She never forgot secretly
seeing, in Newport News in 1932, Clark Gable and Jean
Harlow in *Red Dust*—the movie that twenty years later she
would help remake with Gable himself. She also became an
avid reader of the fan magazines, borrowed from one of her
mother's lodgers. But one September afternoon when she
was ten the lodger attacked her on the second floor landing.
Her mother, ever vigilant, heard her protests and arrived on
the scene as he was trying to pull Ava into his room. By
nightfall, he was looking for another boardinghouse.

At the age of ten, Ava had a cheerful disposition and an
open face brightened by a broad grin and smiling green eyes.
She was the only member of her family to have inherited her
father's green eyes. At thirteen, however, her expression was
solemn and guarded, with her full mouth pulled into a thin,
unsmiling line. The tomboy had grown into a withdrawn
young girl. The previous year, Jonas Gardner had died of his
long illness. Mollie and Ava had moved to Rock Ridge, a
rural community some fifty miles west of Boon Hill, where
Mollie returned to her old occupation of running a teacherage. Ava went to Rock Ridge Consolidated High School.

"Ava and me—we're getting poorer and poorer," Mollie
complained to her other children. In fact, mother and
daughter survived partly with their collective help. Elsie
May, Inez and Jack all contributed to their youngest sister's
upkeep.

Not a dreamer by nature, Ava could not have arrived un-
aided at the possibility of an alternative to marrying a local
boy, settling in or near Rock Ridge, and raising a family.
Then Bappie met and married Larry Tarr, a New York photographer, and followed her second husband to Manhattan.
Tarr had come to Smithfield on a picture assignment for one

of the tobacco corporations. His marriage to Bappie represented another set of footsteps that could be followed besides those of Inez and Elsie May. Bappie was at this time in her late twenties, with all the strength, sureness and authority that Ava lacked. She had remained childless, and during her visits she lavished attention on her young sister. Bappie became, and remains, Ava's staunchest friend and most loyal supporter, the one consistent touch of stability in Ava's stormy career.

When Ava was fifteen, Bappie brought up the notion of a visit to New York. It met with her mother's instant refusal. Since Jonas' death, Mollie had become sullen, and more possessive than ever. Hardened by toil and tragedy, she alternated between fits of disapproval at what she regarded as Ava's immoral life and tender outpourings of motherly love. In fact Ava was not especially active in romance, partly because it was widely known that Ava's boy friends ran the risk of being the target of Mollie's overprotectiveness. Even so, enough young men still thought the game was worth the candle because Ava was a beautiful, leggy brunette with a fully developed woman's figure.

Her first real beau was Dick Allerton, Rock Ridge's football hero. He was a senior when Ava was a sophomore. When he took her on their first Sunday afternoon date, she couldn't open her mouth. As they watched the Bing Crosby picture, her heart was pounding so hard that she was afraid he would hear it. One evening, however, Allerton brought Ava home and, seeing no one in sight, embraced her with youthful passion on the porch. In an instant, the door was flung open and Mollie flew out, ordered the boy away, and poured such a stream of invective at Ava that the girl burst into tears. Another of Ava's beaux, who had the distinction of owning his own jalopy, accompanied her to the movies and to school hops. Occasionally, they sneaked off to Holt's Lake, the local trysting place about four miles outside Rock Ridge. But this proved their undoing: Ava's mother marched to Holt's Lake, literally dragged her daughter out of the boy's car, gave him a piece of her mind, and took her home.

Those who knew the family say that the tension was constant and depressing. Ava loved her mother but was smothered by her overprotectiveness. When she was seventeen, she decided to try to gain a measure of independence by becoming a secretary. Helped by her brother Jack, who owned a diner in Smithfield, she enrolled in the coeducational Atlantic Christian College in Wilson, studying business education and secretarial science. She took typing, Gregg shorthand, composition of business letters, office secretarial practice and the rudiments of accounting.

She was considered shy and withdrawn by other pupils, but this did not prevent her from getting most votes as the most attractive girl in college. However, she was disqualified because she did not live in the girls' dormitory, her mother having refused to permit it, and the award went to the runner-up.

In the summer of 1940, her mother finally agreed to let her visit Bappie and Larry Tarr in New York. This was to be a rare—perhaps unique—feast for Ava and she made the most of it. She saw the newly released *Gone With the Wind*. She also read Margaret Mitchell's colossal novel—by her own admission the first book she had ever read outside of school requirements, for only one book had ever crossed the Gardners' threshold in Boon Hill and that was the Bible. Ava also went to the Stork Club, where she ordered milk, spotted Henry Fonda at an adjoining table and got his autograph on a menu.

Ava was, of course, staying with the Tarrs, in their small apartment over Larry's equally tiny photographic studio at Forty-ninth Street and Fifth Avenue. Larry Tarr, who had not seen her for several years, was struck by her looks and took a number of photographs. So pleased was he with the results that he put one picture on display in the window of his studio. It was a brooding portrait, with her hair pulled up, which gave her face a haunting quality, and it caught the eye of a young runner for Metro's Legal Department, Barney Duhan.

Now, Duhan had a system for getting dates with photographic models whose pictures he saw in studio windows (it worked with magazines too), and he put it into operation. He telephoned the Tarrs. When Bappie answered, he introduced himself as "Duhan from MGM" and asked if the beautiful model in the portrait would contact him in the office as soon as possible.

Here was the secret of Duhan's system. He never sought names and addresses. He merely asked for his call to be returned. Seven times out of ten, the girl in question called back. Duhan invited her out, lacing his invitation with hints that a date with him was a passport to stardom. Four times out of ten, the girl accepted. On this occasion, however, Duhan was unlucky. Bappie replied that the "model" had returned to North Carolina the previous day—"but if you like I can send for her."

No, no, Duhan replied hastily. The inquiry was "just routine." Then he added airily, "Well, send me some pictures of her anyway and I'll show them to Marvin Schenck, who's in charge of talent."

It was a very excited Larry Tarr who delivered a dozen portraits of Ava Gardner to Metro's New York offices on Fifty-second Street that same afternoon. The diminutive, ebullient Brooklynite was all set to bask in the limelight of having discovered a new Metro star. The back of each photograph bore the rubber stamp of Tarr's little studio, together with Ava's name, and Bappie's as Ava's New York contact.

The Tarrs went down to North Carolina for Christmas. At Ava's eighteenth birthday party Larry announced, "MGM is interested in you." When she heard the full story, Ava's first reaction was annoyance that he had displayed her picture without her knowledge. Beyond that, the news of Metro's interest was simply too exotic to have much of an impact on her.

Nothing was heard from MGM after that. Ava finished her year at Atlantic Christian College. Bappie asked her to New York for another visit. Mollie was too ill to argue, and Ava left her reluctantly. Upon Ava's arrival, Tarr telephoned Metro to announce that she was back in town. He was referred to a Metro talent scout, Ben Jacobson, who, of course, knew nothing about Tarr's sister-in-law. But as a professional of ripe experience, Jacobson never turned down a chance to see a new face. He asked Tarr to send another picture of Ava. Tarr took some fresh portraits and once again personally delivered the best ones to MGM. Her impact on Jacobson was strong enough for him to want to put her in front of a camera for a test.

Bappie bought Ava an off-the-shoulder dress at Saks Fifth Avenue, and a bewildered Ava appeared at Metro for an interview and a screen test.

"Why do you want to be an actress?" Jacobson asked her.

"Ah doan't," Ava replied.

"Well, have you had any acting experience?"

Too late, Ava remembered the replies she had rehearsed with Bappie and Larry and mumbled something about school plays.

Jacobson looked doubtfully at the girl sitting in front of him. He handed her a script. "Try this scene," he said. It was a speech in which the heroine confessed her love. When she finished, Jacobson held his head in his hands. "Even if you can act, I couldn't tell it with that accent," he groaned. "We'll have to make it a silent test. If I send a sound track out to the Coast with nothing on it but vocal spoonbread they'll have my head examined."

When they led Ava in front of the camera, she stood stiffly beside a small round table, her arms hanging limply by her sides—not frightened exactly, but awkward and uncomprehending. The test director called, "Action," and began to put her through her paces. "Look up, Ava," he instructed. "Look down. Now smile." He told her to sit down and cross her legs, but the action seemed gawky. Then he handed her some flowers to place in a vase. She dumped them in like potatoes into a saucepan: *whump.* When he told her to face the camera and express emotion, she merely managed to look puzzled. The director and Jacobson looked at each other and shook their heads. She was hopeless. They brought in Marvin Schenck, head of talent and scion of the family that controlled Loew's, Inc., and, through it, Metro-Goldwyn-Mayer. Schenck shrugged. Best to run the test and see what happens, was his suggestion.

Even to the most casual eye, the screen disclosed Ava Gardner as a stunning beauty. Awkward she may have been, but her looks were startling. She had high, firm breasts and prominent nipples and a tiny, tiny waist. She had those green eyes, and her beautiful chestnut hair had a reddish glow. Her skin was intensely pale, like alabaster, and she had a slow, lazy, sexy smile.

They shipped the test to Culver City, where George Sidney and his staff watched it not once but several times. She *was* terrible, yet every time they viewed it she projected an extraordinary combination of freshness and sexuality that simply belonged on the screen. "Tell New York to ship her out," George Sidney said at length. "She's a good piece of merchandise."

It was Bappie who broke the news to Ava that Metro was

interested in putting her under contract. It was also Bappie who met Milton Weiss to make arrangements for her sister's trip to Los Angeles, and who helped her buy her wardrobe (and, in fact, paid for most of it). Even before their mother insisted on it, it was assumed by both Ava and Bappie that the sisters would travel to the Coast together and that Bappie would remain at least long enough to see Ava settled.

One of the ironies of Ava Gardner's "discovery" was that Barney Duhan "from MGM" never did meet her. After the war he was to become a New York cop and to see his name mentioned in stories about Ava Gardner's rise to stardom. But the star would never get to know the man who had unwittingly set her on that path.

# 3

# Marrying an Asset

Lillian Burns had been the acting coach at MGM for nearly ten years. If Ava Gardner was not her greatest professional challenge, she came close. It was not merely that Ava was as green as fresh lettuce, and her accent so broad that it was almost a parody of itself; the woman who had made a plausible screen star out of Lana Turner was clearly accustomed to such challenges. In Ava's case, there was the added problem that she seemed to lack the eagerness which generally propelled Lillian Burns's students. It did not take her very long to identify the root cause of Ava's cool detachment as a defense mechanism. An organic caution had taught this beautiful young Southern girl to cocoon her true feelings against disappointing setbacks. All the same, it made her a doubly difficult subject for acting training.

A small, formidable Englishwoman who had studied under Dame Lilian Baylis, the great London actress, Lillian Burns had developed her own special technique for bringing out the best in Metro's promising newcomers. She would zero in on the essential personality of her subject and help her develop it into a screen persona. Of course, the approach tended to produce performers of limited range, but it had the merit of infusing confidence and developing their personalities, the essence of stardom.

Lillian Burns was smart enough to recognize Ava's *la belle dame sans merci* quality, hardly the girl next door so much in vogue in the forties. This ambiguity was part of her excitement, but it had its drawbacks. The screen personality fashioned for Ava by Lillian Burns required more individual attention than Metro was prepared to lavish on a fifty-dollar-a-week newcomer. It needed special roles to develop it, perhaps special publicity to promote it. Instead, Metro adopted the standard technique of giving Ava screen "exposure" and waiting for her to click, that is, to so arouse the interest of the public that they would begin to write letters to the studio. Every day, Metro received thousands of letters from movie fans all over the country, and the Letters Department acted as a vital popularity gauge in the case of both newcomers and established stars.

The weekly Letters Report distributed to senior executives, which was highly confidential, was carefully studied. Requests for information about the stars, requests for photographs—they were music to the ears of studio executives. They meant that the public was panting for more. "Please could you tell me something about the hatcheck girl who handed William Powell his hat in *The Thin Man*." When inquiries of that nature began to arrive in double figures, it was a promising sign. Hundreds of letters signaled a click of seismic proportions. The original contract would be torn up and a new one offered at three times the money. The sensation would be rushed into a series of roles, each one bigger than the last, usually playing opposite an established star in order to guarantee a big audience and also to invest the rising star with the prestige of the older one. As the process of deification shifted into high gear, the trickle of words about him or her emanating from Howard Strickling's Publicity Department would become a flood.

Ava's first screen appearance can hardly be said to have sent the public flocking to the mailboxes. It came after nearly three months of cheesecake sessions, and it amounted to a one-day walk-on in *We Were Dancing*. Noël Coward's *Tonight at 8:30* had been retooled by Metro to serve as a vehicle for Norma Shearer's return to the screen after her year-long legal battle with L. B. Mayer over the inheritance of her late husband Irving Thalberg's share in the company's profits.

With Thalberg gone, Norma Shearer had lost her position as Queen of the Lot, but she was more than ever the studio's wealthiest star. Mayer's brilliant associate had left her $4,469,013 (half of which went in taxes), and she had increased this handsome inheritance by successfully laying claim to Thalberg's thirty-seven-and-a-half-percent share of Loew's, Inc., profits for another four years following her husband's death, and an annual four percent of production revenues after that. Moreover, Metro paid her $150,000 per picture.

*We Were Dancing* was an attempt at sophisticated comedy about survival at the top. Norma played Princess Vicki Wilomirska, a Middle European aristocrat, exiled, penniless and on the lookout for a rich American husband, and Melvyn Douglas an impoverished smoothie on the prowl for a rich wife. The two marry, each believing the other to be wealthy. But they soon discover their mistake and live by their wits off their witless friends.

It is doubtful that Ava knew much about her first picture. Clad in pants and a silk blouse, she was required to saunter across a hotel lobby, watched admiringly by Melvyn Douglas.

The scene was filmed several times from different points of view, and Ava took the shooting in her stride; Bappie had taken the day off from I. Magnin to lend moral support. Afterward, Ava remained on the set to catch a glimpse of the legendary Norma herself.

An assistant director who had been posted as lookout at the door of Stage Five heralded the star's arrival. Then Norma herself appeared, followed by her personal hair-dresser, makeup man, maid, dresser, and publicity man—the famous Russell Birdwell, an independent agent whose many exploits were overshadowed by his famous nationwide search for an actress to play Scarlett O'Hara in *Gone With the Wind* when he worked for David Selznick. An entourage was a reflection of the star's prestige. Its members were on the studio payroll and not paid for out of the star's own pocket. Some stars were competitive about the size of their miniature courts. Joan Crawford, who always tried to outdo Norma, used to have a gramophone on the set to play appropriate mood music before she filmed a scene, and Metro paid a young man solely to change the records.

Watching Norma Shearer's crocodile making its way across the set, Ava whispered to Bappie, "One day I'm going to have a crowd of people like that to do everything for me." For the moment, however, there was only Bappie, but Ava could have done a lot worse.

The truth was that Bappie was living a vicarious existence through her younger sister. In those early months at Metro, Bappie provided the determination to overcome Ava's grow-ing discouragement. It was Bappie who got her up in time in the mornings, checked Ava's appearance and drove her to the studio. Left to her own devices, Ava would happily have gone to work clad in a loose man's shirt, jeans and saddle shoes, or in a bobby soxer's voluminous skirt and white socks.

It was Bappie who found and rented a larger apartment,

closer to the studio, on Franklin Avenue. Like their earlier one, it consisted of just one room, but the two studio couches could be disguised with cushions during the day, and it also had a small kitchen.

The news that their mother was slowly dying of cancer drew them closer together. Bappie was now indispensable to Ava, and she was even more determined that Ava would never have to face poverty again. Now Bappie's principal purpose in life was protecting and furthering Ava's interests. She learned more about what was required of a Metro starlet than Ava knew herself, and constantly drummed it into her younger, less motivated sister. Ava had the right qualities, but the fire sometimes seemed to burn more strongly in Bappie. She wanted to see Ava a star.

Bappie bought a map of the movie stars' homes and drove Ava around to see them, hoping to stoke her ambition. On some evenings, the two sisters would sit on the bleachers outside Grauman's Chinese Theatre taking in the glitter of a movie premiere and perhaps dream that Ava would one day be arriving in a Cadillac or Rolls-Royce, resplendent in a shimmering gown especially created for her by Irene—a screen queen on the arm of Robert Young, or Robert Taylor, or even, perhaps, Clark Gable.

At first, Ava shrugged off Bappie's talk of fame as wishful thinking. Only one argument seemed to strike home: "But don't you see, Ava, this is the best chance you'll ever get not to have to live in Boon Hill again?" Slowly, Bappie's words began to take hold. Ava showed more determination. She complained less about the cheesecake sessions. Her accent all but faded away, and she strove hard to please Lillian Burns.

Not that the walk-ons and bit parts which Metro continued to give her held much promise of stardom. After *We Were Dancing* (which, incidentally, was a critical and box-office disaster), she was assigned another two days' work in *Joe Smith,*

*American.* Robert Young played a young factory worker kidnapped and tortured by German agents who were after the blueprint of a new bombsight he was installing on U.S. Army aircraft. Marsha Hunt was his distressed wife, and Ava hovered prettily—and anonymously—in the background as a German spy groupie. This gripping picture, deservedly well received, was to serve as a prototype for the propaganda films produced by Hollywood in the early days of World War II.

Though the United States was technically neutral, the catalyst of Pearl Harbor was just around the corner. But the studios had not waited for a declaration of war before identifying the Germans as the bad guys in the conflict. One central reason for this was Nazi persecution of the Jews: Hollywood was full of refugees from Europe, not only filmmakers such as Fritz Lang, but many distinguished figures from the arts, among them Bertolt Brecht and Igor Stravinsky. Another reason for Hollywood's anti-Nazi feeling was that both the German and the Italian regimes had hurt the foreign market for its films by steadily cutting back on their imports in an attempt to extinguish American cultural influences. When the conflict came, Hollywood was already committed (with such movies as *Mrs. Miniver*) to shaping national attitudes.

Like thousands of others in Los Angeles, Ava heard the news of Pearl Harbor over the radio as she was having her Sunday breakfast. The following day at Metro was chaotic, and Ava decided to take advantage of the confusion to play hooky from Lillian Burns and visit a girl friend who was one of the chorines on the set of *Babes on Broadway,* a second-rate vehicle for Mickey Rooney and Judy Garland.

This musical had brigades of vigorous young men and women doing strenuous dance numbers; it also had the now obligatory war angle, provided by a group of English refugee children conversing with their parents by short wave. Judy Garland played a would-be singer: she sang "Waiting for the Robert E. Lee" and "Franklin D. Roosevelt Jones," and a new tune called "Hoe Down." Mickey Rooney was one of a trio of hopefuls billed as Three Balls of Fire. The plot—if you could call it that—centered around a show he was producing for the benefit of the English refugees, who needed a month in the country. Ava's visit coincided with the filming of the benefit, and the chaos between takes was unbelievable. Shrill cockney children were everywhere, playing and fighting, mostly the latter. Rehearsing dancers collided with bustling technicians and scene shifters. The orchestra added to the din by trying out the dance tunes.

Suddenly, a young man dressed up as Carmen Miranda materialized out of the confusion and stood staring at Ava with goggle-eyed admiration. Despite his monumental fruit headdress, false eyelashes and heavy makeup, it was clear to Ava that standing before her was the picture's and Metro's number-one ball of fire, Mickey Rooney. The rest of Mickey's costume consisted of a bra, a slit skirt and the highest pair of platform sandals imaginable.

"Aren't you going to introduce me to your gorgeous friend, honey?" Rooney asked the dancer, never taking his eyes off Ava.

By the time he was called away for another take he had Ava's phone number tucked safely inside his brassiere.

At lunchtime, Mickey Rooney was sitting at his usual table in the Metro commissary, surrounded by his cronies—including his stand-in Dick Paxton, Carey Wilson, producer of the Andy Hardy series, and Les Peterson, his publicity man—when Ava entered. As she searched for an empty seat at one of the unreserved tables, Mickey sent Carey Wilson to invite her over to join them. Ava raised one eyebrow and executed her enigmatic smile. She was flattered by the attention and the speculative looks she received as she crossed the room to Mickey's table. Then Rooney made a mistake: he stood up. As Ava recounted to a friend later, "Jesus, I thought, he seems to have shrunk since this morning. But then I remembered. Of course, the enormous platform shoes."

Mickey had been acting in films since the age of nine. As a kid of thirteen he had already appeared in fourteen movies, including Max Reinhardt's *A Midsummer Night's Dream,* in which he played Puck. At eighteen he won an Oscar for *Boys' Town,* and by the time Ava arrived in Los Angeles he was twenty-one, a kind of national hero, and one of MGM's principal assets. This was largely as a result of having created the character of Andy Hardy. The chronicle of the homey, down-to-earth doings of a gloriously ordinary family in a gloriously ordinary American town was rooted in the assumption that eighty-five percent of the United States was God-fearing and old-fashioned and liked to be reminded of it.

Ardent Hardyites, forerunners of television soap-opera and situation-comedy fans, had come to accept the Hardys as real people. They wrote to Lewis Stone in his capacity as Judge Hardy, Andy's father, for legal advice. They complained that their sons dressed sloppily when Andy dressed sloppily. They rebuked the judge for giving Andy too much spending money. They gave Andy himself advice on his screen romances as well as his real-life ones. When Andy turned nineteen, Henry Ford sent him a Lincoln Continental as a birthday present.

On the strength of Andy Hardy, Mickey Rooney had been voted "King of the Box Office" in the New York *Daily News* poll two years in a row. The Hardy series rested on his shoulders. He had a Catherine-wheel sort of personality, sparkling with energy, zest and self-confidence. Nothing was consid-

ered beyond him: he sang, danced, acted comedy and tragedy with equal enthusiasm, if not always with the same
satisfactory results. But his ebullience hid an acute, indeed
agonizing insecurity; he understandably suffered deep de-
pressions and inner bitterness over his lack of physical
stature.

Against the advice of the "clan," who warned him that she
was not his type, Mickey Rooney began an assiduous courtship of the beautiful Southern starlet. Somewhat to his astonishment, he was rebuffed. When he telephoned to ask for
a date she replied, "I can't tonight, I'm busy," when in reality
she faced another night at home with Bappie listening to the
radio and reading the movie fan magazines.

Her refusal was not coyness, nor was it coquettishness. She
simply was not attracted to Mickey. "Why couldn't he be tall,
dark and handsome like Clark Gable?" she lamented to her
sister. Mickey was blond, his looks were boyish, and he stood
four inches shorter than Ava. But in pursuing women
Mickey was notorious for refusing to take no for an answer.
The following day one of his friends appeared at the Shooting Gallery to relay another invitation from the star. When
Ava declined again, he exclaimed, "You're crazy. Don't you
realize how good it would be for your career in this place to
have Mickey Rooney in your corner?" Ava consulted a Metro
publicity executive: Would it really help her career to be seen
with Mickey Rooney? "Sure it would," he replied.

When Mickey telephoned again, Ava said that she was
sorry, but she had promised to have dinner with her sister
Bappie. Seizing the chance, Rooney promptly invited Bappie
as well.

The three went to Chasen's. He plied them with champagne and caviar, and introduced Ava to crepes suzette,
which were to become her favorite dessert. He was at his
amusing best, full of jokes, imitations and Hollywood stories,

filling every minute with laughter in his eagerness to impress his new obsession. He also table-hopped with Ava to show her off. She met more people that one evening than in her previous four months in Hollywood.

Dancing presented something of a problem: his head rested squarely on Ava's shoulder. But Ava's first big night out since her arrival in Hollywood provided a glimpse of the exciting world she had known existed but had never before seen at such close quarters. So what if her escort was the shortest adult star in the movies? Wasn't it still better than not being escorted at all? That was her initial attitude toward Mickey's ardent courtship. He breathed life into the photographs in her fan magazines. More: he put her into them. They went to baseball games, auto races, the track. Their evenings burned bright with the flames of crepes suzette at the Beverly Tropics, Mike Romanoff's and the Mocambo. Mickey's bills often ran as high as $150 for an evening. They double-dated with Errol Flynn and Lupe Velez, one of the Mdivani brothers and Paulette Goddard, and Peter Lawford and Loretta Young. Everywhere, there were fans, photographers and the welcoming smiles of friends and headwaiters to remind her that her diminutive companion was a powerful star.

There was a curious ritual to their dating. Mickey's Lincoln would pick her up at her apartment and then return with her to his home in Encino, where he lived with his mother and stepfather and where he would be waiting to join her. Mickey Rooney hated to ride alone.

At first Mickey's dominant urge was sexual, and there would be wrestling bouts in the back of the Lincoln on the drive home from a date. Ava had no interest in "going all the way" with Mickey, and perhaps the memory of her mother's disapproval stiffened her resistance. Mickey would drop her off at her apartment, often departing in a huff. But the next

day there would be roses by the hundred, or sprays of or-
chids to apologize and make up. Ava's resistance only served
to increase his ardor, and he began to propose marriage. He
was turned down, but it did not deter him. "I'm going to
marry that girl if it kills me," he told his cronies.

They continued to see each other almost daily, and Ava
began to feel affection for Mickey. She laughed at his antics
and his lively patter. Occasionally, she was too unsophisti-
cated to get the joke. He once told her champagne was produced in France but the bubbles were manufactured in
America and added later. She fell for it, and it was not until
several years later that someone corrected this impression.
"Occasionally, a shrill voice would sound in my brain warning that maybe life with Mickey would be like life on a sound
stage," Ava confided to a Hollywood friend. "He would always be 'on.' But whenever the warning sounded, Mickey
drowned it out with a joke."

But another part of her liked the new deference she was
accorded at Metro as Mickey Rooney's girl friend. Once her
picture at his side stopped appearing in the fan magazines,
she would sink back to the relative obscurity of being just
another starlet. Besides, Mickey had brought out in her an
unsuspected capacity for enjoyment, and untapped reserves
of stamina for late nights and heavy drinking.

On Christmas Eve 1941, Mickey threw a party at Mike
Romanoff's restaurant to celebrate Ava's nineteenth birthday. On the drive home, he proposed for the umpteenth
time, and she accepted. The following day he produced a
diamond engagement ring which he had confidently bought
two weeks earlier. Ava never really stood a chance.

Mickey was elated. He broke the news to the members of
his inner circle, who received it without enthusiasm. "Oh, I
know you guys think she's not the girl for me, but you're
wrong," Mickey told Carey Wilson. "We're in love, and she's

going to be a great wife." Then Mickey phoned Hedda Hopper, the *Los Angeles Times* gossip columnist. Though all Hollywood had been aware that Mickey was dating Ava Gardner, the news of their engagement was still a bombshell to Hedda Hopper. Hollywood's biggest box office star was planning to marry an obscure fifty-dollar-a-week contract starlet!

Puzzled that such sensational news should come directly from the star and not from Metro's efficient Publicity Department, she checked the story with Howard Strickling, who promptly denied it. Sure, Mickey was very fond of Ava, Strickling said smoothly, but in announcing his engagement he was being impetuous. When Mickey was seriously contemplating marriage, Strickling promised, Hedda would be the first to know. Even someone with Hopper's clout dared not go directly against Metro in a matter of such importance: she killed the story.

Strickling quickly tracked down the euphoric Mickey and warned him of the consequences of his intentions. "Mr. Mayer isn't going to like this," Strickling said. "You're the biggest star in the business, and you can't just throw yourself away on anybody. Don't get me wrong, Ava's a very nice girl, but you've got obligations—to the public, and to Mr. Mayer, who believed in you." Mickey doggedly stood his ground. All that Strickling could do was to extract a promise that the engagement would be kept secret until Mickey had spoken to L. B. Mayer.

At Mickey's insistence, Ava was present when he met Mayer. The studio head would have preferred it otherwise, for this gave her some importance. When they were ushered into his vast office, hand in hand, Mayer gave Mickey an icy greeting, ignoring Ava altogether. Benny Thau, the head of talent, stood behind his boss, looking openly hostile. Howard Strickling, his arms folded across his chest, was seated on a window seat.

Mickey's chin jutted out the way Andy Hardy's did when he defied his father. Ava hung back, looking demure and a little frightened. This was her first encounter with the tyrannical boss of her studio. Whether she realized it or not, her future at Metro probably hung in the balance. If Mickey backed down, she could expect to feel the full force of Mayer's vindictiveness: how dare a nobody from the Shooting Gallery turn the head of his hottest star?

Mayer was famous for getting what he wanted at office showdowns. He would rave, wheedle, cajole and plead until his victim surrendered from exhaustion. Continuing to ignore Ava, he now concentrated his artillery on Mickey, ordering him not to marry Ava. When bombast failed, Mayer tried coaxing. "Why do you have to marry the girl? You know all you want to do is to get inside her pants." Mickey remained immovable. Suddenly, tears welled in Mayer's small pale eyes. "Mickey, it would break my heart to see you unhappy," he sobbed, thumping his heart with his right fist. "Please believe me, Mickey, I have always been like a father to you. Believe me: this is not the girl for you."

Since World War II began, Mayer had been dragging patriotism into his fights. There was a war on, he argued. How could Mickey contemplate marriage knowing that he could be drafted at any time, leaving his wife pregnant and alone? It didn't work on Mickey.

Since he couldn't destroy the relationship, Mayer did the next best thing: he took control of it, ordering Strickling to make sure the wedding was arranged as discreetly as possible and held out of town. The job fell to Les Peterson, who located a suitable home for the couple away from the conspicuous Bel Air and Beverly Hills neighborhoods. The Rooneys would live in Westwood at the Wilshire Palms apartment building, owned by Red Skelton and the director Frank Borzage. Peterson also picked out a platinum wedding band, chose the location of the ceremony, planned the honeymoon, and wrote the press release announcing the wedding for distribution to the media after the event.

*Babes on Broadway* was rushed to a conclusion to expedite the marriage. Luckily, MGM had ready for release the appropriately titled *Life Begins for Andy Hardy*, and a promotion campaign exploiting his marriage began on the film's opening day, which had been timed to coincide with the wedding day. Mayer threw a massive stag party for Mickey. There were ribald stories and marital advice from Clark Gable, Walter Pidgeon and Robert Taylor. Mickey replied, "Thanks, you horny bastards. The first guy I see looking hard at Mrs. Rooney gets a right hand to the teeth."

# 4

# Ups and Downs

They were married on Sunday, January 10, 1942, a mere six months after Ava arrived in Hollywood. The wedding party left surreptitiously early in the morning, hoping to avoid attracting attention, and headed for Santa Barbara in two cars. Ava, Mickey and Les Peterson took the Lincoln. Bappie, Mickey Rooney's father Joe Yule, Sr., Mickey's mother Nell Pankey and his stepfather, plus a studio photographer were all squeezed into the second car.

Mickey wore a new charcoal-gray double-breasted suit with a green polka-dot tie and a white carnation in his buttonhole. Ava had bought a dark-blue tailored suit with the wedding bonus that she received from Metro. Her dreams of a white wedding were dashed when the studio ruled that this would complicate the already intricate arrangements and threaten the security of the operation.

In Carpenteria, on the outskirts of Santa Barbara, Mickey called Santa Barbara County Clerk J. E. Lewis and asked him to issue a license. Then the couple drove into Santa Barbara, picking up their marriage certificate without leaving the car. From Santa Barbara they made their way to a small white Presbyterian church in Ballard, tucked away in the foothills of the Santa Ynez Mountains. No one appears to have attached much importance to the fact that Ava had been raised a Southern Baptist and Mickey was a Christian Scientist.

The wedding was performed by the Reverend Glenn H. Lutz, a rotund, cheerful churchman. Mickey trembled nervously, almost dropping the ring while trying to slide it on Ava's finger. As soon as the couple were pronounced man and wife, Peterson found a telephone and called Metro to release the announcement. The studio had already been deluged with phone calls from the press; the Rooney wedding was the lead item in Hedda Hopper's column in that morning's paper. Strickling had kept his promise and given her a scoop.

In Ballard itself the local press had been silenced by Metro's promise of exclusive wedding pictures. The newlyweds were able to leave in secrecy for the Monterey Peninsula for their honeymoon. The Monterey Hotel's advertisements boasted, "People who could go anywhere return again and again." Ava was not one of these people. The honeymoon was such a fiasco that the mention of the Monterey Hotel could make her shudder. After registering, the Rooneys went for a stroll, but Les Peterson quickly retrieved them when the newsreel crew arrived. It dawned on Ava that Peterson was to be their constant companion.

Years later Peterson would say to Ava, "Remember me, Ava? Three on a honeymoon? Ha, ha." Ava remembered him, all right. "When you came down to breakfast, he was there," she said. "When you had dinner, he was there. When you went to bed, he was damn near there." Though spared that indignity, the wedding night was just as traumatic for both Ava and Mickey. Despite considerable experience with women, Mickey proceeded with uncharacteristic shyness. Ava may have felt her mother's stern moralism welling up and was equally terrified. She was also a virgin.

Overcoming her shyness, Ava proved more than a match for Mickey. Overwhelmed by her ardor, Mickey got up in the middle of the night and wrote letters to his parents and friends.

Though Ava resented Peterson's violation of their privacy, she eventually spent almost as much time with him as she did with Mickey, who ran off to indulge his passion for golf or talked on the telephone to his cronies on the MGM Lions, the football squad maintained by the studio so that Mickey could indulge his passion for the game, leaving her to her own devices. Peterson was always there to fill in the waiting hours with long walks, buying her ice cream and chocolate sodas.

The difficult honeymoon merged into a long promotional tour for *Life Begins for Andy Hardy*. In New York Ava and Mickey held a press conference at the New Yorker Hotel, Ava sitting in a deep chair and Mickey perched on the arm to offset the difference in their height. Mickey did all the talking.

Bappie arrived from Los Angeles, and the sisters went shopping for new outfits for Ava to wear when the tour took them to President Roosevelt's birthday celebrations in Washington, D.C. First the party went to Boston, where Mickey entertained at a Red Feather Drive Community Chest function, replete with Cabots and Lodges. Again Mickey did all the talking. After that, he went to Fort Bragg to entertain the troops, while Ava made a side trip to Smithfield to see her mother and family, deeply but silently disappointed that Mickey had not been able to accompany her to meet her folks. Bedridden and close to death, Mollie greeted Ava with characteristically restrained affection and lectured her on the duties of a good wife.

By the time the famous newlyweds arrived in the nation's capital, it was clear that Ava did not share her husband's natural talent for coping with the press—or with fans. Some hesitation was natural in a newcomer, but public appearances invariably reduced her to a state of sheer terror which she would never be able to overcome. Scared of the limelight, she begged Mickey not to force her to accompany him to the President's birthday ball at the White House. Mickey decided they would both stay away, and had to be dissuaded by Peterson: Ava could skip the event, but not Mickey Rooney. He was to represent Metro, along with Lana Turner, Clark Gable and other major stars. They were still arguing when Rooney, in white tie and tails, kissed his wife goodbye in the lobby of the Shoreham Hotel. "Look, you go to the White House," Mickey told Peterson, hoping for a last-minute reprieve. "All I want to do is to stay here with her." Peterson won.

Once the couple moved into their Westwood apartment, the trouble started. Mickey was too young for the obligations of marriage. It was now up to Ava to try to sustain his interest. For a time, her freshness and lack of artifice, in a world in which everyone strove to appear sophisticated and complex, continued to attract him. A friend on furlough from the Army went to dinner one evening at their drab two-bedroom home, with its white walls, white carpet and beige leatherette chairs, and was shocked to find them behaving like school kids, giggling, smooching, and wrestling on the floor. Bored with their horseplay, he slipped out unnoticed into the night in search of adult companionship.

About a month after the marriage, Ava had an attack of agonizing stomach pains which became so excruciating that she had to be taken to Hollywood Hospital where she was operated on for an inflamed appendix. Mickey rushed to the hospital and was at her bedside when she regained consciousness after surgery. For a while after Ava's hospitalization married life in Westwood was idyllic. Mickey was full of concern for Ava, and she seemed to blossom into happy young womanhood in response to his attention. But in April they were separated for the first time. The cause of their quarrel: Ava had danced several times with a good-looking young Metro actor named Tom Drake at a studio party, and Mickey had thrown a jealous fit. While he swore and raved Ava walked out, returning to Bappie on Franklin Avenue, but not before she had given as tough as she got. For the first time, she taunted Mickey about his diminutive size, saying she was tired of living with a midget.

The mounting tension between them was the result of opposite and irreconcilable expectations of married life. Ava's was consistent with her background—a classic vision of the wife as little woman, cooking and caring for her man. Having spent his whole life in the limelight, Mickey was no stay-at-home. He'd pace the house like a caged monkey while Ava, barefoot in the kitchen, cooked elaborate Southern meals. His efforts at conversation fizzled because Ava's frame of reference seemed to be restricted to recent events in Rock Ridge.

Mickey resumed hanging out with his cronies, leaving his young wife at loose ends. She wrote long letters home, listened to jazz, cried and consoled herself with dry martinis. Yet he was available enough whenever she was asked to spend some time at the Hollywood Canteen, serving coffee and doughnuts to servicemen and dancing the jitterbug with them. Mickey would volunteer to play the drums in the band so that he could keep an eye on her.

It should be said in Mickey Rooney's defense that, unlike

the husbands of many actresses, he was ambitious for his wife, perhaps recognizing that movies were their only interest in common. He placed her career in the hands of his own agent and also hustled MGM to give her more and better parts. Thanks to his clout at Metro, Ava began to work regularly. There were more walk-ons: she played a fashion model in Joan Crawford's version of the fall of Paris, *Reunion in France,* one of Metro's spate of war pictures in 1942. She was a Czech resistance fighter in *Hitler's Madman,* the MGM account of the assassination of Reinhard Heydrich, the Nazi "protector" of Czechoslovakia.

In the spring of 1942, Ava landed her first speaking part— the waitress in the drive-in diner who served Marsha Hunt and Lee Bowman in *Kid Glove Killer,* a good but minor mystery picture. As Mickey told her consolingly, you have to start somewhere.

Generously sharing his professional expertise, Mickey swamped her with useful practical tips on how to stand, how to walk across the set, what to do with her hands and how to avoid looking at the camera. He came to the set to monitor her work, whispering last-minute instructions between takes like a trainer in a fighter's corner between rounds. "Keep your chin up, Ava," he would say, or "Remember to keep your eyes fixed on Joan [Crawford]." He could not have been more serious about her one day's shooting in *Kid Glove Killer* if she had been playing Lady Macbeth.

Ava's screen appearances were lighting no fires. If she hadn't been Mickey Rooney's wife, she would almost certainly have been dismissed when her contract came up for renewal after the first six months. Had the other studios failed to sign her on, she would have faced the choice of returning to North Carolina or becoming part of the Hollywood flotsam eking out an existence as an extra, a salesgirl or a secretary.

But L. B. Mayer couldn't antagonize a moneymaker like Mickey Rooney. He agreed to a request from her agent for the removal of the three-monthly option clause in Ava's contract and to treble her base salary to $150 a week. Mayer probably regarded Ava's "reprieve" as a temporary expedient; his spies had informed him that the marriage was not going well.

Metro was feeling the impact of Ava and Mickey's roller-coaster relationship. Shortly after his wedding, Mickey began *The Courtship of Andy Hardy,* full of exploitable parallels with his real-life romance and marriage, and he tried to persuade Carey Wilson to cast Ava as the girl Hardy almost falls in love with. Despite Mickey's coaching and pep talks, Ava's screen test clearly showed her to be too green to cope with the role, and Donna Reed was cast instead. Mickey saw the wisdom of Carey's choice, but the decision still rankled. He blamed himself for Ava's failure.

Their marital separation hit during the filming and sapped Mickey Rooney's acting of its distinctive verve. Worried, Carey Wilson consulted Eddie Mannix, the burly Irish head of production at Metro. Mannix viewed the footage and was alarmed at what he saw: there were dark shadows of sadness on Mickey's youthful face. Subdued, Mickey Rooney was like flat champagne.

"Dammit, Carey, he looks as if he's at his own funeral," Mannix said. "If we don't do something to pull him out of it, we're going to have a terrible disaster on our hands."

Mannix summoned Mickey and Ava to his office, shrewdly including Bappie after enlisting her support, and talked them into a reconciliation. To cheer them up, he promised Ava a good part, but one that was not too demanding. Ava moved out of Bappie's apartment and back into Westwood. The couple reappeared on the nightclub circuit, which they had deserted since their marriage, and became regulars at the Mocambo.

It was at the Mocambo that she first met Frank Sinatra. Most of the forties big bands and singers were by now signed to movie contracts, including Sinatra, a handsome, hollow-cheeked young crooner from the East. When the Rooneys met him at the Mocambo, Ava, as she confessed later, found him dangerously attractive. To avoid another jealous fit by Mickey, she feigned indifference to Sinatra's open attentions. When he was asked to sing with the orchestra, he dedicated the song to her.

Eddie kept his word. Ava was loaned out to Monogram to make a B picture with the Dead End Kids, *Ghosts on the Loose*. Friends who dutifully went to see it were surprised by Ava's flair for comedy.

But there was nothing comic about her domestic life which had not been improved by the reconciliation with Mickey Rooney. His gossip about baseball, football and high-powered movie figures was over her head, and her lack of repartee exasperated him. Had he been less self-involved at this time he might have noticed a slight change in Ava's attitude. She no longer insisted on cooking dinner for him and in fact asked for a live-in cook/housekeeper. This meant moving to a larger home. Mickey turned to Metro, and the reliable Les Peterson found an attractive cottage on Stone Canyon Drive in Bel Air, a newly fashionable district on the hilly periphery of Beverly Hills.

Ava's emergent spirit of independence was the result of her growing friendship with other Metro girls—for example, Lana Turner, who was much further along the road to both stardom and notoriety. In her starlet days at Metro Lana had been posing in the Shooting Gallery in a blouse and sweater "twin set" for a fashion layout when the publicity girl on duty, Emily, said, "Lana, why don't you take off your blouse?" Lana removed the blouse from underneath her sweater—and the Sweater Girl was born. Shapely, child-voiced, she was launched as one of the forties bad girls—critic Ian Cameron calls them "dames"—along with Lizabeth Scott, Veronica Lake, Rita Hayworth, Barbara Stanwyck and Shelley Winters. They played women of dubious ethics or unconventional femininity who were often on the wrong side of the law, and whose presence the audience knew meant trouble, big trouble.

Lana Turner had a reputation for being a handful off screen as well as on. When she met Ava she was divorcing her first husband, Artie Shaw, and Ava was impressed with Lana's coolness while maneuvering through court hearings and packs of pushy newspaper reporters. She was flattered when Lana, an established star, poured out confidences to her, a raw starlet. Lana confided that she was having an affair with Howard Hughes. In the long sequence of Hughes's Hollywood women, which would soon include Ava herself, Lana Turner came after Katharine Hepburn and immediately before Yvonne De Carlo. Like many of her predecessors, she confidently considered herself the end of the line for the eccentric millionaire. When Hughes told her that marriage was out, Lana pouted, "But, Howie, I have all our sheets monogrammed HH." Hughes's reply shows either a quick wit or unusual thrift: "Why don't you marry Huntington Hartford?"

Such stories had an impact on Ava. They were a reminder that other options might be open to her beyond her present marriage. Her strict upbringing made her block out divorce as a possibility in her own situation, at least for the moment, but Lana's example encouraged her to be less submissive to Mickey. One night Mickey came home from a late poker game to find Ava still out: she had accepted an invitation from Lana to join a group of her friends at the Copacabana. When Ava returned and the couple were settling into bed, Mickey suggested that having a child might save their marriage. He made a tentative pass at Ava, but she sprang back, protesting in characteristically colorful language.

The quarrel continued to simmer for several days. When it flared up again, Mickey moved out, returning to his mother's home in Encino. Ava also left the Bel Air cottage and went back to the Westwood apartment, which the studio still retained.

Mickey called constantly, pleading for another chance. When Ava remained adamant, he turned ugly, threatening to reclaim her by force. Ava was terrified. She asked Leatrice Carney, a close friend from the studio and the daughter of John Gilbert, to move in with her. She threatened Howard Strickling that she would expose their marital mess to the press unless the studio restrained Mickey immediately. Strickling reported the crisis to Mayer, who ordered, "Keep them away from each other—and keep them both busy."

Mickey's new film, *A Yank at Eton,* was rushed into production on location in distant Connecticut. To keep her in California, Ava was pitchforked into one walk-on part after another. Mickey telephoned every evening, but Ava had Leatrice say she was not in. Actually she went out very little, spending her evenings with new friends like Fran Heflin, wife of Van Heflin, Minna Wallis, the agent, Ava's lawyer Jerry Rosenthal and his wife, Ruth, and actor Tony Owen and his wife, Donna Reed. Ava cooked for them herself— steaks or chicken with Southern trimmings.

By mid-April 1943 shooting on *Yank at Eton* was completed. Mickey raced back to Los Angeles, and one of Ava's quiet evenings was violently interrupted. When she refused to let him in, he broke down the door.

Emotionally, Mickey was close to a crisis. Besides his wrecked marriage, he now faced the prospect of being drafted; he was classified 1-A. He was not afraid of going to war, but he knew that if he went his marriage would be over. He pleaded with L. B. Mayer to have the draft board decision reversed. It was an emotional scene, with both of them weeping and embracing. Mickey called Mayer the father he had never had—though he had a perfectly adequate father in Joe Yule, Sr., and Mayer knew it. Mayer called Mickey his son, and for the first time the studio appealed against the conscription of one of its stars. Its argument was that Mickey's contribution to the national morale through his pictures, especially the Andy Hardy series, was indispensable. The draft board was not impressed. In a brusque reply, Metro was accused of putting its own commercial interests before the national war effort.

Another reconciliation attempt was engineered by Bappie and Mannix. Ava appeared for the appointment wearing a skirt and sweater à la Lana Turner. Mickey lectured her on the mode of dress to be expected from Mrs. Rooney. Ava told him what she thought of being Mrs. Rooney in strong language and left.

On May 2, 1943, she filed suit for divorce in Los Angeles City Court, claiming half Mickey's property. The grounds: "grievous mental suffering" and "extreme mental cruelty." The undefended suit went before Superior Court Judge Thurmond Clarke on May 21. Ava wore her blue wedding suit and a hat borrowed from Bappie, the suit being the only outfit she had that was serious enough for the occasion.

In the witness box she was subdued but in control as always. Mickey, she testified, "wanted no home life with me. He told me so many times."

Her attorney, Alo G. Ritter, asked her, "Is it true that he left you alone much of the time?"

"Yes, he did," Ava replied. "He often stayed away from home. Twice he stayed away for long periods. He spent a month with his mother once, and when I protested he told me he simply didn't want to be with me." Then Bappie took the witness stand to substantiate her sister's testimony.

Judge Clarke granted her a divorce decree and upheld her claim for $25,000, a car, and the furs and jewelry Mickey had given her—all this instead of half his property. Originally she had asked for more than $25,000, but Eddie Mannix persuaded her to take less, again dangling before her the carrot of better roles. The studio's intervention, of course, also contained the implied threat that things would not go well for her at Metro if she took Mickey to the cleaners.

Next morning, Ava received news of Mollie Gardner's death following a long fight against breast cancer. Ava flew home—her first plane journey—and arrived just in time for the funeral. The *Smithfield Journal* carried a front-page story about her divorce with a picture of her sitting in the Mocambo, evidently out on a date with Errol Flynn. Mickey Rooney and Flynn's wife, Lily Damita, had also been present at the table that night, but they had been cropped out of the photo. The paper mentioned that Ava was to attend her mother's burial, and when the funeral party arrived at the small Baptist graveyard a sizable crowd was waiting. Ava sobbed as her mother was lowered into the ground; but not many of the others present had come to mourn the unfortunate Mollie Gardner.

# 5

# A Tub of Ice Cream

In the fall of 1943, Ava was yanked right up the cast list to fifth place in *Three Men in White*, one of the famous Dr. Gillespie pictures about a lovable old curmudgeon whose popularity foreshadowed a whole genre of television medical soap operas. Like Andy Hardy, Dr. Gillespie had a huge following. Moviegoers wrote to him for medical advice, just as they appealed to Judge Hardy for help with legal problems. Ava's "promotion" was a real break, guaranteeing her an enormous audience.

For the first time in her career, she received a full script (written and directed by Willis Goldbeck, whose career as a film writer went back to the silents). She was to play the part of a girl who is used by Dr. Gillespie to try to seduce Van Johnson, a young intern who wants to become Gillespie's assistant. It was the old doctor's way of testing the younger one's strength of character.

The role did not call for great acting, but the sight of those printed pages intimidated her. In a panic, she instinctively turned for help to Mickey Rooney, who had instructed her so effectively in the past. Mickey leaped at the chance of re-establishing contact and advised her throughout filming.

It was only a short step to dating again. Interviewed with Ava at a restaurant table, Mickey said, "I love Ava a great deal. Maybe we'll be reconciled. We're young yet and both of us are glad that we caught our domestic error in time to correct it for a long and happy life together." Ava clutched his hand and said, "I couldn't get along without Mickey. And I guess he couldn't get along without me." The new mood of reconciliation did not survive the picture. When shooting ended, they were at each other's throats again.

The preview at the Village Theatre in Westwood was a success. Men in the audience gave loud wolf whistles every time Ava appeared on the screen. That the women in the audience did not seem to resent her was of enormous inter-est to studio executives in attendance that night. Standing in the foyer later, Mannix overheard several women comment-ing on Ava's sensual looks enviously but not vindictively. With women making up sixty-two percent of the wartime audience, their approval was an important factor in Ava's continued progress at Metro. More than one promising star-let had been dropped by the studio because of a perceived hostility among women moviegoers.

The *Hollywood Reporter* said Ava Gardner and Marilyn Maxwell (who played the other would-be seductress engaged to test Van Johnson) were "superb and should delight the studio with their histrionic conduct here." In one scene Ava pretends to be a lush dragged into the hospital in the middle of the night. Johnson discovers she is in fact a sweet girl who supports her invalid mother. Ava was convincing as a bat-tered alcoholic, and played the seduction scene with skillful comic timing.

Metro followed up *Three Men in White* with a supporting
role in *Maisie Goes to Reno,* another successful series. Ava
played a rich divorcée friend of Ann Sothern, who, as usual,
was the scatterbrained blonde Maisie. The part required little more than a haughty manner, but it too added to Ava's
remote enigmatic screen style.

Mickey Rooney hadn't been around to help her this time.
On June 15, 1943, he left Los Angeles for Fort Riley, Texas,
as a buck private, hauling a five-foot duffel bag about the
same size as himself. Les Peterson, Eddie Mannix and a host
of cronies showed up at the station to see him off. To
Mickey's deep disappointment, Ava was not among them.
They had dined together the previous evening at the Palladium. Mickey had asked her if she would come to the train
and she had replied, "Maybe."

From boot camp Mickey wrote long letters begging Ava to
come back, but the letters went unanswered. His phone calls
were equally unsuccessful. Bappie had the task of keeping
Mickey at bay. He learned from a newspaper story that
Ava—*his* Ava—had become Howard Hughes's regular date.
He wept, and for the first time in his life began to drink
heavily. Desperate, he went AWOL to fly to Los Angeles.
MPs were waiting at Los Angeles Airport to take him back to
Texas, and Metro had to pull strings to prevent serious trou-
ble. Strickling also succeeded in keeping it out of the papers.

Hughes's relationship with Ava began late in 1943, after
her name had been linked with a long list of Hollywood
bachelors and unhappily married men. Mickey had awak-
ened in Ava an urge for the high life. She continued to dance
at the Mocambo and eat crepes suzette at Romanoff's, acquiring a reputation as a Hollywood party girl, photographed arm in arm with Peter Lawford one night, with
Greg Bautzer, the attorney and social gadfly, the following
night, and with Billy Daniels, the dancer, the night after that.

The young Argentinian Fernando Lamas taught her to tango. Irving Reis, the director, took her to Santa Anita racetrack with Bappie in tow, for Ava's sister was a racing addict.

With fashion advice from MGM's Anne Strauss, Ava acquired a veneer of elegance to go with her straight-backed model's posture. Even so, she could still cause a stir by kicking off her shoes at a nightclub or a party and going barefoot as she had done in the tobacco fields. She was never around her house longer than a few minutes with her shoes on, no matter what the company. Once, she showed up at a party at Lena Horne's Beverly Hills house wearing an evening gown and carrying her shoes in her hand. She had walked barefoot down Nichols Canyon from her own home, and one of the other guests would later recall that "her feet were black with dirt."

She had a friend at Metro who kept telling her that she had aroused the interest of Howard Hughes. He had seen her on the screen in *Three Men in White* and wanted to meet her. One evening after work, when Ava was feeling particularly low, the friend casually invited her home for an impromptu dinner. Other guests appeared as if by magic, and among them was the shy, awkward millionaire bachelor. He ate nothing, said little, and stuck to Ava's side like glue.

A couple of days later, he telephoned to ask her for a date. Ava squeezed into a black strapless figure-hugging party dress and nestled into a mink wrap. She did not know that Hughes's conception of an evening out differed radically from her own. Hughes hated wearing formal clothes; he hated crowded, fashionable restaurants and "in" night clubs; above all, he hated the limelight. So when Ava began to see him regularly, she stepped into a social backwater of out-of-the-way chophouses and quiet, unknown bars.

On a typical evening they watched two movies alone in the

screening room of his green stucco Hollywood office on Romaine Street off Sunset Boulevard. Then they drove in his battered Chevy to a Pico Boulevard steak house, where Hughes ate a butterfly steak and tiny peas, as he invariably did every night. He would produce a small silver rake and began to sift the peas through it. If a pea did not go through, he rejected it immediately, fearing that his delicate stomach wouldn't absorb it. The meat was cut into minuscule pieces for the same reason.

When Ava moved into the eccentric world of Howard Hughes his fetish for hygiene, based on his physical frailty and constant fear of infection, was already a dominant factor in his life. But so was his high sexual appetite. He would have his women stashed in apartments or houses within easy reach any time he wanted them. Bodyguards followed them everywhere and brought them home at once if Hughes signaled that he wanted to go to bed with them. Hughes never dallied after sex. He was afraid that if he romped around too long he would get tired and catch something.

Ava Gardner appealed to him because she refused to regard being his girl friend as a full-time job. He picked out a house for her on Mulholland Drive, but she preferred to remain in her Westwood apartment. She also continued to report to the studio every morning, and to take the small speaking parts Metro was offering her. There was something deliciously challenging about her detachment. But the novelty wore off. The core of remoteness in Ava began to frustrate and anger him, and her frequent attempts to assert her independence now ended in rows.

In December 1943, when Hughes was away on business in New York, Ava slipped out to the Mocambo, danced the night away, and returned home in the small hours of the morning. When Hughes returned, Ava's night bodyguard—she was watched around the clock—dutifully reported her

night on the town. Hughes summoned Ava to his mansion in
Beverly Hills and told her he was disgusted. When Ava
cursed him out, he slapped her so hard that he dislocated her
jaw. In retaliation, she grabbed the first large object that
came to hand and hit him with it. It happened to be a heavy
brass bell, and it laid him out cold.

Such dingdong battles would eventually be patched up,
however, and the peace settled with a lavish gift from
Hughes, such as a new Cadillac or a piece of jewelry. But Ava
also discovered that he was a dangerous man to cross. Shortly
after the bell incident, she took the Cadillac he had given her
to the Hughes Tool Corp. to have it serviced. She was driving
away later when the car lurched to a noisy halt. The engine
had been loosened from its moorings (she was convinced on
Hughes's instructions) and had fallen out. At the root of
their clashes was the simple fact that Ava was not in love with
him. But in the brash, macho movie industry, the shy, nervous thirty-eight-year-old tycoon, who made no secret of his
poor health, was an ideal target for female sympathy. For all
his great height, Hughes was a scarecrow, weighing 160
pounds, with arms and legs like sticks and disproportionately
large hands and feet.

But there was more to Ava's fascination than mere mothering. Hughes's unpredictable nature and enormous wealth
made him an exciting suitor for any woman, especially a still
relatively simple girl from North Carolina. There were sudden jaunts to Mexico in his private Boeing Stratoliner, which
was equipped with a bedroom, a cocktail bar (stocked with
cola only), easy chairs, and couches. Most of the time,
Hughes piloted his own plane. Ava, wearing a flying suit and
aviator's goggles, sat beside him in the co-pilot's seat.

On her twenty-first birthday Hughes asked Ava what she
wanted as a gift. "Just tell me, and you can have it," he told
her. "How about a big tub of orange ice cream?" Ava replied

mischievously. Two hours later, an enormous limousine pulled up outside Ava's apartment, and a uniformed chauffeur delivered a giant tub of orange ice cream. There was an accompanying card, but it read, simply, "Love, Howard." As a lover Hughes was totally devoid of romantic eloquence. His most articulate moments were when he talked about his grand design for living in which he intended to devote a specific number of years each to science, to the movies, to aviation and other pursuits worthy of his genius.

During this period Hughes was developing a near-paranoid preoccupation with Communism, reflecting in exaggerated form the political climate that was building up in the movie industry. At RKO, Hughes instituted a secret procedure for testing any star or director who he thought might be a "red." The artist was offered a film entitled *I Married a Communist*, which had a strongly anti-Communist theme. Anyone who turned it down confirmed Hughes's suspicions and did not work at RKO. The picture was turned down by thirteen directors before it was finally made by Robert Stevenson. It died at the box office, but can still be seen on television with the title *The Woman on Pier Thirteen*.

Politics led to more heated arguments between Howard and Ava. Hughes supported Thomas Dewey in the 1944 Presidential race. Ava sang Roosevelt's praises. In defiance of Hughes's edict, she was present when Secretary of the Interior Harold L. Ickes spoke at the Ambassador Hotel to a glittering assemblage, and again when Vice-Presidential candidate Harry Truman appeared at the Shrine Auditorium before a throng which included Edward G. Robinson, James Cagney, Orson Welles and Lillian Hellman.

For all Hughes's generosity, his interest in Ava was oppressive. To escape from the suffocating weight of their relationship, and very much against his will, she began to go out alone on her free evenings—one of the few women in Hollywood who would dream of appearing at Ciro's or at the Mocambo without an escort. Often she would be with Lana Turner. They would dance with male acquaintances, talk to the bandleader, and drink—but somehow without actually getting drunk. Sometimes the two of them would close Ciro's at three in the morning and then pile into their cars and go to the house of the club's owner, Herman Hover, with other party-loving stars. When all the others dragged themselves off at dawn, Ava would still be looking as good as new.

Ava's growing addiction to night life was also brought on by her depression over what MGM was doing to her—or not doing. The studio had not wasted much time and effort trying to discover the key to her screen personality before her marriage to Mickey Rooney; it was even less inclined to do so after her divorce. MGM brass blamed her for the breakup. They held her responsible for Mickey's lack of spark now that he was back from the Army.

This bad feeling between star and studio was not helped by Ava's late-night carousing. However late she stayed out, and however much she drank, Ava never made a public spectacle of herself. But that was not the basis of Metro's complaint. The studio preferred its stars to be more circumspect in their public behavior. Clark Gable's discreet life was held up as a model for others to copy: Ava became the figure in a cautionary tale about the consequences of bucking the system. As a result of the studio's hostility, her career was stuck faster than a cart in deep mud. She simply did not possess the star status to get away with nonconformity.

Metro relegated her to the loan-out list, its catalog of artists available for rental which was discreetly circulated among the other studios. She was offered at the reasonable price of $5,000 per six weeks' shooting. (Since Ava was earning $300 a week, the studio stood to make a profit of $3,200.) At that price, she was an attractive proposition, and early in 1945

Ava's partying came to a stop because at last she had landed an important role and was filming *Whistle Stop* at United Artists.

The best-selling novel was intended as a vehicle for George Raft, the quintessential movie gangster, who was making a belated attempt to widen the scope of his screen personality. But clearly nobody at UA had bothered to read the novel before buying it. This torrid story centered on an incestuous brother-sister relationship which, given the strictness of the Hays Code, was problem enough. Worse still, the brother was a blond Adonis in his twenties. George Raft was in his middle forties, balding and paunchy. Undaunted, UA hired a young screenwriter named Philip Yordan to blend these irreconcilable elements of star and story into a viable film.

Yordan threw out everything in the novel except the title and the characters' names and wrote a completely different story which was persuasive, gripping—and would pass the censor. Ava was signed to play Mary, a girl with a mysterious and shady background who returns to her whistle-stop Illinois industrial hometown, where her lover, played by George Raft, has become a loafer and a drunk. The owner of a local hotel and saloon becomes obsessively attracted to Mary, while Raft is nearly forced into theft and murder by a bartender (Victor McLaglen). But the ending shows Mary rescuing her downtrodden friend from a life of crime.

The director was Léonide Moguy, a French refugee with an unerring instinct for handling actresses. His technique was to draw them aside and, with great charm, explain to them how they must allow their natural animalism to release itself without shame. With Ava, he worked hard at stripping away the veneer which Lillian Burns had worked equally hard to construct. The unconscious animal grace she had possessed before being put through the MGM mill could now resurface.

Luckily, Ava had enough native intelligence to see his point. Bit by bit, both before and during the shooting of the picture, he wore away her stilted manner and revealed instead the faint glow, the temperament, of a star. The role was the biggest challenge Ava had faced in her screen career, and the emotional toll was considerable. From the first day of shooting until the last, she was a bundle of nerves. She began to suffer from insomnia, which was to trouble her for the rest of her life. Insecure, and often out of her depth, she clung to the friendship of Moguy and his Danish wife, Daan. Yet in moments of panic she would instinctively turn to Lillian Burns—the very person whose influence Moguy was trying to undo—to help her with her lines. Much of the dialogue in her scenes had had to be rewritten in simpler language in order for her to cope. Endless retakes were required before she gave a convincing performance.

When the picture was finished UA executives viewed it dubiously and then decided to preview it in Pomona. Ava donned a cheap scarf and sunglasses and went to the preview. She shuddered at her stiff and mannered acting. But then she had an extraordinary experience. The phenomenon that had occurred at the Westwood preview of *Three Men in White* was repeating itself. All around her, her impact on the men in the audience was electric, and she suddenly saw the sexual and commercial power she exerted on the public, especially the male public.

The opening shot of Ava on the station platform wearing a mink coat and a diamond ring was more than the start of her most important role. In a larger sense, it marked the arrival of her screen personality. This was the role she was to play in her most successful pictures: a sensual, well-heeled woman of the world who was likely to be evasive about how she came by her mink. *Whistle Stop* also introduced Ava's sultry love-making style. She kissed George Raft with her mouth open, which was not at all the way the Hays Office liked stars to kiss each other on the screen.

The critical and commercial success of *Whistle Stop* strengthened Ava's confidence in herself as a movie actress, and she reported back to Metro hoping that the studio would now think of her as something more than a clothes horse. But nothing changed at Metro. Despite the critical praise, she was cast in yet another Maisie movie.

Intensely disappointed at Metro's indifference, she decided to quit movies altogether. To buttress her decision, she embarked on the second of her three mismatched marriages. On October 15, 1945, she wed Artie Shaw in the living room of his house on South Peck Drive in Beverly Hills.

# 6

# Artie

Artie Shaw. The name evokes the Swing Era, big bands, and immortal Shaw renditions of "Begin the Beguine" and "Dancing in the Dark." At twenty-one he was internationally famous as the most gifted clarinetist and bandleader in America. In 1944, at thirty-four, he was a mental and physical shambles.

He had been stricken with granulocytopenia, a rare blood disease that weakens the white cells and is often fatal. He had fought it, but before he had had time to recover completely the war broke out. Right after Pearl Harbor he joined the Navy and set off on a grueling tour of military bases and installations in the South Pacific with a uniformed band.

The ensuing two years of hit-and-run performing with no respite shattered his nerves, and his state of mind when he received his medical discharge in California is vividly recalled in his autobiography, *The Trouble with Cinderella*, written six years later.

I was pretty much washed up. This was in 1944 and at that point I wanted nothing more than to lie down somewhere in a deep hole and have someone shovel enough dirt over me to cover me. I was really beat—not only physically, but completely. The war was, of course, still on; but I was out of it . . . I had no idea what I wanted to do, what I could do, what would make sense for me to do—and I wasn't in any state to do any constructive thinking about it.

In short, I'd had it—or, as the psychiatrists would say, I was in a state of dysfunction. As I would put it, I was nowhere. For a while I hung around Hollywood, hoping I'd snap out of whatever it was I was in—but nothing happened. Nothing would have happened right up to this moment, I guess, if I hadn't somehow, from somewhere inside myself summoned up enough energy to see someone about what was going on with me.

That someone he went to see was the Los Angeles psychoanalyst May Romm.

Highly strung, argumentative, not an easy personality before his illness, Shaw was now, after it, more difficult than ever. The man who visited May Romm three times a week at eight in the morning talked nonstop, ramming home his opinions with all the subtlety of a piledriver. The fact that his musical career had come to a standstill as a result of his emotional state did not diminish his brashness.

He had the typical autodidact's urge to show off his wide-ranging book knowledge. His autobiography is strewn with literary references as it recounts his progress from David Arshawsky to Artie Shaw, from humble Bronx origins to big-band fame and the psychiatrist's couch.

But it is conspicuously reticent about the five women he had married and divorced by 1950. Not one of them is mentioned, as though Lana Turner, Ava Gardner, novelist Kathleen Winsor and the others had left no mark whatever. At least they were spared the hostility he directed at his possessive widowed mother, presented as the bane of his life. When she had threatened to jump out the window during an argument with him, Shaw said, "I walked out of the room, down the stairs, and went across the street so I could watch her do it."

How this attitude affected his relationships with other women can only be guessed. Women were drawn to his unusual combination of dark good looks, quick wit and extraordinary arrogance. Movie stars had the looks, but rarely the wit and even more rarely the intellect. Writers had the intellectual capacity, but not often the looks. So it was no problem for Artie to get the women he wanted. He was constantly being photographed with one Beverly Hills beauty or another hanging on to his arm, including his analyst's daughter.

Before she loved Artie Shaw, Ava loved Artie Shaw's music. Growing up in North Carolina, she had been swept up in the swing craze just as teenagers of a later generation went wild over rock 'n' roll. She had swayed to his music on his coast-to-coast radio program, and Artie Shaw records had kept her company when she was a lonely newcomer to L.A. in a Westwood apartment.

One evening she had gone to a theater to hear him perform in person, and she was immediately smitten. She found out that he lived at the Garden of Allah, and sometimes she would drive slowly past the old apartment complex in Hollywood late at night, trying to work up the courage to call on him.

Her nerve failed her, but strange forces were at work. Artie had seen a cheesecake picture of Ava in the color section of the *Los Angeles Times* and pointed it out, drooling at her extraordinary beauty, to his friend Frances Heflin. "Oh, that's Ava," she remarked. "We're good friends. I'll introduce you."

Two days later, Ava was Artie's date at a Count Basie concert in the Paramount Theatre in Hollywood. Artie took her backstage and introduced her to Basie and members of his band. Ava was impressed. They finished the evening dancing to Ernie Coleman's band at the Mocambo.

After the diminutive Mickey Rooney, and the secretive Howard Hughes, this tall, handsome charmer was a breath of fresh air to Ava, even if—from the start—his conversation gave her a feeling of being out of her depth. A few more dates, and she was completely under his spell. Artie said, Move in. She moved in. Artie told her being a Metro starlet was degrading, and she began to seriously consider giving up movies altogether. Bappie was appalled, sensing impending disaster for her sister. Metro was shocked, but the studio's opposition only encouraged her.

The problems of being the mistress of someone with intellectual pretensions did not take long to surface. Artie's friends included William Saroyan, Robert Benchley, S. J. Perelman, John O'Hara, Gene Fowler and Dorothy Parker. And at Shaw's house on Bedford Drive, north of Sunset Boulevard, sandwiched between the homes of Greta Garbo and Marion Davies, the conversation more often centered around books and writers than on movie gossip.

Shortly after Ava moved in with Artie, the discussion at dinner one evening concerned the missing opening chapter of Hemingway's *The Sun Also Rises*, dropped from the novel by the author on the advice of Scott Fitzgerald, who had found it nasty. Artie had argued that the chapter should be restored to the book. "When is Hemingway anything but nasty?" he argued. Ava had sat silently beside him, dismayed and mystified.

When their guests had gone, she said, "What am I doing here?" and burst into tears. "I don't belong here. I didn't have any idea what any of you were talking about."

Artie tried to console her. "For Christ's sake, honey, you look beautiful, you don't have to know. Look at all those ugly women who were here tonight. They would give anything to look like you."

She refused to be consoled. Artie handed her a copy of *The Sun Also Rises* and said, "There's one remedy—here's the book. Read it."

And so Artie earnestly began to try to transform Ava through education. She had read only one book in her life, *Gone With the Wind,* but now Shaw launched her on a cultural crash course. Before a trip to New York, where they were to meet Artie's friend Sinclair Lewis, Artie gave her *Babbitt* and sat down with her while she labored through it—then handed her the rest of Lewis' work. When they were invited to a party for Aldous Huxley, Ava was expected to do her homework. She read *Brave New World* and detested the soulless, scientific vision of the future Huxley painted.

But Ava lacked *Sitzfleisch,* the stamina to remain seated, and however forcibly he tried—and Artie could be forcible—Ava was too restless to sit and read a book when she could play tennis, phone a friend, drive to the beach, raid the refrigerator or have a drink. At her reading rate she was hardly likely to get through *Buddenbrooks* or *The Magic Mountain,* two of Artie's favorites, and the truth was that she rarely finished any of the books Artie gave her.

In a fit of remorse, she once tried formal education. She told MGM that she wanted to take an English literature course at the University of California, Los Angeles. Metro balked at the idea of one of its starlets mixing with the public and told her to sign up for a correspondence course. Ava lost interest. Ironically, MGM added to her official biography that she had been an external student at UCLA.

In his postwar doldrums, Artie Shaw somehow decided to form a new band. It would be similar to his big swing band, but, curiously, it would perform transcribed versions of classical compositions. Never one to do things by half, he began to prepare his new venture by totally immersing himself in the classical idiom. Instead of Benny Goodman, Artie Shaw and Tommy Dorsey, Ava now heard nothing but Mozart, Beethoven and Ravel.

She was disappointed. These were totally new sounds to her ears. But she was naturally musical and soon developed a lifelong taste for the more popular classics. Under Artie's guidance, she also discovered that she had a good singing voice, and she began to toy with the idea of concentrating on a musical career in movies, à la Kathryn Grayson. She even began to badger Artie into letting her play the part of Billie Holiday in a movie he hoped to make about the black blues singer's life.

Meanwhile, Ava and Artie had become the subject of widespread gossip. It was still relatively rare in Hollywood for a couple to live together openly, as they were now doing. Hedda Hopper, Louella Parsons and the other purveyors of studio-approved gossip could only hint at the real situation for fear of incurring Metro's anger. The studios insisted on preserving a facade of respectability no matter what. Hollywood was just another American town, and Hollywood people just folks.

A few years earlier, a leading *Photoplay* writer got himself and his monthly fan magazine into hot water for having had the audacity to hint very strongly in print what was widely known in the movie community. His article, entitled "Unmarried Husbands and Wives," was a thinly disguised catalog of leading stars who were living together—Barbara Stanwyck and Robert Taylor, Gable and Carole Lombard, and Paulette Goddard and Chaplin. The writer was declared persona non grata by the studios, and *Photoplay* was forced, under threat of advertising cancellations, to print an abject, full-page apology to the stars, ostensibly for casting their friendships in the wrong light.

Since then, columnists had stuck to publicity-department euphemisms; Ava and Artie were "inseparable companions" or "good friends," and of course they were planning to get married. Most of the gossip was coming from Ava's friends, who considered Artie to be a brash, bossy outsider. They resented the way he corrected her for swearing—"There must be another word, Ava"—or complained about her going barefoot in public, which was by now her trademark.

The gap between rumor and reality in their relationship was often enormous. One afternoon at their home, Ava playfully suggested, "Let me fix your toes, let me manicure them." Shaw declined. "C'mon—you can go on reading," she insisted. Artie sat back with his book while Ava knelt at his feet, giving him a pedicure. A friend came to call, took in the scene, and the following day all Beverly Hills was talking about Artie Shaw forcing Ava Gardner to give him pedicures.

It was true that Shaw found her ignorance appalling. He rightly perceived that she possessed a native intelligence and was a quick learner, but wrongly saw himself as the man to set things right. As a teacher, he lacked patience and human understanding. He had a short fuse, and he erupted—violently—and occasionally in public. Once, after a dinner party at their home, Ava slipped off her shoes as usual, tucking her feet under her on the couch. In an instant, Artie bounded to her side and frog-marched her out of the room in front of their embarrassed guests, raving against her uncivilized ways.

Whatever the root cause of the quarrel, it was nothing as trivial as Ava's bare feet. The relationship was under great strain because of pressure on the couple to marry. In reality, both were ambivalent about marriage. Ava was still gun-shy after her breakup with Mickey Rooney; as for Artie, no one makes four attempts without accumulating plenty of scars.

"Have you fixed the date yet?" Hedda or Louella would harp, and out of the couple's evasive replies they would weave fresh examples of journalistic wishful thinking. "Ava Gardner and Artie Shaw have not set the date yet," Louella reported on September 14, 1945, "but close friends of the beautiful star and her dashing beau say it could be any day now." The "close friends" were of course Metro publicists trying to put up a respectable front.

Ava made a desultory attempt to start analysis with May Romm, Artie's psychiatrist, but it lasted about as long as her university enrollment. Artie was afraid that if he continued his own sessions he would talk himself out of marrying Ava and abruptly broke off his own analysis.

On her wedding day, Ava woke up to find Artie quietly getting dressed. The trees outside the bedroom window were like a pencil drawing in the dawn grayness.

"What's the matter?" Ava asked, fully awake.

"I don't know. I can't sleep," Artie said.

"What are you going to do?"

"I'm going to get in the car and drive," Artie said.

"Can I go?" Ava asked, leaping out of bed.

In Artie's Cadillac they drove along Sunset Boulevard to the ocean. It was encased in its customary thick morning mist. They listened to the roar of the waves for a while without getting out of the car. Then they drove back, this time along Santa Monica Boulevard.

Neither spoke. Each seemed to be waiting for the other to

break the silence. Artie concentrated on the driving. Ava seemed deeply engrossed in the scenery.

The weight of the conversation they had not had hung oppressively between them and continued to as Ava left to keep an appointment with hairdresser Sydney Guilaroff. Artie went into his study to brood. The precious chance of decisive action had been lost.

Artie phoned a close friend to unburden his misgivings. "I can't go through with this thing," he burst out. "It's just ridiculous." But both knew there was no turning back. The affair was so notorious now, in flagrant violation of Ava's contractual morals clause, that marriage was mandatory, if only as a step toward a divorce that could at last end the relationship. For Ava to have ended such a widely publicized liaison in any other way could have destroyed her reputation and her career.

They were married nearby in Frances Heflin's Beverly Hills home. They honeymooned in New York, where Artie was performing at the Paramount Theatre. He had returned to personal appearances because he needed money to give to his mother. When Ava purchased Kathleen Winsor's run-away best-seller *Forever Amber,* Artie snatched it from her and threw it out. "Why do you have to read such shit?" he said. Ava stood shocked, almost in tears, realizing that her only hold on Artie was her physical attraction. Whether it was worth all the emotional effort, the fact remains that in her months with Artie she acquired a finish. She grew sleeker and more self-possessed, shedding the last awkward traces of North Carolina.

She learned to handle her marital frustration in novel ways. One evening shortly before her twenty-third birthday she slipped away from her own dinner party—where the talk was considerably over her head—and out of the house.

When the guests departed she had still not returned and Artie made up a story about her being tired and having gone to bed. Thoroughly he searched the house and then retired himself.

At that moment, the doorbell rang. Artie went downstairs and opened the door. There stood Ava, barefoot, with her hair soaked and clinging to her face. She looked ravishing—a nymph out of the sea.

"What the hell have you been doing?" Artie roared.

Ava was slightly breathless. Her little girl voice quivered with excitement. "I just had to get a little air, so I took a walk. And, Artie, you know the house just round the corner in Beverly Canyon Drive?"

"What about it?"

"Well, I looked over the hedge, and there was a swimming pool. There were statues around it, and it was absolutely beautiful—dark, and Southern, and . . . I don't know, I just had to do it. I took off my clothes and went in."

"You mean you stripped naked and swam in the pool?"

"Yeah, it was wonderful."

"But what if someone had come out of the house?"

Ava shrugged. "Well, nobody did."

He found it enchanting, primitive, moving. Unable to cope with heavyweight intellectuals, Ava had sought consolation in nature, going naked in the water. Artie liked the story and told it frequently, often in the presence of Ava herself.

He was still telling it ten years later when Ava suddenly added a shattering postscript. Reminiscing with him in Madrid, Ava said, "Artie, I never went into the pool. I couldn't stand feeling left out, so I got in the car and drove around. I knew you would be mad, so I found a garden faucet and wet my hair and my dress. And I made up that story."

# 7

# Turning Point

It is not unusual for a role to take over the personality of the screen actress playing it. This phenomenon was often true of Ava and was to reach its peak when she played Lady Brett Ashley in *The Sun Also Rises* in 1957. The picture took three months to make, but Ava remained Lady Brett out of choice for years afterward. At the time of the garden hose escapade, she was playing Kitty Collins, the beautiful but deceitful gangster's moll in *The Killers*. Kitty Collins was a mythomaniac and a liar. The tale Ava fabricated for Artie was nothing compared to the inventive fantasies of Kitty Collins. The black satin gown Ava wore that evening was one of her costumes for *The Killers*.

Success has many parents; failure is an orphan. Many have claimed credit for casting Ava as Kitty, the big break of her movie career—Artie Shaw because he lobbied the director, his friend Robert Siodmak; producer Walter Wanger and his wife Joan Bennett because they had seen *Whistle Stop* and recommended Ava to *Killers* producer Mark Hellinger; John Huston because he wrote the script with his friend Ava in mind.

But Mark Hellinger was the kind of man who made his own casting decisions. He saw *Whistle Stop* and immediately rang Ava's agent. A colorful, independent producer, Hellinger had made his mark with Humphrey Bogart's gangster hit *High Sierra*. He had talked Hemingway into letting him buy the film rights of the short story, and then signed a deal to make the movie at Universal. *The Killers* was to be Hemingway's favorite film from his work. He had a generally low opinion of the screen versions of his novels, especially something which he called *The Snows of Zanuck*.

In his sinister classic "The Killers," a pair of professional hit men ask some people in a lunch wagon about a man they say they want to see. Young Nick Adams (Hemingway as a boy) manages to warn Swede, their quarry, but Swede stays in bed, knowing he cannot escape. The picture reproduced the short story virtually as Hemingway wrote it. In the opening sequences, Swede's tragic predicament became the frame for the movie's ambitious overall design. An insurance investigator zeroes in on the inexplicable assassination through a series of flashbacks of ringside and gangster life. The result was a crisp and lively melodrama, full of suspense, and perforated with cynicism and harsh, violent action.

Hellinger was able to invest the milieu of *The Killers* with an authentic touch drawn from personal experience. In the 1920s Manhattan teemed with bootleggers, big spenders, lovable drunks, and chorines with hearts of gold, and Hellinger immortalized them as a columnist for the *New York Mirror*. *The Killers* is packed with scenes, characters and dialogue straight out of Hellinger's New York. The transplanted producer, who was forty-three, had retained a number of colorful personal touches in Hollywood—midnight-blue shirts worn with white silk ties; a black Lincoln limousine (a gift from a former gangster acquaintance) equipped with a siren, white bearskin rug, New York license plates (MH 1, of course), and bulletproof glass. As for the chorines, Hellinger was married to former Ziegfeld Follies beauty Gladys Glad.

To add further authenticity to the picture, Hellinger picked a cast of unknowns. He chose a husky newcomer named Burt Lancaster to play Swede, the slow, vulnerable, natural-born fall guy, a failed boxer turned gangster. Opposite Lancaster he needed a very special feminine screen personality to play Kitty, and he found her in Ava.

Summoned to Universal to be interviewed by the producer, Ava was struck by his energy and intelligence. There was something else which she found electrifying yet could not identify until they had met several times to discuss the project. Then it came to her: Hellinger treated her as an actress. Half apologetically, he asked her to test in a love scene with Lancaster. She was so perfectly convincing in her simulated passion that he never bothered to finish the test. He had absolute confidence in her. After the uncertainties of life with Artie, her ego was receiving a welcome boost, but in fairness to Artie, it was he who had urged her to read the Hemingway short story and had rehearsed with her before the interview.

At first, Metro dashed her hopes by refusing to loan her out to Universal for *The Killers;* she had already been cast in a Metro production, and the shooting schedules of the two pictures overlapped. Ava was nearly hysterical with disappointment and threatened not to report for work on the MGM picture.

Universal, on Hellinger's behalf, spoke to MGM in a language they understood. The studio was offered a loan-out agreement of $1,000 a week for the $350-a-week actress, with a seven-week guarantee and a penalty clause for running over schedule, plus an option to loan out a Universal contract player of Metro's choice within the year. *The Killers* was to run over the contracted seven weeks, and Metro's net profit would be $4,608.34.

Once again, Ava was lucky in having a director who recognized her limitations as an actress and at the same time had the patience and skill to make the best of her narrow range and charisma. This was the German refugee Robert Siodmak, an intelligent filmmaker who specialized in gangster and underworld films. He was so excited by Ava that he let her dominate scene after scene. In one shot devoted to a poker game, he focused the camera entirely on her boredom and restlessness as she stood by a window gazing at a sudden downpour of rain.

With *The Killers* Ava arrived as a screen actress, but the picture also represented the best of what film historians now refer to as the "film *noir*." The genre had its heyday in the 1940s and early 1950s. Its characters live in the night and make their fearful way through darkness.

The gangster is only one of these people. He shares his world with cops, private eyes, molls, murderers, psychopaths and other lone-wolf variants. Film *noir*'s tortuous plots, treacherous relationships, unpredictable events and dark frames mirrored the bewildering adjustments of returning soldiers at the end of the war. They provided a disenchanted view of how the networks of social and personal life functioned. Those who had remained behind had formed their relationships, made their compromises, and now closed ranks to keep out the newcomers.

The gangster movies of the 1940s were also full of seductive women of deceitfully angelic appearance. The men always bought them a drink, and life suddenly became a nightmare. A critic wrote that these women were signs of a collective male desperation about the world as something that can be understood and put right. They are society's misogynist fantasy—woman as an object to be feared, woman as a scapegoat for the world's ills.

It was in the role of one such siren—and a particularly unwholesome specimen—that Ava made her mark on the screen. Watching her in *The Killers*, it is not clear whether she had thought out and understood the character of Kitty or had *become* Kitty by some kind of instinctive process, or, again, had perhaps followed Siodmak's instructions, which were minute, to the letter.

In her biggest scene, she handled herself with the skill of an experienced actress. Toward the end of the film, having triplecrossed Swede, Kitty has transferred her affections to Colfax (Albert Dekker), a thief with a touch of class. When he is fatally shot Kitty begs him to swear her innocent, but the dying Colfax cannot bring himself to lie to the police for her benefit. Faced with arrest, Kitty goes to pieces.

Worried that she might not be up to the required emotional pitch, Siodmak had been preparing Ava for days. Every day he would say to her in his heavily accented English, "Ava, if you don't do zat scene right, I vill hit you, I vill *kill* you!" On the morning that the scene was scheduled to be shot, Siodmak bore down on her, hissing his familiar threat like a vaudeville Nazi: "Zis is the day. If you don't do the scene right, I vill hit you, I vill *kill* you." Ava was so nervous that her hysteria in the scene was only half simulated; the rest was genuine fear of Siodmak.

Ava returned home so rattled that evening that Artie protested to Siodmak. "But, Artie, you should see the scene I got afterwards," Siodmak countered. Both men found this sufficient justification for the director's behavior.

Ava received high critical marks for her portrayal of Kitty and won the *Look* magazine award for the most promising newcomer of 1947 as a result—an odd accolade for a starlet who had been under contract in Hollywood for five years. Her fan mail increased from an intermittent trickle to a sizable flow. Most of the letters were mailed to Universal Studios, a clear indication that the new surge of interest was due to the release of *The Killers*. Universal rather smugly forwarded the letters to Metro.

Normal practice now called for Metro to rush her into a succession of films in order to build on that initial advantage, but MGM failed to capitalize on the impact of *The Killers*. The problem was an old one—Ava never really fit into the MGM mold. Films such as *The Killers* which used her sensuality and aesthetic appeal to advantage were simply not L. B. Mayer's style. Metro never jumped on the film-*noir* bandwagon; such a pessimistic vision of America was hardly compatible with the studio's Andy Hardy tradition. The end of World War II ushered in a new era of moral vigilance, and at Metro observance of the Hays Code went beyond the minimum requirements considered sufficient by other studios. Metro's new stars were Debbie Reynolds, Elizabeth Taylor, Deborah Kerr and June Allyson, and Ava was out of synch with Metro's heavy commitment to musicals and family whimsies.

Her problem was eloquently demonstrated by her first MGM assignment after *The Killers*, the prestigious Clark Gable film *The Hucksters*, in the second female lead. The starring role went to the wholesome, peaches-and-cream British import Deborah Kerr. Ava was not impressed, but Metro saw the assignment as an honor, despite the King's failure on his return from the service to recapture his public in a turkey called *Adventure* with Greer Garson.

*The Hucksters* cast a critical eye on the advertising business, which had burgeoned into "Madison Avenue" in the wartime economic boom. The hero of Frederic Wakeman's hit novel was a bit of a rotter, the heroine an adulteress. The thought that Metro would consider such a picture suitable for him affronted Gable's sensibilities. To appease him, the studio ordered the book castrated. Writer Luther Davis produced an acceptable screenplay that was largely a satire on soap commercials. He made the hero a scoundrel with a heart of suds who strikes at his ludicrous, power-mad boss by emptying a pitcher of water over his head; the heroine was a genteel English widow.

When Ava at first turned down the role of the sexy singer who is jilted by Gable in preference for Deborah Kerr, Strickling's Publicity Department said it was because she was awed by the prospect of acting opposite the King. But Gable did not frighten her; no man ever did. She was holding out for a better role in a better movie. Metro threatened her with suspension if she refused to comply. To sweeten the pill, *Hucksters* producer Arthur Hornblow, Jr., persuaded Gable to phone her and talk her into playing the role.

Gable overcame her opposition by confiding that he wasn't thrilled to be doing the picture, either—at least they could have "a few laughs" together.

MGM persisted in calling him the King, but the Clark Gable who played opposite Ava Gardner in *The Hucksters* was not the triumphant star of *Gone With the Wind*. He was still adjusting to the death of his wife, Carole Lombard, and to civilian life, which he found hollow. He was drinking too much. Like many of his fellow film stars, he found acting pointless and demeaning after the peak experience of fighting World War II. He probably also felt that he had reached the pinnacle of his career as Rhett Butler and thus had nowhere to go except down.

The only security he had ever felt about acting seemed to come from the momentum of going straight from one picture to another. That momentum gone, he suffered real stage fright. He perspired when he was working, and his head shook whenever there was tension on the set. Victor Fleming, who had directed *Adventure,* had taken few close-ups because of the shaking; now the same problem resurfaced on *The Hucksters.* The shaking was not the result of Gable's drinking but of the Dexedrine he was taking to fight the weight his drinking was putting on him.

His jitters transmitted themselves to Ava, who fluffed line after line and was bawled out by Gable's friend Jack Conway, who had been assigned to direct the picture and who vented on Ava some of the frustration he really wanted to take out on his friend. To Ava's astonishment, Gable also fluffed lines, and their mistakes created a bond between them. Ava was Gable's kind of no-bullshit buddy. But they were never to be more than friends. Gable claimed not to be physically attracted to brunettes, once confiding to Anita Colby that he thought brunettes looked dirty.

If *The Killers* was an artistic landmark in Ava's career, *The Hucksters* was a financial one. Early one morning, halfway through the filming, Ava rebelled against the difficulties of the production and Artie said, "Stay in bed." When the phone calls began to come in from the studio Artie answered them. The first one was from the production office demanding to know why Ava had not reported for work. Artie replied that she was not feeling up to it. Was she ill? the office asked. Not ill, Artie replied: overtired.

The calls escalated. And by midmorning Eddie Mannix himself was on the line. "What's the problem?" the Irishman inquired.

No problem, replied Artie. Ava had preferred to relax in bed.

Mannix pointed out that Ava's absence was costing the studio thousands of dollars in lost working hours.

For the amount of money she was getting, Artie replied, why should Ava feel obligated to get up at five-thirty every morning? "It's ridiculous—I give her as much as Metro does anyway."

Mannix immediately arranged a meeting between Louis B. Mayer and Ava's husband. Artie drove to Culver City alone and was immediately ushered into Mayer's office. The studio head made one of his typical speeches about Metro being a family in which no dispute was too great or too bitter to be resolved through discussion.

Artie said, "This girl's not interested in the parts you are giving her. Either she is going to be an actress, and you take that into account, or she will quit."

Mayer testily pointed out that if Ava refused to appear in a movie she could be suspended.

"But, Mr. Mayer, suspension doesn't mean anything if she doesn't want to be in pictures anymore."

"What do you think she should get?" Mayer asked.

"What would she have to get for you to take her seriously?"

"A thousand a week."

"I don't think you would take her seriously for a thousand a week, do you?"

Mayer agreed to raise the figure to $1,250 a week. A new three-year contract was drawn up, with two consecutive renewal options of two years each, plus the promise of a $10,000 bonus at the satisfactory completion of the third year. A subclause in the contract gave her the right to borrow up to $25,000 from MGM for the purchase of a house at the very favorable rate of four percent interest.

The new contract was signed with appropriate flourish in Mayer's office on December 21, 1946. Artie Shaw was not present. Two months earlier, Ava had obtained an interlocutory divorce on the grounds of mental cruelty. In fact, Artie was in Mexico getting married to Kathleen Winsor, whom he had met in the emotional slump of Ava's departure.

Strangely, she was the author of the novel Artie had earlier tossed out as trash—*Forever Amber*.

When his relationship with Ava began to corrode, Artie had decided to try his hand at writing; that had only made life at home more tense as Artie wrestled with the novice writer's inaugural period of utter paralysis before the blank page.

Ava had the misfortune to interrupt an afternoon of gloomy creative constipation. She had been playing tennis and she entered swinging a tennis racket. "Hi, honey, what's for dinner?" she piped.

It was a standard greeting, but this time Artie said, "Ava, sit down, I want to talk to you."

"Of course, darling," she said. "What about?" She dropped on the couch beside him with a happy flounce and waited.

"Ava, look, I do certain things for you, do I not?"

"Darling," she said, "you do everything."

"No, wait, not everything. But certainly some things. Let's start from scratch. I pay Amos [the butler] and Mary [the maid], right? I own this house—you live in it. The Cadillac—I bought it. That tennis racket—I bought it too. In other words, I support you."

"Oh, darling, I know you do—"

"Ava," said Artie, "what do you do?"

"I love you," Ava said, surprised at his reaction.

"I love you. You love me. Wash. Now let's start again. I own the house. I pay the maid. I own the car. I buy the food. What do you do? Can't you at least go down and tell *me* what we're having for dinner?"

Artie wanted an intellectual who was also a competent mistress of the house. But Ava's sole training, as a movie sex goddess, did not equip her to be either. She liked to cook but she was utterly devoid of any sense of domestic responsibility. Children might have helped to make her more domesticated, but she never felt sufficiently secure in her marriage to Artie to consider starting a family. In a repetition of the closing phases of her marriage to Mickey Rooney, Ava began to say to Artie, "You never wanted us to have a child." He replied, "If you wanted a child so much, Ava, what were you doing in the bathroom before we made love?"

He was once asked, as an old hand, how to go about getting a divorce. He replied, "First call a cab and get the hell out of there, then let the lawyers argue." On September 12, Artie called a cab. On October 24, six days after their first wedding anniversary, the Shaws received an interlocutory divorce. To speed up the proceedings, Ava asked for no settlement.

Artie's next marriage, his fifth, lasted twenty-one months, and the divorce was not nearly as civilized as the split with Ava. Kathleen Winsor filed a searing thirty-two-page affidavit in a Nevada court that made lurid reading. She alleged that Artie beat her and came home drunk, abusive and belligerent. He boasted that he had beaten his previous wives (including Ava) and found it an effective method of keeping them under control. In Norwalk, Connecticut, Kathleen Winsor complained, he "knocked me down" at the railroad station and he also threatened to kill her.

The novelist demanded $116,326, claiming that it was her share of their joint bank account, plus $500 a week alimony. Shaw struck back with a twenty-eight-page countersuit charging that she had refused children and even suggested that he undergo an operation which, as the New York *Daily News* gleefully phrased it, would have made him *Forever Sterile*.

Shaw complained, "She is trying to blackmail me. I know the defendant to be a money-mad extortioner." Money mad or not, when the divorce decree was granted in December 1948 Kathleen Winsor received her alimony.

Artie's immediate reaction to the breakup of his marriage to Ava had been to resume psychoanalysis. He tried making a fresh start by going to a new therapist, one who didn't know him, but the analyst firmly sent him back to May Romm. She had kept the 8 A.M. slot open since he stopped his weekly consultations. "You mean you knew I'd be back?" Artie asked her. "Of course," May Romm replied. Ava did not immediately follow Artie's example, though later she would. Nor did she break off all contact as she had when she split from Mickey Rooney.

On the contrary, Artie would remain her occasional adviser and for years close enough to make at least one of her subsequent lovers insanely jealous. She turned to Artie for advice on her career, boy friends, money and even clothes. Artie arranged for the former manager of his band, Bennett Cole, to become her business manager (and, incidentally, Lana Turner's as well).

Ava attended Artie's concerts. She was on hand to witness the disaster of his first experiment in conducting classical music at New York's Bop City in January 1947.

Flashbulbs popped when she arrived on Manhattan's Upper East Side at the old jazz cellar that was enjoying a new lease of life as a haunt of teenage beebop addicts. She was at last a glamorous movie star, recognized everywhere. She was one of the "nine out of ten" movie stars who endorsed Lux Toilet Soap. Her portrait in the glossy magazines advertised Max Factor beauty products. The Coiffeurs Guild of Los Angeles had crowned her queen of their 1947 convention. The organizers of the Harvest Moon Festival for the Purple Heart Fund in Chicago had specifically asked MGM to send Ava Gardner to be their main attraction. She was a regular guest on radio shows—*Hollywood, USA;* Bob Hope; Louella Parsons; *Command Performance; Hollywood Calling; The Prudential Summer Show.*

Even before she had finished work on *The Hucksters,* Universal again tapped Metro for her services. The studio was in a jam because the female lead in *Singapore* had fallen ill. Could Ava possibly step into the role immediately? Metro agreed to loan out Ava for ten weeks at $5,000 a week. She was rushed to Universal and onto an oriental set, introduced to the star of the picture, Fred MacMurray, and told to make passionate love to him. Only after that was she taken aside and told the plot of the picture.

Ava played a woman suffering from amnesia who married a rich British planter (Roland Culver), forgetting that she was already married to poor American pearl-smuggler-turned-spy Fred MacMurray. A bang on the head restored both her memory and the matrimonial status quo ante. After a hectic first week to make up for lost time, the filming settled down to a normal schedule.

During the shooting of a fire sequence, part of a burning ceiling caved in without warning, narrowly missing her and setting Fred MacMurray's white tropical suit on fire. Bullfrogs on the Universal back lot kept up such an obbligato to her dialogue that many of the outdoor scenes had to be shot at four in the morning when they fell silent, presumably from exhaustion. The film had a well publicized Manhattan opening at which the first hundred women at the box office were awarded one string of pearls each. Four hundred forty women tried. The pearls were synthetic, and so was the picture.

With the escalation in Ava's loan-out price and her rise in status came a corresponding assertiveness. It was too early to say that Ava had become difficult. But Metro executives found her harder to deal with in their daily contacts. On March 5, Ava instructed her manager to phone Frank Hendrickson, Benny Thau's long-suffering deputy at MGM, and report the loss of two caps for her teeth from her studio dressing room.

"According to Miss Gardner," Hendrickson reported in a memo to his boss, "she placed the caps on her dressing room table and she feels that they were probably thrown away by the person cleaning her dressing room. The cost of replacing these two caps is $175.00. She wanted to know if the studio is covered by insurance on a loss of this kind and in any event she would like to know if the studio will pay for replacing the caps."

Metro tried to ignore the request, but Ava began to telephone personally for a reply. Benny Thau ruled that it was not studio policy to pay for lost tooth caps, especially when the star was earning $1,250 a week.

After her divorce, Ava had moved back into her old Westwood apartment. Bappie moved in to help pick up the pieces, as she had done in the post-Rooney phase. The breakup of this second marriage scarred Ava deeply. Her spirits were at a low ebb, and when not filming *Singapore* all that she wanted to do was sit at home listening to Benny Goodman and Artie Shaw records—the kind of music Artie himself would not let her enjoy.

She was a stronger person now, better at coping with emotional crises. She also had a large circle of friends to buoy her up and help rebuild her shattered ego.

There were Beverly Hills socialites such as Walter Wanger and Joan Bennett and Mark Hellinger to take her to Romanoff's, where Prince Mike himself now greeted her with kisses on both cheeks and David O. Selznick stopped to ogle her. Men back from the war flocked to date her and amuse her, some no doubt hoping for marriage, but it was too soon for that—David Niven, who made the war sound like a drawing-room comedy, and John Huston, out of his major's uniform and deeply involved with Evelyn Keyes but still game for a gambol on his front lawn or a frolic in his pool when Evelyn wasn't around.

There was also Lana, coincidentally between husbands herself. With their names and pictures constantly in the press, the two women sought ways to escape the limelight—but never for very long.

Ava, Lana and some of the other girls would meet for lunch and gossip about men and complain about the way the studio treated them. Industry talk made them feel grown-up. Or they would go "cruising." A few girls would pile into somebody's convertible and ride with the top down to a drive-in to flirt incognito with boys in other cars. Occasionally they went to a big dance hall in the San Fernando Valley and jitterbugged and danced the Big Apple, pretending they were just ordinary girls chasing ordinary boys. Inevitably, someone would ask, "Say, aren't you Ava Gardner?" And Ava would reply, "No, but I've been told I look like her."

For R and R they flew down to Acapulco for constant parties. Dolores Del Rio had a house nearby, as did Teddy Stauffer, who was living with Hedy Lamarr. Ava found him attractive for a while—and vice versa. Hedy was not amused and remained hostile to Ava on her Mexican trips for years afterward.

There was nightly jai alai, and Ava met one of the players, a Spaniard from Madrid, not a Mexican. He looked the way a Spaniard is supposed to look—dark curly hair and black flashing eyes, slim waist and muscular body. When he introduced Ava to bullfighters, he slipped to second place in her list of male preferences. Bullfighters' waists were even narrower, for one thing, and Ava was fascinated by the interaction of skill and danger in the ring. "Can you imagine living with a bullfighter?" she said to Lana. "What a life it would be."

# 8

# Doesn't She— Don't I?

By now the highball glass was like a skin graft onto her right hand. Gin, vodka, tequila, rum, scotch, rye, bourbon, beer, champagne—or "shampoo," as she persisted in calling it—brandy, crème de menthe: you name it, she guzzled it. Straight, on the rocks, in Bloody Marys, daiquiris, Alexanders, stingers, whiskey sours, or in lethal concoctions of her own creation. Would you believe a Drambuie-and-tequila cocktail? Touch of Venus, she called it, in honor of her latest picture.

Ava's drinking was an antidote to her insecurity, a salve to her personal problems. But everyone drank, and everyone in Hollywood more than most. Alcoholism made rapid and widespread strides in postwar American life, increasing by nearly twenty percent to 3,750,000 chronic alcoholics in 1947. It was estimated that in Hollywood incidence levels were twice as high as in the rest of the nation.

The saving grace of Ava's drinking was that her capacity for booze matched her consumption; she was never drunk in public. She prodded herself into periodic dry spells, which she called "health kicks"—usually when she was working on a picture.

Ava always got her sleep—her daily routine was shamelessly self-indulgent. A night bird by nature, she slept very late whenever she could, and woke up slowly, savoring the luxury of not having an early call at the studio. A glance at the morning papers—in other words, at Hedda's and Louella's columns—was part of the waking ritual. So was a phone call from her bed to her current male interest.

Above all, Ava ate. She liked to start the day with a steak or fried chicken for breakfast. Lunch was frugal by her standards, perhaps another steak, salad, ice cream, but she made up for it with a vengeance at dinner, which was a three-course affair culminating in a no-nonsense dessert. Before going to bed, which could be anytime between midnight and dawn, Ava unwound with a snack, prepared by her maid Maerene Jones, known as Renée—maybe spaghetti, or an omelette, washed down by a large glass of milk, or a shake.

But Ava was touched by an enviable kind of good fortune: this monumental intake had no effect on her waistline. Her weight remained more or less constant at around 120 pounds, no matter what she ate. Even when it climbed to 130 pounds, and padding had to be added to the curves of her tailor's dummy in the MGM Wardrobe Department and she was forced to cut out desserts for a few weeks—even then her figure on the screen was still sleek and catlike.

Ava's figure was at its fullest when she posed for an Italian sculptor named Joseph Nicolosi in preparation for the filming of the Ogden Nash–S. J. Perelman musical *One Touch of Venus*, in which she started off as a marble statue of the Anatolian Venus. Nicolosi immediately complained that she was wearing too many clothes. He needed to see more of her figure to get a good likeness, he said. Ava took off her dress and stood in her panties and brassiere. Not good enough, Nicolosi said. Ava whipped off her bra and rolled down her panties until they were a hardly visible bikini. "Is that enough?" she said cheerfully.

Nicolosi was delighted with the wonderful life-size nude he was able to produce. William Seiter, the director, was horrified. "We'll never get away with that," he said.

"Why not? It's only a statue," Nicolosi said.

"Because the statue is supposed to come to life right on the screen, that's why not," Seiter said.

In the movie, Ava's statue of Venus, which is on display in a department store, turns into a woman when a handsome window decorator kisses it. Reluctantly, Nicolosi was forced to clothe his creation in a skimpy classic Grecian robe, off one shoulder and tied at the waist with a cord. The robe, reproduced in a flimsy material, was all Ava wore throughout the picture, with nothing underneath, in the interest of preserving "classical" lines. Wind machines were used in Ava's key scenes to heighten the dramatic effect, and the word quickly spread around the studio whenever the wind was about to blow on the Gardner set. Large crowds would gather to ogle. Ava was chilled to the bone. Portable heaters were stationed on the set, and her maid stood just outside camera range with a heavy mink coat and a brandy flask.

Dick Haymes did what singing had been retained from the musical; Tom Conway was the department store boss, and Eve Arden played Conway's cynical secretary. The window decorator whose kiss melts the marble into ardent flesh was Robert Walker. Life briefly followed art when, halfway through the filming, Ava drifted into an affair with Walker, estranged from his wife Jennifer Jones and already on the road toward alcoholism and self-destruction.

Though Walker was a man of enormous charm, it was his helplessness that appealed to Ava. But their evenings together almost always ended up as benders. No matter how late they stayed up, Ava, the indestructible, bore no signs of wear and tear on the set in the morning, but Robert Walker showed plenty. Scenes had to be put off because he was in no condition for close-ups. As a result, Ava's face was favored in many of their embraces on the screen, with Walker seen from behind. Once the first mothering impulse had subsided, Ava's interest diminished. Walker went wild when he discovered that Ava was dating actor Howard Duff and on one occasion tacked an unprintable sign to her dressing-room door.

Filming ended at Universal—the picture was another loan-out—and Ava walked out of Walker's life, the way Venus disappears in the movie. She changed her phone number, moved in briefly with the Van Heflins until Walker gave up trying to see her. Her brief affair with Howard Duff was now in full swing.

*One Touch of Venus* was disappointing, a success neither at the box office nor with the critics. All the same, the title role was tailor-made for Ava, and she made the most of it. Considering her lack of experience in comedy, she showed a surprising command of the timing. *Newsweek* actually called her "a natural comedy actress." And she never looked more beautiful, her profile alone establishing her physical credentials for the role of Venus.

This newly revealed promise in a comedy role could have been an interesting avenue for Metro to explore. Ava seemed to have the glimmerings of Lauren Bacall's blend of sexiness, glamor and sardonic humor, reflecting the way her own personality was developing as she said goodbye to twenty-five. She was acquiring a knack for funny, self-deprecating put-down lines. To a fan-magazine reporter who interviewed her on the set of *The Great Sinner* she said with a perfectly straight face, "Deep down, I'm pretty superficial."

Yet the powers at Culver City continued to miss the point. Not that Ava's movies at Metro lacked importance. Artie Shaw had been right: $1,250 a week turned out to be the figure at which she would be taken seriously. But on the whole Metro made poor use of the qualities she had demonstrated when other studios borrowed her.

In other respects, Ava now received the star treatment at Metro. She was allotted Norma Shearer's old dressing room on the lot. This three-room suite on the third floor of the dressing-room building was the largest of the women's quarters. Norma had ruled as Queen of the Lot from it for nearly eight years. The door opened onto a vestibule; then came the dressing room itself, with its expanse of mirror along one wall, encircled by naked light bulbs, and its big built-in cupboard for Ava's clothes. Beyond that was a boudoir, a bathroom and a kitchen. On the walls were photographs of Ava with L. B. Mayer, Ava with G. B. Shaw, Ava with Clark Gable, Ava at lunch in the Metro commissary with Archbishop Francis Spellman of New York. There were also a record player and a stack of records, mostly Artie Shaw and Frank Sinatra.

Her apotheosis was marked by a Metro press release put out by Howard Strickling's office and proclaiming her "Hollywood's glamor girl of 1948." In MGM's official account, her rise to stardom was entirely due to MGM pictures and no mention was made of the essential contribution of her two most important loan-outs, *The Killers* and *Whistle Stop*.

The year has brought this beautiful and talented young actress signal honors by the score [the press announcement said]. As the climax, it brought her first starring roles at her home studio, Metro-Goldwyn-

Mayer, opposite two of the screen's foremost leading men—Robert Taylor and Gregory Peck. She went from Taylor's arms in *The Bribe* to Peck's in *The Great Sinner*.

These developments were prefaced by the impressive manner in which the year opened for her. After a number of Hollywood's young actresses had been tested, she won the role of the glamorous night club singer in love with Clark Gable in *The Hucksters*. Her performance opposite the King placed her on the threshold of stardom, and had every studio in Hollywood asking for her services.

It is questionable how much *The Bribe* and *The Great Sinner* contributed to Ava's progress to stardom. More likely, they set it back, for both films flopped. Though it starred Gregory Peck, Hollywood's newest heartthrob, as well as "Hollywood's new glamor girl," *The Great Sinner* turned out to be box-office poison and was dropped from Loew's circuit of first-run theaters after only two weeks instead of running the standard five to seven.

It was based on Dostoevsky's novel *The Gambler*, and Ava was cast as the daughter of a Russian general. Opposite her, Peck was cast as Fedja—an autobiographical character—a compulsive gambler whose weakness brings him to the verge of ruin. The assignment of the principal roles to Ava and Peck brought co-scenarist Christopher Isherwood to the brink of despair. He had expected better of the newly enthroned head of production at MGM, Dore Schary, who had arrived full of promises to treat the work of studio writers with more respect.

Literacy was not widespread among studio brass at the time. Mayer could barely read. There was a widely circulated story that someone had asked him to read the short story "The Wizard of Oz." The following morning, Mayer arrived at work uncharacteristically late. "I stayed up most of the night reading that story," he explained, "and I'm going home early tonight to finish it."

Mayer usually left the reading to his staff. The books that the studio was interested in buying were narrated to him in condensed form by a woman storyteller, hired by MGM expressly for this purpose—a sort of modern Scheherazade, except it was not her fate that hung in the balance, but the book's. Mayer based his decision whether or not to purchase on her synopsis.

Dore Schary could not only read, he could write. Later, his *Sunrise at Campobello* was to be a successful Broadway play. He succeeded in getting a few unusual films made over Mayer's objections—notably *The Red Badge of Courage*—but the writers at MGM continued to be brutalized. Isherwood had written a moving script about Diane of Poitiers, only to discover that the studio had cast Lana Turner as the tragic French duchess. When Ava Gardner was given the role of the strong-willed Anya, who saves Peck from his gambling weakness, Isherwood, thoroughly disillusioned, quit MGM.

Ava took little interest in the picture. As a result she was pleasantly relaxed on the set. Once, a large group of extras was sitting around between takes wearing their heavy period costumes. Ava walked by in a magnificent black ball gown with a skirt that seemed to billow for miles around her. As the extras stared admiringly, she suddenly began drawing her skirts up as far as they would go. The onlookers held their breath in anticipation—only to discover that Ava was wearing rolled-up jeans under the skirts. "Get a good eyeful, fellahs," she laughed as she walked away.

*The Bribe* was MGM's attempt to emulate the success of Warner's recent hit *To Have and Have Not,* with Bogart and Bacall, but, without the wit and whimsy of the original, MGM's heavy-handed imitation flopped. Even the presence in the cast of Charles Laughton didn't help: *The Bribe* was the worst picture of Ava's heyday. *East Side, West Side,* in which she duplicated her other-woman role from *The Hucksters,* was not much better. Smooth, glossy, meaningless, this MGM concoction, based on a novel by Marcia Davenport about well-heeled New Yorkers, required her yet again to lean on a piano wearing black satin and looking vampish.

Ava had developed a resigned indifference to such roles. She was punctual, faultless in her delivery of her lines, and completely uninvolved. In private, she complained that she seemed to have been sentenced to the perpetual role of the heavy, which was a poor use of her talents as she now perceived them. *One Touch of Venus* had brought home to her the impact of her true screen persona and boosted her confidence.

Shortly after the film was released, she took a close friend to see it in a Westwood theater. Ava sat quietly until the moment the statue of Venus comes to life. As the music soared and backlighting suffused the figure on the screen, she nudged her companion. "Doesn't she—I mean, don't I look great?"

It was a kind of epiphany. She was looking at a goddess, and it was rapidly sinking in that the goddess was herself. After the movie Ava took her friend home to supper, and the latter noted that Renée the maid had taken to addressing her mistress as Venus—"You want some more fried chicken, Venus?" Furthermore, Ava accepted this without any sign of embarrassment.

If Ava was not the goddess of love, she was certainly a busy practitioner of the art. In the year following her breakup with Artie, she flitted from one liaison to another like a bee on a pollen-gathering foray. Escorts and lovers followed each other in rapid succession. Howard Duff forsook Yvonne De Carlo, his steady girl friend, for Ava. He abandoned a quiet life to indulge Ava's fondness for dancing, nightclubs and late hours, particularly at Ciro's, the "in" place of the moment. Ava's whim was Howard's command. When she heard about a terrific tennis pro in La Quinta, near Palm Springs, they drove down from Los Angeles for tennis lessons. But after the first day, Ava tired of tennis and wanted to go home. Eventually, her mercurial nature wore down the durable, good-natured Duff and they parted company.

Duff was followed by Jerry Wald, the bandleader at Ciro's, and a table close to the band was reserved for Ava every night. After Wald came a brief fling with impeccable and urbane Peter Lawford, followed by a second go-around with Howard Hughes.

Once again, as he had done three years earlier, Hughes fed and encouraged Ava's capricious streak. She would jump up and say, "Howie, let's go to this wonderful cafe I know in Mexico City and drink anis!" Half an hour later they would be taking off in Howie's plane from Burbank Airport. In Mexico City, Howie would, of course, order cola.

In this way, with Hughes's help, the restless, kinetic quality in Ava's nature grew like Topsy. A small weakness burgeoned into a reckless tangle of moods, fits, starts, changes— like the jungle, colorful, surprising, and frequently dangerous to those who ventured inside.

When Ava and Hughes broke up, he sent her a tiny ivory fist with a pointing middle finger which she strung on a gold chain and wore around her neck as a charm necklace. Depressed, she tried to drop out of a picture she was due to make at RKO, Hughes's studio, entitled *My Forbidden Past*. Hughes consulted with her home studio, MGM, and Benny Thau, recalling Gable's intercession during *The Hucksters*, suggested that Hughes might try the same technique.

Ava received a call from Robert Mitchum, who was to be her co-star in *My Forbidden Past* (earlier entitled *Carriage En-*

*trance*) while she was dining at Lucey's restaurant in Beverly Hills. She had never met Mitchum.

"Listen, Ava, I think the script is worse than you'll ever think it is, but I want you to do it with me," Mitchum told her. The film was important to him in only one respect, he said. He needed the money to pay the defense attorneys in his drug rap.

A year earlier two detectives had raided a three-room house in Laurel Canyon. In the living room they found dancer Vickie Evans, Lila Leeds, a pert blond movie starlet whose home it was, a real-estate man named Robin Ford, and Robert Mitchum. The star quickly tried to get rid of a marijuana cigarette, without success. The detectives searched him and found two "reefers" in his coat pocket. The quartet were hauled off to Los Angeles County Jail.

With three Mitchum pictures unreleased, David Selznick and Howard Hughes, who jointly held Mitchum's contract, were worried about the impact of the drug bust. But there was more riding on it than that. The arrest of a rising young star threatened the town's respectable image. So the studios quickly closed ranks. Mitchum, a self-confessed grass smoker "since I was a kid," had been talking freely about the effects of the drug. Suddenly, he, the others and even the arresting officers went mum. Studio publicity agents—and not just RKO agents—whispered "confidentially" that the case looked like a frame-up. Who would want to frame Mitchum was never revealed.

With the star out on $1,000 bail, coverup statements began to flow smoothly out of the front offices. Having persuaded his eccentric partner in the Mitchum contract to remain in the background, David Selznick issued an earnest plea to the American public and the press not to prejudge Mitchum but to "wait until the facts are known."

Dore Schary, speaking on behalf of the whole industry,

called on the public "not to indict the entire working personnel of 32,000 well disciplined and clean living American citizens [in the movie industry]" and called reports in the press of widespread drug use in Hollywood "shocking, capricious and untrue."

Mitchum was ordered to return to his wife, from whom he had been separated for several months. The Mitchums were reconciled in front of the press, and vowed never to part again. Sympathetic and intrigued, Ava agreed to make *My Forbidden Past,* and when the trial came up during rehearsals it lasted less than ten minutes. Mitchum and his companions entered a plea of guilty and were fined $250 apiece. In return for absolute silence from all concerned, David Selznick personally footed the entire bill. Lila Leeds made a couple of brief appearances in Selznick productions after that and then dropped out of sight.

Mitchum's career seemed unaffected by the revelation of his marijuana smoking habit. The anticipated boycott of Mitchum films by the Legion of Decency or one of the other guardians of public morals never materialized. The Bob Mitchum Droolettes, the star's national fan club, claimed that it had gained hundreds of new members. Once again, the public had proved less moralistic than the industry's view of it. Soon leftist political lapses would float to the surface in Hollywood, and America was to prove less tolerant. But infidelity, alcoholism and even drug use did not seem to harm a male star's standing with the public. If anything, they invested him with a welcome human dimension, and he could be forgiven. Women, however, had a harder time defying convention and getting away with it.

Mitchum continued to smoke his reefers. He tried to introduce Ava to marijuana during the filming of *My Forbidden Past,* but Ava continued to prefer booze.

The two of them hit it off instantly. The sleepy-eyed star

had Clark Gable's appreciation of earthy, buddy co-stars. But Ava ceased to qualify as a buddy the moment they began to film the love scenes in the picture. When she was attracted to her leading man, a very realistic style crept into her screen embraces, and her kisses quickly shook the drowsiness out of Mitchum's eyes.

He was trying his best to be a model of propriety on the set following his drug scandal, but he was soon giving her a full-blooded response. Just as their passionate encounters were about to spill over into daily life, Mitchum decided to check with his boss, Howard Hughes. Without telling Ava, he telephoned Hughes and said, "Listen, how would you feel if something happened between Ava and me?"

"What do you mean?" Hughes replied.

"Well, I heard she used to be your girl, so I'm asking you," Mitchum said.

"Bob, if nothing does happen everybody's going to think you're a pansy."

The following morning on the set as Ava and Mitchum waited in front of the camera to start filming, she stood on tiptoe and whispered in his ear, "Well, what have you decided? Do we have an affair, or don't we?"

Mitchum knew that an affair with Ava was one further complication he did not need in his troubled life, and he stood firm. A brief but real friendship developed. He'd drive her home after the day's shooting, and they'd sit in the car outside the house as Ava unburdened her problems.

Her face scrubbed clean of film makeup, hair pulled back from her fine-boned features, wearing Levi's and loafers, she was again a fresh young country girl. Her problems, however, could not have been more rooted in the fishbowl existence of a notorious movie star. Her second marriage had broken up in public and her career lacked direction.

Though she had by now come to regard herself as an

actress, Ava still did not have much judgment in selecting pictures, making little use of the narrow margin of maneuverability available to her in the studio system. Artie, who was a good judge of scripts suitable for her, was no longer there with his overpowering but frequently sound advice. She was left to the devices of MGM, which she quite correctly felt was primarily interested in serving its own interests.

When she sought Mitchum's advice he told her to take the money and run. The star's philosophy was simple: if his career soured there was always trucking, his previous occupation. But Ava didn't want to return to anything. So she did what movie stars always did in moments of uncertainty; she switched agents.

For some time she had been pursued by the prestigious, much-loved Charles Feldman, who specialized in women clients. Feldman was top-drawer Hollywood, a good-looking man whom his friends called "the Jewish Clark Gable." His wife, Jean Howard, was the only woman over whom L. B. Mayer was known to have lost his head. When Jean married Feldman, L.B. attempted to blackball all his clients and tried to get other studios to do the same. By then Feldman represented such a large slice of Metro's talent that had the order been obeyed the studio would have ground to a standstill.

The move to Feldman not only put Ava's career in better hands, but it brought her into the upper reaches of movie society, which was enjoying a period of postwar lavish living. Ava began to decorate the famous Sunday brunches at the David Selznicks'; she went to formal dinners at William Wyler's Beverly Hills house, which had Utrillos on the walls. She played croquet on David Niven's lawn and watched Darryl Zanuck play polo at Will Rogers Park.

For all the merriment, there was an undertone of gloom about these social rituals, for the sun was slowly setting on the Hollywood of *Gone With the Wind* and the huge, busy prewar studios. Television, of course, was cutting a swath in movie audiences and causing ripples of concern in the industry. Movie attendance in the Los Angeles area was down thirty percent, and in southern California alone, 134 movie houses had closed in two years. One chain of more than five hundred theaters across the country had registered an overall decline of forty-three percent in its audience from its 1946 high. One exception in the chain's overall pattern of shrinking box-office returns left no doubt that television was the culprit: audiences had increased slightly in its Rocky Mountain houses, where television still had not penetrated.

Even more immediately frightening was the political witch-hunt then gathering momentum and spreading the poison of suspicion and betrayal in the movie community. Lastly, runaway productions—Hollywood films made entirely in Europe to take advantage of lower production costs—were siphoning off work from the studios at home.

In 1948, Darryl Zanuck, then in full power as head of 20th Century–Fox, started the runaway production trend by sending Tyrone Power and Orson Welles to Italy to star in *The Prince of Foxes,* a costume epic about the Borgias. The film was to be shot on location in Tuscany, its natural setting, with studio work in Rome. There was great skepticism in Hollywood that the facilities existed anywhere in Europe to make a major motion picture. Zanuck not only finished the picture but claimed to have done so at $118,000 less than it would have cost at home.

What Zanuck started was nothing short of a mass migration across the Atlantic, and the tax implications of living and working in Europe for part of the year had become a constant topic of conversation not only among stars but also among technicians. The names of Cinecittà in Rome and Shepperton Studios in England rapidly were soon as familiar to film people as Culver City and Burbank.

As one of the top women stars Ava inevitably found herself cast in a European movie. She came close to landing the lead in *Quo Vadis*, which was to be filmed in Rome, but director Mervyn LeRoy's final choice was the more ethereal Deborah Kerr. A few weeks later, director Albert Lewin offered Ava the starring role in *Pandora and the Flying Dutchman*.

Lewin, a tiny, partially deaf former MGM staff director, had written the role of the flippant, willful playgirl specifically for Ava, and she had fallen in love with it at first reading. The surrealist implications of the role fascinated her. The prospect of going to Spain on location made it doubly exciting. The fact that *Pandora and the Flying Dutchman* was another loan-out added to the attraction.

Before going abroad Ava accompanied Robert Mitchum to Chicago on November 14, 1949, for personal appearances in conjunction with *My Forbidden Past*. At Hughes's insistence, she was accompanied by a bodyguard, a former Los Angeles District Attorney's investigator named Kemp Niver, otherwise known as Shamus. Niver was to prove his worth when Ava, piqued that Mitchum continued to hold out, took off on a tour of South Side jazz dives. Swathed in a strapless black cocktail dress, with a small hat on her head, and wafting Chanel No. 5, she caused a stir as she went from club to club, all alone, ordering scotch on the rocks at every stop.

In the morning hours Niver received a call in his hotel room. It was Ava. "Come get me, Shamus," she said. Niver drove to a club and found her locked in the powder room, where she had taken refuge from a mob of overenthusiastic fans.

To "punish" Mitchum, Ava decided to board the train for New York instead of returning with him to Los Angeles. In New York, she accepted a last-minute invitation to the premiere of *Gentlemen Prefer Blondes*. Her escort was Frank Sinatra.

# 9

# Frank

Ava knew a lot about Frank Sinatra: "the Voice," "the Verce," "the Sultan of Swoon," or—as Jimmy Durante once called him—"Moonlight Sinatra." It was difficult not to know *something,* for his personality imposed itself on a fascinated American public. But Ava knew more than most. Both were notable figures in the colorful fresco of Hollywood life. More than that, they were linked by one of those sequences of interlocking relationships typical of the movie community. Ava had been married to Artie who was previously married to her friend Lana, whose relationship with Frank had posed the one serious threat to date to Sinatra's marriage to Nancy.

When Frank's name began to be publicly and persistently linked with Lana's, Nancy Sinatra, the daughter of a plasterer from Frank's home town of Hoboken, New Jersey, said *Basta!* Her husband wanted "freedom without divorce," Nancy complained to Hedda Hopper. Well, it was going to be both or nothing. Frank moved out of the family home in the Holmby Hills district of Beverly Hills and into an apartment of his own.

But the couple were reconciled shortly afterward by Phil Silvers, of all people, at his opening night at Slapsie Maxie's. Silvers had invited Nancy without telling her that Sinatra would be appearing as an invitation artist. Then, when Frank had sung his song, which was "Going Home," Silvers led him over to Nancy's table, and as the couple embraced the audience gave them a standing ovation.

Frank's brashness had always grated on Ava. Somehow, there had always seemed to be too much macho for too little man. Whenever she was invited to his home he invariably had his own records playing in the background. His treatment of Lana naturally did little to improve her view of him.

But the Sinatra she met in New York in November 1949 was different. He seemed more subdued, more vulnerable, and Ava found herself warming to him. Their evening together was electric, and they parted promising to see more of each other on the Coast.

Back in Los Angeles, Ava began to have second thoughts. For a week she avoided Frank's calls. To buttress herself from his attentions she again sought the company of Robert Mitchum. The burly actor warily took her to dinner at the Brown Derby on Vine Street and told her she would be crazy to get involved with such a different, complex character as Sinatra—just as he, Mitchum, would be crazy to embark on a relationship with her. But Frank was very persistent and single-minded in the pursuit of Ava. After more soul-searching, Ava finally agreed to accompany him to a party in Palm Springs.

Clearly, she could not ignore the fact that Frank was a married man if only because it could result in bad publicity. But Frank's domestic situation was his problem: if he wanted to fool around on the side, she was not going to judge him.

Probably the last thing on her mind when she began seeing him regularly was the thought of marrying him. What she had to decide was whether her attraction for the emaciated crooner was strong enough to overshadow what she was sure, given both their characters, was going to be a stormy affair.

Ava's more perceptive friends realized that at the root of her fascination with the singer were a number of parallels between Sinatra and Artie Shaw. Physically, there was no similarity. Compared to Shaw's solid good looks, Sinatra was hollow-chested, scrawny-limbed—a stringbean who looked as though a breeze would blow him over. But they were alike in their spiky, difficult personalities, their extraordinary vitality, and most of all in the state of their careers just at the moment when Ava happened along.

Though still a major talent, Frank was losing the Orpheus-like power he had exerted over millions through his songs for the past five years and appeared to be on the slide toward total eclipse. Ava's thwarted motherly instincts found new scope in a man undernourished, frightened and desperate. She had a deep-seated urge to help him out.

Women in hordes had been yearning to mother Frank Sinatra for years. That was the magic of his appeal. But changing musical tastes had cut into Sinatra's record sales, which had been falling steadily. The world of pop was moving toward a harder sound, the full, muscular voice of Frankie Laine, the country traditions of Nashville's Hank Williams. Tony Bennett ("Cold, Cold Heart") and Perry Como began to steal Sinatra's crooning, bel-canto audience, and Nat King Cole his clubland status. The week of his New York meeting with Ava, the 1949 *Downbeat* poll showed that Sinatra was out of the top spots for the first time since 1943.

Billy Eckstine headed the poll. Frankie Laine was second. Bing Crosby and Mel Tormé tied for third place, and Sinatra could only manage the fifth spot. Moreover, the singers who figured in that year's Best Discs compilation were Eckstine, Doris Day, Frankie Laine, Perry Como, Vic Damone, Nat King Cole, Sarah Vaughan, and even Metropolitan Opera star Dorothy Kirsten—but not Sinatra.

Early in 1950, the passing of the Sinatra craze would be complete with the arrival of Johnnie Ray out of Detroit cabaret. Following the Sinatra pattern, Ray not only conquered the teenage market of theater, radio, and record sales, but won over the swells and sophisticates of the Copacabana. He was to reign more or less intact until the arrival of Elvis Presley six years later.

Even Sinatra's film career was in a slump. In 1948, MGM pushed him into a terrible musical picture, *The Kissing Bandit*, then finally reteamed him with Gene Kelly in a pair of song-and-dance movies. The first of their 1949 pictures, *Take Me Out to the Ballgame*, set no box-office records. Gene Kelly and director Stanley Donen had conceived a thin story which never managed to come to life, and the picture amounted to little more than a string of brilliantly executed but disconnected song-and-dance routines.

The next Donen-Kelly film was the smash-hit musical *On the Town*—three sailors on a twenty-four-hour furlough in New York—based on a successful Broadway show. MGM did not publicize it as a Sinatra picture but as an all-singing, all-dancing extravaganza, giving Gene Kelly first billing. The decline in Frank's fortunes was now in full free-fall. Even the beautiful performance which he gave as Kelly's shipmate could not help. Despite the success of *On the Town*, the press began to carry stories that Metro was thinking of terminating Sinatra's contract.

Sinatra was too smart a man not to be fully aware of the extent of the setback to his fortunes. In 1951, *Time* magazine approached him for an interview in connection with a projected cover story on Ava. The singer's reply was that he did not want to become entangled in anything involving Ava's career. He was trying to avoid tainting her bright prospects with his own disastrous ones.

The motion picture press corps could have been a useful ally in these difficult times, but the press was Sinatra's nemesis and would remain so. The columnists huddled over their typewriters like the witches in *Macbeth* around their caldron, stirring up more toil and trouble, and contributing to his decline. His long war with the press had its origins in his temperamental outbursts against photographers and reporters, usually outside nightclubs and restaurants late at night; his political activism; and the stories of his unsavory connections.

Defying the studios' unwritten law against stars becoming publicly involved in politics, Sinatra campaigned for Roosevelt in the 1944 Presidential elections. At a Madison Square Garden rally he declared that Roosevelt was "good for me, and my kids, and my country." In a predominantly Republican industry his continued open support of Roosevelt irritated Hollywood's power elite. Worse, it earned him the enmity of the influential Hearst newspaper chain, and Hearst papers all over the country never lost a chance to trumpet his problems, tantrums and setbacks. Westbrook Pegler, the aggressive Hearst columnist, used to call him "the New Dealing Crooner." Later, following an outburst against the Franco regime in Spain which proved very unpopular in the Catholic community, Sinatra's most loyal constituency, the label gave way to the more topical one of "Pinko." When Senator Jack Tenney of Ohio came out with one of the first lists of alleged pro-Communist movie stars sometime later, including Gregory Peck, Danny Kaye and Katharine Hepburn, Sinatra's name was on it.

The stories of his underworld connections—particularly

his friendship with Chicago's Fischetti brothers, Rocco and Joe, who were Al Capone's cousins and prominent in what was left of his mob—had recently returned to the headlines. Sinatra had shown up in Havana, Cuba, seemingly on the fringes of a summit meeting of syndicate bosses chaired by Lucky Luciano, then already barred from reentry into the United States. Sinatra's subsequent explanation of how he came to be seen there in the company of some of gangland's leading figures was that he had gone to Havana knowing nothing about the meeting.

At this juncture, the vagaries of Ava's shooting schedule intervened, with far-reaching repercussions. *Pandora and the Flying Dutchman* was postponed from January until April because James Mason, who was to play the Dutchman, first had to complete another picture. Consequently, Ava's departure for the Spanish location was postponed until March.

Without the delay, her affair with Sinatra might well have petered out when she left for Europe. Given those extra three months, it took root. Ava and Frank were careful to avoid being seen alone in public. In restaurants and night-clubs and at boxing matches—a shared passion—they sought safety from gossip in groups. But rumors were soon flying about the true nature of the relationship. Then, after the New Year, Frank accepted a two-week inaugural engagement at the newly completed, mammoth Shamrock Hotel in Houston, and decided that Ava should go along with him. His friends strongly advised him to change his mind, or at least to wait until after the Shamrock's opening celebrations, which were to last several days. Planeloads of celebrities had been invited, and the press was sure to be there in full force. Inevitably, Ava and Frank would become the focus of a lot of attention, and the minor scandal now surrounding their affair would burgeon into a major one. But Frank was determined to show off Ava, and she to be flaunted. Following the usual practice, she asked MGM's permission to leave Los Angeles. With no film commitments pending, MGM had no valid reason to withhold consent, but Eddie Mannix, fearing the adverse publicity, said no.

Ava insisted on appealing to L. B. Mayer, who endorsed his aide's decision. Mayer even pretended that she had to remain in Los Angeles because he had decided to star her in a new film, forgetting that she was already lined up for *Pandora and the Flying Dutchman*. Characteristically, he also lost his temper, unleashing a string of synonyms that passed in those days for the word "whore." Ava sat impassively through his tirade and then drove straight to the airport and took the plane to Houston to join Sinatra, who had already departed. "Neither Metro nor the newspapers nor anyone else is going to run my life," she said.

Metro's worst fears were borne out almost from the moment the two lovers were reunited. The Shamrock, built by a Texas oil millionaire with the specific intention of dwarfing the Waldorf-Astoria, was a massive pile surrounded by seven acres of grounds. It had a huge, fan-shaped swimming pool, and five hundred original paintings in the guest rooms, which included four luxuriously furnished penthouses available for rent at $2,100 a month. The photographers had a field day chasing Ava and Frank around this lavish setting, and Frank was soon on the warpath.

He and Ava were eating at Vincent's Sorrento restaurant one evening as guests of Mayor Oscar Holcombe. Edward Schisser, a photographer for the *Houston Post,* came over to the table while they were tackling a large bowl of spaghetti and asked Sinatra if he could take a picture. Later Frank said, "I refused graciously." According to Schisser, however, he said, "Beat it, you bum." Whatever he said, there was no mistaking what he did when Schisser did not move away. Frank sprang to his feet and seemed on the point of smashing the camera and punching Schisser. When Ava screamed and hid her face, Frank abruptly sat down. The incident was to characterize their relations with the press. Frank's outburst was self-defeating, since it made them even hotter news.

By now Ava knew that Frank's qualities did not include an ability to keep his cool. This was true in private as well as in public, and the tensions did not stop outside the door of their hotel suite. Their relationship swung like a pendulum between moments of passion and eruptions of bitter argument. Both were intensely jealous of each other, quick to take offense and mercurial in their behavior.

Frank had plenty of reason to be tense. In the space of that fortnight in Houston the underpinnings of his world suddenly crumbled. George Evans, his long-time publicist and friend, died of a heart attack, and Frank had to fly to New York for the funeral, leaving Ava alone briefly in her opulent surroundings. Manny Sachs, Sinatra's steadfast ally in the recording world, resigned from the board of Columbia Records, Sinatra's studio. In the middle of his personal crisis, he was bereft of the only two associates whose voices counted for something in his public and private situations.

At the same time, Metro began negotiations with MCA, Sinatra's agents, to sever his movie contract, and a liquidation of $85,000 was agreed on. Before it could be paid, Nancy filed for separate maintenance in Santa Monica District Court, and at the preliminary hearing the judge instructed the studio to pay the money over to her directly, in three installments, as interim support. The break with Nancy affected Frank deeply. He began having trouble with his voice, and some people in his circle remembered George Evans' assertion during a similar bout with voice problems that these crises were caused by nervous stress—the "guilt germs."

Ava for her part was badly shaken by the public reaction to the affair. Some of the columnists turned on her, calling her a home wrecker, and she began to receive anonymous phone calls and poison pen letters. One correspondent who was to plague her persistently for years and who always managed to find out where she was, anywhere in the world, invariably began his or her letters: "Bitch . . . Jezebel . . . Gardner."

Another shock was her first contact with some of the unsavory characters of Frank's circle. Many of his former friends and hangers-on had begun to give him a wide berth, but not by any means all of them. Through Ava, Rocco Fischetti met one of her girl friends and began to date her, until one day he flew into a rage and threw a cup of coffee in her face in Ava's presence. Ava also discovered that Frank had received a telegram from Quarico "Willie Moore" Moretti, a childhood friend, but now a *capo*, reminding him in a paternalistic Sicilian way that he had "a decent wife and children." But it was when she found herself drinking in the Copacabana with Sinatra and mobster Frank Costello that Ava protested mildly. Sinatra snapped back with a reply straight out of a gangster movie. "Don't cut the corners too close on me, baby," he said.

No one, either at the time or since, has ever actually linked Sinatra with the illegal activities of his underworld friends. Possibly, he needed the aura of toughness and violence these associations lent to his personality to compensate for doing something as intrinsically precious as crooning for a living. Going around with an escort of bodyguards and drinking with dubious characters in nightclubs somehow enhanced his macho image. Or did it? "Are you as tough as you sound?" Artie Shaw has said that he asked when Sinatra warned him to stop seeing Ava. "Yeah," Frankie replied. "Then why do you need him?" Artie said, pointing to the bodyguard standing behind Frank. There was, of course, no answer to that.

The confrontation took place in New York, where Sinatra was singing at the Copacabana throughout March, his first Copa date since his years of peak success. For the sake of appearances he and Ava had traveled to New York on different planes and checked into separate suites at the Hampshire House, the Central Park South hotel that was home away from home for Hollywood personalities. In New York, Shaw has said Ava sought him out and poured out the story of her trials and tribulations with Frank. Ava now sought reassurance from Artie. How had the sex been between us? she wanted to know.

"Christ, if everything had been on a par with that, we would have been together for eternity," Artie replied.

"It was fine for me, but was it all right for you?"

"What are you talking about? You were one of the great sexual things in my life," Artie insisted.

Artie commented that sexual incompatibility was often a signal of other problems in a relationship.

"He wants to marry me," Ava said.

"What about you? Do you want to marry him?" Artie asked.

"I've got to," Ava replied.

"What do you mean, you've got to?" Artie said.

"How would it look if I didn't? I pulled him away from Nancy. Now he's having a tough time. He's having problems with his voice. The studio has dropped his contract. I've just got to, that's all."

There was no doubt that Frank loved Ava. For all his romantic escapades, he was deeply devoted to his family, and in separating himself from his children to be with Ava he was paying the supreme price. In her own way, Ava loved Frank. But the memory of her two failed marriages was still too fresh to make the prospect of a third very attractive. Still, she was deeply moved by his plight and filled with a sense of mission to see him through his dark days to a resurgence which she was convinced waited round the corner.

As he struggled with the tensions of the only significant engagement he had had for many months, Ava was constantly at Frank's side. Fear of failure made him more jumpy than ever. On opening night, his hands shook and he seemed on the verge of collapse. Ava insisted a doctor be called to give him a mild sedative. After doing what she could to soothe him, she went out front, where the atmosphere was unfriendly, as if the audience had come to see him fail. As she took her place all eyes were upon her, but she focused only on Frank, willing him to succeed. It did not help when he was either foolish or unthinking enough to sing "Nancy with the Laughing Face" and there were snickers from the Park Avenue sophisticates. Ava brazened out the scene, but she was badly unsettled by it.

At a late supper hosted by Manny Sachs she confronted Sinatra. "Did you have to sing that fucking song? It made me feel like a real fool."

"It's been a good-luck song for years, I sing it in almost every big show," Frank replied defensively.

"Well, don't expect me to sit out there and get laughed at every night," said Ava. "Either the song goes or I go."

Frank dropped the song. For the first ten nights of the engagement, Ava attended, fervently hoping her presence would bolster his courage. His performance was well received, but he continued to be extremely nervous, often venting his tension on Ava. The news from Hollywood was not good. No major studio had expressed interest in giving him a film contract. Calls from his children asking when he was coming home reduced him to tears. Nancy herself said nothing, pressing on with the separation proceedings.

Ironically, considering the history of their own relationship, Ava sought to escape from her problems by visiting

Artie Shaw at his Manhattan apartment. Frank had made it clear that he was jealous of Shaw, but Ava made no attempt to conceal the fact that she was going to see her former husband. The publicity surrounding the affair upset her. "They won't leave me alone," she complained to Shaw. "I wish they'd leave me alone."

"Leave you alone?" Artie echoed. "But, Ava, look at the swath you're cutting."

"I don't need that, I'm an actress."

"Oh shit, Ava, I know girls who can act rings around you and they can't even get arrested, but you—you're making five thousand a week. I'll tell the shortest short story in the world. I just made it up, two sentences. First sentence: Once upon a time there was a little girl who said, 'Why don't they leave me alone?' Sentence two: And, one day, they did."

It was true that Ava enjoyed the limelight and the other trappings of stardom and wasn't going to give them up in a hurry. But her conception of publicity was the controlled, comparatively nuisance-free kind orchestrated by Howard Strickling and his capable staff, not the white-hot glare surrounding her affair with Sinatra, which was beginning to take its toll. Unwilling to admit even to herself that high tension was endemic to both the nature of the affair and the personality of the protagonists, she shifted the full weight of responsibility to the press. She had originally tried to persuade MGM to assign a publicist to travel with her, as Les Peterson had traveled with her and Mickey Rooney, but the studio had refused, washing its hands of the rapidly growing scandal.

Ava confided to Artie that she was tired of sharing every evening with Frank's Sicilian cronies and wished they had more opportunity to meet "normal people." Artie invited Sinatra and Ava to dinner with some of his New York intellectual friends. But Ava appeared alone, making Frank's excuses. She did not add that she had defied Frank's orders not to come herself.

They had just begun dinner when Ava received a phone call. It was Frank. "Well, I just called to say goodbye," he said.

"Where are you going, Frank?" Ava asked. "Why can't I come, too?"

"Not where I'm going, baby," Frank replied.

Then came the unmistakable sound of a pistol shot, followed by a pause, and then another shot.

Terrified, Ava ran out of the apartment and into the night, leaving the dinner party in disarray. Hailing a taxi, she rushed back to the Hampshire House to find a small crowd in the corridor outside Frank's eighth-floor suite watching several firemen break down the door, which had been bolted from the inside. David Selznick, who had heard the shots from his nearby suite, was directing operations. "Ava, I think the son-of-a-bitch just shot himself," he said. But Ava was too terrified to reply.

Soon the door was flung open, and they surged through the living room into the bedroom. Frank was sitting up in bed in his pajamas, alive and unhurt. When Ava recounted what had happened to the police who were on the scene, Frank denied firing any shots. His story was that he had called Ava to say good night and then gone directly to bed. The next thing he knew the door had been broken down and his bedroom was full of people.

The truth was that Frank and Ava had quarreled sharply over whether or not to accept Artie's dinner invitation. In the end, Ava had sailed out of the room, leaving him in a fury. Coincidentally, the papers that day headlined a story referred to as "the Telephone Killings." A young engineer named Emory Holt shot and killed his unfaithful wife, her lover and himself in their Manhattan apartment while his mother listened on the telephone in Burbank, California, 2,500 miles away.

A few days later, on Sunday, March 26, Ava flew to London, en route to Spain, in a dejected mood. During the drive to the airport, Frank talked grandly about his plans for movies and records. Both knew, however, that things were destined to get worse before they got better. It was a strained, nervous parting.

A PORTRAIT
GALLERY

*The Killers*

Ava Gardner, age four

Ava at fourteen

A family portrait: back row, brother Jack, Mom, sisters Elsie and Inez, and Inez' husband; front, sister Myra and husband, Ava, Bappie and child

Ava with Artie Shaw on their wedding day

An early publicity still

With husband Mickey Rooney, following Ava's
emergency appendectomy

With Mario Cabre

Ava with friends Mrs. Van Heflin, Lana Turner's husband
Bob Topping, Lana Turner, and Van Heflin, attending a premiere

Ava talks, Howard Hughes listens

Cover girl

Ava kisses husband
Frank Sinatra

Lester Glassner Collection

UPI

Jorge Tablada Collection

With Deborah Kerr and Richard Burton in
*Night of the Iguana*

*The Barefoot Contessa*

UPI

Spanish bullfighter
Luis Miguel Dominguin

Italian actor Walter Chiari

Ava bullfighting. A month later in the same bullring she was
thrown from her horse and was injured

Ava today

# 10

# In Spain

Ava fell in love with Spain on the evening of her arrival in Barcelona on March 27. One reason she was attracted to the script of the movie was precisely because Pandora is hotly pursued by the greatest matador in Spain. She spoke no Spanish, but the men stared at her with undisguised admiration and suddenly she felt completely at home.

Spanish music reached down and stirred the depths of her being. At the first sound of the flamenco she wanted to leap up and dance. The ocean location, the stretch of coast eighty miles north of Barcelona, and the solitary beaches south of the city near Sitges—all excited her. In 1950 the Costa Brava was untouched by tourism, a far cry from the hectic playground of today.

It was inevitable that Ava and Mario Cabre, the Spanish bullfighter who was to play the matador in *Pandora and the Flying Dutchman*, would become lovers. Mario Cabre was not the country's greatest bullfighter, but he was arguably the most popular. He was a moderate performer in the ring, but his flashy style appealed to the gallery. In the ring or out, he had a gift of keeping himself in public view. He dated celebrated international beauties, which kept his picture in the paper, and he wrote poetry with a strong, sentimental flavor.

To Ava, he seemed the ideal Latin type: proud, fierce, moody, tall by Spanish standards, dark-skinned, broadshouldered, narrow-hipped and wasp-waisted. He dressed to perfection in dark suits with slim, elegant ties. He had impeccable manners and immense charm. In Spanish, he had a highly cultured line of conversation. He spoke very little English, but the language barrier did not inhibit him, and Ava was left in no doubt of his feelings and intentions. Nor, for that matter, was anybody else, for Cabre produced a stream of passionate verse declaring his undying devotion—verses which found their way into the popular magazines. He wrote of caresses sprouting from her fingers, vibrating kisses, and rapturous lips.

To the poetic matador, his friendship with the American movie beauty was a dream that had arrived on a breeze. To the Spanish press, the affair was manna from heaven, and reporters made the most of it, considerably helped by Cabre himself with his unerring instinct for self-promotion. An accomplished guitarist, he serenaded Ava underneath the window of her rented villa, and somehow a photographer always happened to be within camera range.

Ava did not remain immune to the handsome Spaniard's ardor. What American girl of her generation, visiting Europe for the first time, would have? But she was not overwhelmed either. She accepted Cabre's attentions with a cool sophistication worthy of her current screen character, Pandora Jones. In the movie, the Dutchman, found guilty of killing his wife, is condemned to roam the seven seas, putting into port once a year, until he finds a woman prepared to die for him. Until that moment of loving self-sacrifice for the Dutchman, Pandora streams through life like his ship, the *Flying Dutchman,* trailing a flotsam of rejected suitors in her wake. Even the suicide of a jilted racing driver does not shake her; she views it as the inevitable upshot of his failure to capture and hold her affections.

Not for the first time, nor the last, a film role had captivated Ava's imagination and was shaping her behavior. Fantasy and reality merged into one. Basking in the attention of the Spaniard while Frank Sinatra wrestled in New York with his "guilt germ," she *was* Pandora Jones. Occasionally the real Ava surfaced, and then phone calls crisscrossed the Atlantic as she lay sleepless at night.

She had taught herself to repeat parrot fashion, *"Por favor, quiero hablar con Nueva York,"* and to give Frank's Hampshire House number. Sometimes, Frank called her. "Gimme my big girl," the famous voice would intone. Usually his big girl was not in and her carefully coached maid told him Ava was shooting. By mutual agreement, it was usually Ava who placed the call. The production company was paying the phone bills at her rented villa.

Ava was too canny not to realize the dangers of a double life. On one romantic evening with Cabre, they dined at a small restaurant where Cabre grabbed a guitar and sang to her as she ate, afterward driving along the coast in the moonlight to a hilltop nightclub outside Barcelona where Ava joined the flamenco dancers, capturing the spirit—if not the steps—of this difficult Spanish dance. As she and Cabre left, hand in hand, they ran into Harold Warrender, who also had a role in *Pandora.*

"Having a good time?" Warrender asked.

"Wonderful, but now I'm going home to sober up," she said. Then Ava, who was not drunk, asked Cabre to drive her home. Cabre sulked all the way. Back at her villa, she put on one of Frank Sinatra's long-playing records, picked up the telephone to call the Barcelona operator, and spoke the familiar words, *"Por favor, qu:ero hablar con Nueva York . . ."*

Ava's affinity for the role of Pandora helped her overcome the tedium of working with a director known for being slow. Lewin took hours to prepare a shot, arranging her as carefully as an ornament, and then spent more hours shooting the same scene a dozen times because of some imaginary wrinkle in her dress, a hair out of place, or the suspicion of a fluffed line or to get the desired number of angles and "cover shots." Ava bore it all with characteristic unflappability. She even made jokes about it. When Lewin seemed bent on spending the entire day on a close-up, she said very loudly and with exaggerated sweetness, "Al, do you think I could go to the bathroom after the eighty-first take?"

Ava insisted on doing her own swimming in the picture, even though she could have had a double. She wrote to a friend that, as a result of having to spend hours in the still-cold Mediterranean in the nude while Lewin shot and reshot the sequence in which Pandora swims out to the Dutchman's anchored schooner, she had "the bluest tail in Spain." But the situation, swimming in the night to meet the unknown, captured her imagination. She found the scene, with its surrealist overtones, exciting. And part of the excitement was the prospect of appearing in the nude on the deck of the schooner in the following scene, Pandora's first meeting with the Dutchman. With the restraints of the Hays Code still in full force, the idea of exposing herself to the view of millions, even if it was only from behind, appealed to her rebellious streak.

Lewin cleared the set and shot a rear view of Ava scrambling onto the Dutchman's boat, with the silvery moonlight casting shadows on her nude body. In the reverse shots filmed from James Mason's viewpoint, a bulkhead obstructed

Frank arrived on May 10, pale and weak, and the lovers were reunited in Ava's villa. He brought her six bottles of Coca-Cola and a large pack of Wrigley's chewing gum. The gift delighted Ava more than the expensive Van Cleef & Arpels diamond necklace he proffered shortly after his arrival.

That night they slipped past the waiting photographers and went for a long drive down the coast, retracing the route Ava had taken on several occasions with Mario Cabre. As they returned, rain sprinkled the car windshield. By next day, it had become a raging storm which wiped out the day's shooting, and the next, and the one after that. Frank and Ava moped indoors, marooned from the *cordon insanitaire* of persistent photographers huddled under the trees outside.

Frank suffered from the time change. His throat was like an open sore. Worse, he had forgotten to bring one of his medicines, and a doctor had to be found to prescribe a substitute. Ava cooked spaghetti, which Frank could not eat.

Ava enlisted Frank's help as a singing coach. She had heard that MGM was to film *Show Boat,* the Oscar Hammerstein–Jerome Kern musical, and hoped to try out for the part of Julie, the tragic half-caste played by Helen Morgan on the stage.

Despite his sore throat, Frank harangued her endlessly about being "unfaithful." Ava protested that Cabre meant nothing to her. "If I hear that Spanish runt has been hanging around you again I'll kill him *and* you," Frank warned in a painful whisper in the middle of a dinner she gave for him.

Ava snapped back, "Be reasonable, Frank. We're in a fucking movie together, and he's supposed to be my lover—how can he avoid being near me? Besides, I haven't raised hell about Marilyn [Maxwell], have I?"

"That's different. We're old friends, and you know it," Frank whispered.

"Well, Mario and I are new friends," Ava said.

The local Associated Press reporter reached Sinatra on the phone and asked him to comment on Mario the matador's confident assertion, made to reporters on his thirty-fourth birthday, that "after Sinatra's visit is over and Ava and I are alone again, I think you will find that our love has survived." After insulting the reporter, Sinatra turned to Ava and there was a scene. It was the first time she had borne the brunt of his rage. It would not be the last.

On the third day, there was a break in the weather and Ava and Frank gave the photographers the slip and drove to Tossa del Mar, where they spent the afternoon shopping, unnoticed by passersby.

But after five uncertain and uncomfortable days together came an uneasy parting, Ava back to *Pandora* and Mario Cabre, Sinatra to his disintegrating career. Just as he was leaving for Barcelona Airport, Ava learned that she must immediately film a scene in Tossa del Mar, ironically the triumphal entry into the town of the victorious matador. The rain had cleared and the local Festival of San Ysidro made it possible to recruit a large and excitable crowd.

As Frank's plane was taking off, Cabre was borne into the town square in a horse-drawn carriage through streets lined with cheering, flower-throwing villagers and peasants. In the front row was Ava. When the carriage passed, she shouted, "Mario *mio*, Mario *mio*," blowing kisses. Resplendent in his glittering matador's costume, Cabre beamed.

When the scene was over, he strutted over to Ava and presented a bouquet to her. The crowd in the square applauded as he kissed her on each cheek and hugged her, at the same time using up almost his entire English vocabulary. "Hello, baby," Cabre said. "Okay, baby."

Baring his chest, he showed where the bull's horns had penetrated during the previous day's filming. "I was thinking of Ava," Cabre declared, "even when the bull had me up against the rail. I think of her all the time. She is sublime." The extras went wild, and there was still more cheering at the end of the day's work when Mario and Ava left arm in arm. "We are going to dinner," Cabre announced; the onlookers nodded enviously.

Details of Ava's public reunion with Cabre were immediately relayed to the States by a Metro publicist on the set. Frank Sinatra arrived in Los Angeles in time to read all about it in the *Los Angeles Times.* "I hadn't counted on that bullfighter," he confided to his friend and collaborator Manny Sachs, putting on a brave face. "He was an added starter they ran at the last minute. I never did meet him. I assume that what he said was just a publicity stunt." Frank drove directly from Los Angeles airport to Nancy's house and spent the evening and night at home with his wife and children before flying back to New York—his voice somewhat improved by now—to complete his Copacabana engagement.

In June, location work on *Pandora* ended and the cast flew to London for studio work on the picture. Cabre brought over three notebooks containing eighteen love poems to Ava: "The night was of one color/ Yet when she appeared the sky held a rainbow/ For Ava was the dawn and when our hands touched, the air was filled with tenderness." When his scenes ended, Cabre hung around for as long as he could, but bullfighting commitments eventually forced him to return. He mournfully presented to her an ancient Spanish gold doubloon, which she affixed to her charm necklace, next to Howard Hughes's middle finger.

Ava shrugged off her friendship with Cabre. What about those goodbye kisses at London Airport? she was asked. "I kiss a lot of people goodbye," Ava said. As for Frankie, "He's a wonderful guy, but I'd rather not say anything." She did add, however, that she had had no contact either by phone or by letter with Sinatra since his return to America.

She moved into a beautifully furnished flat in London's fashionable Berkeley Square and continued working on the closing sequences and interiors at Metro's Boreham Wood studios. She reveled in her first taste of London living. She began to date a titled Englishman. She forgot about Mario Cabre.

MGM, however, did not. Pleased with the flow of exotic news stories Mario had generated and with the corrosive effect he'd had on the unpopular Gardner-Sinatra affair, MGM shrewdly began to contemplate a movie loosely based on Ava's Spanish adventure.

*Montes the Matador* it was to be called; unsurprisingly it would star Ava Gardner as a glamorous movie star on location in Spain who has an affair with a bullfighter. Fortunately for MGM, public announcement of the project was delayed until studio executives had had a chance to see Cabre on screen and assess his movie potential.

One glimpse of his *Pandora* footage was sufficient to scuttle the project. Dore Schary remarked, "Let's sign up the bull, we'd get a better performance." The matador was so hammy on screen that his *Pandora* debut had to be cut to the bone. MGM didn't jettison Cabre instantly; someone would resurrect *Montes the Matador* every time Ava's fondness for bullfighters manifested itself, which was to be often.

Ava was living it up in London, a city still shaking itself free from wartime suffering and deprivation, and already displaying the vigor that would later set the pace and style of the 1960s. Ava prowled the streets at the wheel of a low-slung blue Cadillac loaned to her by the studio, taking in the patched-up beauty of her surroundings. London in 1950 was like a boxer who had just won a tremendous fight—bruised and punchy and triumphant.

One of Ava's haunts was the Screenwriters' Club in the West End. She became a fixture in the downstairs bar, sipping vodka martinis while a procession of Hollywood acquaintances stopped by her table. Nunnally Johnson, writer of the screenplay of John Steinbeck's *Grapes of Wrath,* invited her to dinner in the restaurant upstairs, where she talked happily about Spain and London and—soberly—about Frank Sinatra. When she laughed, it was a throaty roar, with head thrown back. She gave an order to the waiter: steak. It was at a premium in heavily rationed postwar England, and she grimaced at the size. "Bring two more," she shouted to the departing waiter. Johnson looked at her in astonishment.

Sinatra arrived for his first singing engagement in England, and an apartment was found across Berkeley Square from Ava's. The enthusiasm of the London audience at the Palladium put the clock back to his sensational appearances at the New York Paramount. Sinatra responded with an exhilarating performance. His voice was back in top form, and he regained his self-confidence.

For once, their interlude was a happy one. The British press were atypically restrained, respecting their privacy. It was an exceptionally mild fall, and they roamed hand in hand through the city's parks and gardens. In those days, you could still—as the saying goes—walk across London on grass. Their open affair raised some English hackles. One London clergyman delivered a scathing sermon on declining moral standards among modern young women, calling them "painted trollops who worship at the shrine of Saint Ava Gardner."

Socially, Ava and Frank were in demand; the high point was their presentation to Princess Elizabeth and Prince Philip after a movie charity performance. Ava received lessons from a titled Englishwoman hired by the studio to teach her to execute the mandatory, straight-backed deep curtsy to royalty without falling over. The stars were presented in alphabetical order. Ava preceded Stewart Granger. By coincidence, Frank followed Granger's steady girl friend and future wife, Jean Simmons, another rising British star.

Encased in an ivory silk strapless gown hastily designed for her by Irene, who had flown to London to supervise its manufacture, Ava stood out among Englishwomen still coping with postwar austerity. She was shaking with nerves, but she curtsied without a wobble.

# 11

# A Battling Courtship

On August 14, 1950, Ava ran out of excuses for delaying her return to Los Angeles and wrenched herself from London. After her European initiations, she expected to find life in the movie colony dull and provincial. She found much worse—a mood of fear and political and industrial uncertainty. Television was a bigger attraction now than the movies, with disastrous results at the box office. The golden age was ending; it could no longer be taken for granted that most Americans would go to the movies on Friday and Saturday nights.

The McCarthy hearings descended on an already demoralized industry, poisoning long-established friendships and creating feuds which in some instances would last over a decade—or forever. An unofficial studio boycott list, which no one had ever seen but which everyone could recite, circulated in the industry. Cautious as ever, MGM told Ava to avoid certain old friends because of their involvement in the hearings. Agents and informers were everywhere. She and Frank may themselves have been under surveillance by the FBI as suspected Communist sympathizers. The mere fact that Sinatra had courted political visibility as an active Democrat was enough to make him a target for 1950s paranoia. On September 8, agents were watching the home of Ida Lupino, who had loaned her backyard for a meeting of the dissident left-wing faction of the Screen Actors Guild. The session ended in an uproar when antileftists Ronald Reagan and William Holden challenged the principal speakers.

In Los Angeles Frank kept up a facade of discretion to avoid hurting Nancy. Ava resented this. He had had no compunction about dating her openly in New York, Spain and London, but in Los Angeles he now refused to appear alone with Ava. When they went out to restaurants or nightclubs, they traveled in a group. Afterward, Ava either was taken home by friends or had to drive herself.

In Frank's mind Los Angeles was Nancy's turf and would remain so until their marriage ended in divorce, which he now sought but which Nancy refused to give him.

Nancy had won her separate-maintenance suit on September 18. She was awarded one-third of her husband's annual salary on the first $150,000, ten percent of the second $150,000, and a descending scale thereafter. She retained the house in Holmby Hills, some shares in her husband's corporation, and the custody of their three children, Frank Junior, Nancy and Tina. Throughout the hearing in Santa Monica Court, Mrs. Sinatra was in tears.

She refused to discuss divorce, clinging to the conviction that Frank always came home after his flings and that Ava, like the others before her, was a passing fancy. Frank's insistence on a clandestine romance could not have helped Nancy in coming to terms with the breakup of her marriage. Mike Romanoff had a table set up for Frank and Ava in a small

George Sidney, who had made her first Hollywood screen test.

Ava was anything but the studio's first choice for the role of Julie; the search was concentrated on finding a more mature actress. Ava was tested at her own insistence and instinctively resumed her North Carolina accent for the test. To her disappointment, she was asked to mouth to Lena Horne's recorded voice, although she had meticulously learned the songs while on location in Spain.

The test was outstanding. She identified with Julie, not only as a Southern girl but also because Julie was the girl on the margin of her man Bill's life, the "second best," and that too was something Ava understood. On the strength of her test, Metro had no hesitation in assigning her the role, postponing *Scaramouche* to allow her to appear first in *Show Boat*. The flow of approving mail told the studio executives they had made a popular choice. The public's approval was a source of intense relief to Metro, for it meant that the publicity of her affair with Sinatra, which was proving so damaging to the singer himself, had actually enlarged her following. By the end of 1950, the Publicity Department was mailing out three thousand black-and-white portraits of Ava every week—signed by a team of three staff members who worked from a sample of her autograph—placing her second only to Esther Williams among Metro's popular women stars.

She was bitter that the studio insisted on dubbing in the songs by a professional. It embarrassed her to have to mouth the lyrics while Kathryn Grayson and Howard Keel, her co-stars, were singing their roles, but she grumblingly complied with the decision. Then the singer dubbing her voice was dropped by George Sidney because she lacked the emotional quality he felt he needed for Julie. Now Ava saw her chance to persuade MGM to let her use her own voice.

Sinatra rallied to Ava's cause with characteristic energy, cajoling his musical director, Axel Stordhal, Columbia Records's Manny Sachs, his music-publishing partner and former Tommy Dorsey arranger Ben Barton, and other influential friends in the music business to lobby MGM executives. In the end the studio relented, giving director Sidney the green light to assess Ava's capacity to sing the role. She was tested a second time, without the help of Lena Horne, and the results were remarkable.

She had worked out a half-singing, half-speaking style which proved extremely effective. When she finished singing "Can't Help Loving That Man of Mine," the film unit applauded, and Ava started to cry. It was one of the most satisfying moments of her life.

But her satisfaction was short-lived. Less than a week later, Ava reported for work to find George Sidney waiting for her in her dressing room. The usually genial director seemed grim and uncomfortable; the studio had developed cold feet about Ava's singing, and Sidney had to break the news that a second professional singer, Annette Warren, was replacing the one fired earlier.

Ava stormed out of the dressing room and out of MGM. She drove home to Nichols Canyon, vowing never to set foot in the studio again. When she failed to return to work for three days, the roles were reversed and it was Metro's executives from Benny Thau to L. B. Mayer himself who were appealing to Frank Sinatra and his circle to persuade Ava to return to the set. "Frank, she was wonderful in the singing test," Thau admitted. "But she doesn't have the range, and with such a well-known property, the studio simply couldn't take the chance." Ava eventually cooled down and went back to work—but not before she had extracted a written commitment from MGM that she would sing the role in the soundtrack album.

Ava never forgave MGM for reneging on their commitment. Her future dealings with the studio brought out an aggressive streak in her nature. She frequently warned her agents to protect her interests vigilantly; more than one found himself her *former* agent for failing to take her admonishment seriously.

*Show Boat* ended up being a pleasant experience for Ava, anyway. She got along well with Grayson and Keel, and the picture earned her good notices. Unknown to the studio, reality clashed with image on the set of the picture; in defiance of Metro's strict ban on drinking on the job, Ava, Kathryn and Howard smuggled tequila sunrises into the dressing rooms. They were happily sloshed by the end of the day's work.

Oddly, MGM did not build on Ava's personal success in the picture. After *Show Boat* the best they could offer her was *Lone Star,* an undistinguished Western except for the fact that her co-star was Clark Gable. Even the pleasure of working with Gable again did not compensate for the mediocrity of the Borden Chase script. When Ava protested, she was advised that Mayer personally wanted her to play Martha Craden, a Texas newspaperwoman of the 1840s; refusal would mean certain suspension. Ava's protracted London interlude had made a sizable dent in her bank balance, and she could not afford the financial setback of a suspension. She meekly agreed to film this trivial, flag-waving Western in which she and Gable seemed to be costumed in hand-me-downs from *Gone With the Wind,* and the dialogue rejoiced in lines like:

GABLE. You're a lot of woman. . . . You're a strange woman . . . but still a lot of woman.
AVA. You know, you're a strange man, but quite a lot of man.

Gable was drinking heavily following the breakup of his marriage to Lady Sylvia Ashley—although probably more out of relief than remorse, since the marriage had been unfortunate. The effects of his drinking showed in his face; memos were exchanged in the Publicity Department lamenting that "Gable doesn't look like Gable anymore," and requesting heavy retouching on the publicity stills. The King's head was shaking as it had in *The Hucksters*, and the love scenes were difficult to film.

Another source of irritation for Ava was being forced to portray a *journalist*, a species she had come to loathe since the start of her affair with Sinatra. She was partly taking her cue from Frank, and partly giving vent to her own distaste for the gossip writers.

"What in the name of Christ are you doing this [movie] for?" she asked the director, Vincent Sherman.

Sherman shrugged. "God knows," he said.

Ava liked the straightforward, reserved filmmaker. But when he started giving her books on psychology she shied away as though she'd been bitten by a hornet. When he handed her *Our Inner Conflicts*, by Karen Horney, she yelled, "Oh Christ, Vince! I don't want to read any more books on neurosis. Artie fed me that crap and I'm so damned mixed up as a result I don't know what I'm doing."

Sinatra usually joined her for lunch and they ate in the privacy of Ava's dressing room while Sherman, Gable and his close friend Spencer Tracy ate in the commissary. Not without a twinge of guilt, she looked forward to the days when Sinatra was unable to come to the studio; then she could eat with "the boys" and enjoy Tracy's wit. One day, she complained that the prim Dore Schary had cut a scene in which she walked joyfully down the street after spending the night with Gable. Tracy said, "Since Schary took over, nobody gets laid at MGM."

The new production chief was rapidly gaining control of the studio. His power struggle with Mayer had complex corporate ramifications, but the crux of it was Schary's success with several films Mayer had not wanted to make. The two men were in conflict over most potential properties—*Lone Star* had been Mayer's choice, not Schary's—and now that Schary had proved himself right on several key occasions, he was able to go over Mayer's head for authorization. Their fights were now open, and abusive. On June 22, 1951, midway through the making of *Lone Star*, Mayer found himself isolated in the corporation and resigned, effective August 31. There was shock in the industry, but little sadness anywhere, except in the offices of such Mayer stalwarts as Mannix, Thau and Strickling. Mayer was severed with close to three million dollars of MGM's cash; he hung on to seventy-five percent of it through clever work by his tax lawyers. Schary was proclaimed head of the studio. A three-man executive committee, composed of Mannix, Thau and producer L. K. Sidney, was appointed to serve directly under him. In the clinch, Mayer's people prevailed. The old guard was unanimous in its dislike of Schary, a bespectacled, owlish, cerebral, generally courteous and refined man, and united in its effort to prevent any decline in MGM's preeminent position in the industry. *Their* lion must roar proudly on. It didn't, and after two years of failure, Schary's office came to be known as "Hollywood's Panmunjom" before ceasing, in 1955, to be Schary's office at all.

Shortly after taking over, Schary lunched Ava. He extolled her value to Metro and promised her better parts. "No more *Lone Star*s," he said. It seemed to her, Ava replied, that her next scheduled picture, *Scaramouche*, was nothing but another *Lone Star* in period costume. Then no *Scaramouche*, Schary decreed. The role of the actress who loses Stewart Granger to Janet Leigh went to Eleanor Parker.

In an attempt to win Ava over, the new management gave Ava a voluntary bonus of $20,000 "in appreciation of your cooperation and of the excellent services rendered by you," and granted her a hiatus for the remainder of 1951. In August, she celebrated by going to Mexico with Frank, hoping that the trip would repair their collapsing relationship. The conflicting pull of his family and his love for Ava, plus his professional slump, was tearing Sinatra apart. By the time they left for Mexico, he seemed to be on the verge of a nervous breakdown.

At Los Angeles International Airport, he looked pale, drawn, and ill with sleeplessness and strain. He refused to board the American Airlines *Mexico Clipper* until all the photographers were removed from the tarmac and the ramp. The photographers refused to leave and became menacing when attempts were made to dislodge them; their jobs were at stake, after all. Finally, Ava made a dash for the plane, a copy of *Life* magazine over her head as a shield from the cameras. Frank finally agreed to follow her some thirty minutes later, and rushed into the plane scattering photographers and cameramen as he went.

Depressed and exhausted, they sat miserably, holding hands, until they reached El Paso for a forty-five-minute stopover, where the press once again swooped down. Arriving in Mexico City, they decided to confront the press in an attempt to avert more scandal. Frank denied that they were going south of the border to arrange a divorce from Nancy, echoing a statement Ava had made during the El Paso stopover that the trip was "purely for vacation purposes." It didn't work; photographers continued to hound them wherever they went.

On August 4 they left for Acapulco in an attack bomber, the private plane of the former baseball magnate Jorge Pasquel. At the airport Frank got into another fight with a photographer who advanced too close to them. An armed bodyguard threatened to execute the photographer with his revolver unless he handed over the film. Frank shouted to the pressmen: "This is a private affair of my own, and I don't have to talk to anyone, you sons-of-bitches."

They spent the first evening at a nightclub owned by Hedy Lamarr's husband, Ted Stauffer. Lamarr, never one of Ava's admirers, pointedly ignored her even though the couple were supposed to be her guests at the club. Furious, Frank threatened "reprisals." At one point in the evening, Frank and Ava walked onto the elaborate stone balcony of the club and necked passionately in the darkness, attracting a large audience. A nightclub patron said later, "They thought nobody could see them when they went out there to smooch in the dark. But they were wearing white clothes and it was better than the floor show."

On the night of August 8, Ava and Frank flew back to Los Angeles in Jorge Pasquel's bomber. The plane landed in a secluded corner of the noncommercial area of the airport, but half a dozen newsmen had been tipped off and stood in wait. Frank and Ava, who had been bickering on the flight, dashed to a waiting car. Frank got behind the wheel and stepped on the gas. Bill Eccles, the KTTV cameraman, shone a spotlight on Frank's face through the car windshield. The car came straight at the reporters, almost pinning them against a wire fence, narrowly missing them. "Next time I'll kill you, you son-of-a-bitch," Sinatra screamed as the car disappeared in a cloud of dust.

# 12

# Mrs. Frank Sinatra

After the breakup of her marriage, Nancy Sinatra, who had always been a homebody, became almost a recluse, retiring into her Beverly Hills home, seeing only a few relatives and friends, and lavishing attention on her three children.

She refused to agree to Frank's repeated requests for a divorce, partly on moral grounds as a practicing Roman Catholic and also because she remained convinced that he would one day come back to her. She perceived him as a man possessed by some private demon and she prayed for him daily at mass in her parish Church of the Holy Savior on Santa Monica Boulevard. Whenever reporters approached her, she smiled wanly and said nothing.

Frank continued to have free access to the children. Indeed, Nancy encouraged his visits, knowing that he adored them and hoping that the strong family ties would act as a form of exorcism and bring about the miracle of reconciliation. Sinatra often stayed to supper, which Nancy cooked. A true Italian wife, Nancy knew Frank's favorite dishes and cooked them superbly.

They would sit around the dining table, Frank, Nancy and the children, Nancy Junior, Frank Junior and little Tina, barely a year old, making domestic small talk about school, and music, and old friends—forcing back the clock to the days when no clouds marred their sky. In the end it was usually Nancy who shattered the make-believe scene by bursting into tears and running into the kitchen to hide her sadness from the children.

Ava always knew when Frank had been visiting his family. It was not difficult: a vicious, black mood enveloped him and he criticized everything she said and did.

It was the turbulence of a Catholic conscience in full cry. But Ava, whose two previous marriages were now completely forgotten, never understood the depth of Sinatra's inner torment. Like most Catholics contemplating divorce in the 1950s he was feeling the heat of widespread disapproval. Public criticism did not deter him. What was unnerving was that friends, relatives, priests and cronies whose love and respect he prized were urging him to give up Ava and go back to Nancy; their argument was always the same: was it really worth breaking up the family?

Sinatra nonetheless kept his sights immovably fixed on marrying Ava. No doubt he loved her and no doubt the attention surrounding their well-publicized relationship served as a psychological counterweight to his artistic decline. Ava was a rising star, Frank a falling one, but whatever else was going wrong for him, the old sex appeal was still there.

Ava wanted to quit the screen and have babies and raise a family with Frank. She could not have picked a worse time to contemplate retirement. With the release of *Show Boat*, MGM proclaimed her the studio's number-one female star.

Howard Strickling's hyperbole machine was working overtime on her behalf. In the still photographers' barnlike studio on the lot, Clarence Bull was grinding out scores of glamorous nine-by-twelve glossies of her.

But Ava still got no real enjoyment out of moviemaking. She had no illusions about her limitations as an actress. On top of that, she died "a nervous death," as she put it, whenever she had to face a live audience, and reporters, with their prying questions, confused her and gave her a constricted dry throat. MGM had broken her spirit over the *Show Boat* dubbing fiasco. Now she was twenty-eight and she wanted children before it was too late.

Ava's refrain in private conversation as well as press interviews was, "I like the simple life, I'd like nothing better than to be a housewife and mother."

The Legion of Decency warned MGM that Ava was skating on thin ice and risked a boycott of her movies. Then at the height of its power as the nation's watchdog of movie morality, the Legion of Decency had banned films for less. MGM decreed, "Sabotage the relationship before it sabotages us." Ava was deliberately paired with Metro's handsomest, most eligible stars as escorts to premieres and studio social functions; clearly the studio hoped that one of them would become a habit. But aside from Sinatra's fits of jealous rage every time Ava sailed off on the arm of a Richard Greene or a Stewart Granger (not without justification at times, especially in the case of the former), their romance survived—and continued to be a thorn in Metro's side.

Letters from fans poured into the studio requesting "the truth." The official explanation emanating from Culver City was: Sinatra, a married man legally separated from his wife, was one of Ava's large circle of friends.

That captured as much of the flavor of the real thing as calling Romeo and Juliet teenage chums or Abelard and

Heloise nodding acquaintances. It was one of the most tempestuous love affairs Hollywood had ever witnessed, by turns magnificent and petty, tender and vicious, and always furiously paced. It would be inaccurate to say that they found happiness in each other. But what was happiness? A dog asleep in the sun? Frank and Ava could go from ecstasy to despair in a single encounter.

The wear and tear of their romance showed clearly in Frank. His nerves stretched taut as catgut on a well-strung tennis racket. While he hurled himself at reporters and other windmills, Ava sat quietly, an amused, cynical smile in her eyes, fingering her charm necklace. Seeing them together at Romanoff's one day, Hedda Hopper remarked to her lunch companion, "I predict that a year from now, when their romance is over, Frank Sinatra will be as thin as your backbone, and Ava will be more beautiful than ever."

At the end of March 1951, Sinatra recorded his intensely moving version of "I'm a Fool to Want You," a song for which he shared the writing credit. The agony and uncertainty echoed in that song lasted through spring and early summer. Frank was filming *Meet Danny Wilson* at the time, and a constant procession of priests and psychiatrists visited the set trying to dissuade him from divorcing Nancy. Sometimes Frank's children would appear for lunch with their father, accompanied by a priest from the Catholic Counseling Service.

Frank's understandable edginess began to affect the rest of the cast. He got into a dispute over one of the musical numbers with his co-star Shelley Winters, who promptly slugged him and walked off the set. For two days, the picture was shut down. Then Shelley received a phone call from Nancy. "Shelley, [if] Frank doesn't get the $25,000 for this picture, the bank might foreclose the mortgage on the house," she said. "My children are going to be out on the street. Please finish the picture or they won't give me the $25,000." Shelley Winters went back to work.

At the end of June, Nancy capitulated. She told Louella Parsons, the only gossip columnist to win her confidence, "I'm convinced that a divorce is the only way for my happiness as well as Frank's." She surely meant peace of mind, because happiness would continue to elude Nancy for some time to come. It was not until August 18, after the infamous trip to Mexico, that Frank filed for divorce in Reno, where he was appearing at the Riverside Inn. He called a press conference to announce what was already common knowledge. "Miss Gardner and I," he said, "will definitely be married."

Part of the proceeds of Frank's Reno gig went to pay legal fees connected with the lengthy divorce negotiations. The rest paid for a new motor yacht called *Tina*. Ava was disappointed that it was not named after herself. Frank's fortunes afloat soon proved as dismal as they were ashore. After taking possession of the boat, he rammed it into a pier on Lake Tahoe and damaged the prow. A second accident within the same month was more serious. On August 29, Ava, Frank, Bappie and a group of friends went to Lake Tahoe for a picnic on the *Tina*. A freak storm blew up suddenly, hitting the boat and drenching the picnic party. Frank threw the anchor into the soft shale and the party jumped over the side and waded ashore soaked. A violent gust of wind caught the vessel midships, capsizing and sinking her. The couples were badly shaken up by the accident; had the yacht been caught in deep water the consequences could have been fatal.

Henceforth, they confined themselves to dry land. As they impatiently marked time waiting for the Nevada divorce to become final, the tensions between them mounted. In early September, newspapers reported that Sinatra had attempted to commit suicide following a quarrel with Ava.

Sinatra vehemently denied the suicide attempt. "This

would be a hell of a time to do away with myself," he said. "I've been trying to lick this thing for two years and I've practically got it licked now." It was simply that he had made the mistake of mixing sleeping pills and alcohol, he explained. "Tuesday night, Miss Gardner, my manager Hank Sanicola, and Mrs. Sanicola dined at the Christmas Tree Inn on Lake Tahoe. Ava was returning to Hollywood that night. We came back to the Lake and I didn't feel so good. So I took two sleeping pills. Miss Gardner left by auto for Reno and the plane trip back to Hollywood. By now, it was early Wednesday morning. I guess I wasn't thinking, because I'm very allergic to sleeping pills. Also, I had drunk two or three brandies. I broke out in a rash. The pills felt kind of stuck in my chest. I got worried and called a friend who runs the steak house here. He sent a doctor, who gave me a glass of warm water with salt in it. It made me throw up, and I was all right. That's all there was to it—honest."

True or not, the episode raised a lot of eyebrows in Hollywood. Ava was summoned to the office of Eddie Mannix, who told her MGM wanted a wedding—and fast. Mannix fixed the date, September 19. Metro's lawyers were to take over the divorce negotiations to ensure against further legal delays. Two days before the planned wedding, Ava and Frank "went public" in Hollywood at the premiere of *Show Boat* at the Egyptian Theatre, and Metro made the reassuring discovery that Ava's personal popularity had not suffered as a result of her affair with Sinatra. If anything, it had enhanced her allure.

The theater had been given an elaborate "Southern" look with black children jumping up and down outside to the sound of banjos, bales of cotton piled high, and a reproduction of the helm room of the great showboat *Cotton Blossom* itself. Ava looked stunning in an emerald-green satin and black-lace gown designed by Irene, a diamond necklace and a Sydney Guilaroff hairdo. The crowd stacking the bleachers screamed, *"Ava!"* and *"Frankie!"* Photographers swarmed around them, and they behaved impeccably, smiling and waving.

"It gives me great pleasure and pride to be able to escort Ava publicly," Sinatra announced, savoring the moment. "I've cared for her for a long time—almost a year now. I'm very much in love with her and it's wonderful to know we can be seen together without hurting anyone. There's no ill feeling about it anywhere—with anyone."

Despite good notices, Ava's success was overshadowed by the disappointment and frustration of having to postpone the wedding once again because—Metro's lawyers notwithstanding—the interlocutory decree was still not available.

On September 26, she was trying on costumes at MGM when she collapsed and was rushed to St. John's Hospital in Santa Monica, where doctors diagnosed a severe virus infection and extremely low blood pressure. Ava lay in the hospital for almost three weeks, most of it without the comfort of Frank's presence because of a New York singing engagement. The illness robbed her of the female lead in an MGM remake of *Flesh and the Devil;* its famous antecedent had starred Garbo and John Gilbert and had led to their celebrated affair. The second time around, the film was to star Ava, Ricardo Montalban in the John Gilbert role, and Fernando Lamas.

Ava's doctor, William Webber Smith, said she was "tired, exhausted and had lost a lot of weight." The drama of her affair had taken its toll after all. She was still shaky when she joined Frank in New York on October 28. But the news, four days later, that the divorce from Nancy had finally been granted on terms close to those of the previous year's maintenance suit did wonders for her recovery. She flew with Frank to Las Vegas for a closed final hearing before Judge A. S. Henderson, lasting all of four minutes.

Then they checked into the Sands Hotel, posed smilingly for photographers, and ordered champagne and dinner in their suite. But the divorce cut Frank adrift from his cultural roots. His sense of isolation not just from his family but from his very being was greater at that moment than any comfort Ava could provide.

Still, the way was at last completely clear for them to marry. But where could they marry quietly? Los Angeles was out of the question. Press and fans could turn the whole thing into a circus. New York was not much better in that respect. So they settled on Philadelphia, where they could count on the help of close friends from the recording industry.

To Howard Strickling's chagrin, Ava shut MGM out of her marriage plans altogether. Anxious to avoid a clash between Sinatra and the reporters on her wedding day, she refused to reveal either the time or the place of the ceremony. She did not trust Metro's Publicity Department not to leak the secret venue to their friends in the press. Anne Strauss, the publicity girl who often worked with her on fashion layouts, tried hard to get her to promise to send the studio a telegram. "Ava, you owe it to Metro to tell them the minute you are married so they can release it first," she said. Ava was adamant.

Predictably, the secret got out. On November 4, reporters tailed Ava and Frank to Philadelphia City Hall, where, in the chambers of Orphanage Court Judge Charles Klein, they filled in the marriage license application. Ava lied about her age, which she gave as twenty-four, while Frank correctly stated that he was thirty-five.

Then came the bad news. Judge Klein told them that Philadelphia had a three-day minimum waiting period before the license could be issued. Their hopes of marrying later that day shattered, they fled through a rear exit while the judge diverted the attention of reporters with an impromptu press conference.

For the next several hours, they drove around the city with Axel Stordhal in a rented limousine, trying to find a judge who was willing to waive the waiting period and marry them immediately. When that failed, they took the train back to New York. Sinatra's fury was not assuaged when he discovered more reporters and photographers clustered at Pennsylvania Station. Assuming that the couple were now married, they said, "Let's have a wedding-day smile, Mr. Sinatra. Kiss the bride, Mr. Sinatra. Just once, Mr. Sinatra."

"Get out of my way, you sons-of-bitches," Frank shouted as a railroad detective and a bodyguard swung their umbrellas to hack a path through the crowd, then fought a rearguard action while the couple sprinted the last quarter of a mile to yet another waiting limousine.

Frank literally shoved Ava inside and dived in after her. "Christ, why are we always on the run?" Ava reflected as she breathlessly rearranged her clothes and groped for her composure.

It was back to the Hampshire House, separate suites, and a deep, divisive depression. Some couples are brought closer together by adversity, but Frank and Ava were not. Crises brought out the worst in both of them. In an attempt to ease the tension, they accepted an invitation to make up a foursome with James and Pamela Mason. The evening ended in disaster.

Frank was unsociable, Ava broody. She was in no mood to ignore Frank's admiring glances at an attractive woman sitting nearby. Colorful invective flew across the table. As Ava gathered her things to make her exit, she said to the Masons,

"It looks like I'm through with him. I can't even trust him on the eve of our wedding." Frank followed her into the night. The quarrel continued all the way to the Hampshire House, where Ava flung her diamond necklace out the window of her suite and locked the door against Frank. It took the combined efforts of Axel Stordhal, James Mason and Bappie to make peace.

The wedding was on again, and so was the elaborate secrecy surrounding it. Questioned by reporters, Nancy Levy, wife of Isaac Levy, a member of the board of Columbia Records and a close friend of Sinatra, confided that the wedding would probably take place at her home, 3333 West Schoolhouse Lane. The more skeptical newshounds checked with a leading Philadelphia florist, and with the top caterer, both of whom revealed that they had been engaged for a wedding on November 7 at the home of Lester Sachs, 1445 Maple Drive. Lester Sachs was Manny Sachs's cousin, and reporters smelled a rat. When Ava and Frank arrived at the Sachs home for the afternoon ceremony, they walked straight into a stakeout. "How the hell did you creeps know where to find us?" Sinatra snarled.

At the last minute, Frank's parents, whom Ava had met only once, joined the small party. Others included Bappie, still not thrilled at the prospect of Sinatra as a brother-in-law, Stordhal and his wife, the Sachses, Ben Barton, and Dick Jones, Sinatra's arranger, who played Mendelssohn's Wedding March on the piano.

Once again there was no white wedding for Ava, but she looked resplendent in a Howard Greer cocktail-length dress of mauve-toned marquisette stiffened like brocade, with a strapless top of pink taffeta. Around her neck was a double strand of pearls, with matching pearl-and-diamond earrings.

As she started down the stairs on the arm of Manny Sachs, who had been chosen to give her away, she hesitated a split second too long, causing him to lose his footing and slither down several steps before recovering his balance. Ava retained her composure throughout the ceremony, but Sinatra was taut and kept fluffing his responses. They exchanged plain platinum rings and were pronounced man and wife. As they embraced gently, Sinatra sighed, "Well, we finally made it." Then Ava edged warily across the room to Sinatra's mother, Dolly, and took the hesitant woman in her arms. Dolly burst into tears.

During the champagne buffet, Ava remembered to send off a one-line telegram to Anne Strauss at Metro, signing herself "Ava Sinatra." Anne Strauss immediately alerted Strickling, who released an announcement to the wire services. The Publicity Department was thus spared the embarrassment of hearing the news from reporters calling the studio for details and reaction. Meanwhile, outside the Sachs house, a steady drizzle had begun to fall on the waiting newsmen in the darkness and the six detectives hired by Frank to keep them at bay.

At 8:30 P.M., Ava and Frank emerged into the rain arm in arm, laughing and slightly sozzled, and without a word to the waiting cluster of wet figures in the dark drove quickly away. Ava wore a mink stole, Frank's wedding present to her. She had given him a gold locket with a Saint Christopher medal on one side and a Saint Francis on the other, and her picture inside. Frank had opened his shirt and hung it on the gold chain around his neck along with the silver Saint Francis medal he had worn since boyhood and the gold medal of Our Lady of Lourdes—Nancy's wedding present.

As the couple were leaving, Manny Sachs had taken Ava aside and told her quietly, "Look after him, Ava. He's had some hard knocks and he's very fragile. It isn't going to be easy living with a man whose career is in a slump."

Ava glanced over at Frank, who was baring his teeth at the

press. "I'll do anything to make him happy," she said, ingenuously but sincerely.

"Then help him get back his self-confidence," Sachs said.

Determined to avoid another scene at La Guardia Airport, Sinatra had chartered a twin-engine Beechcraft to fly them directly to Florida for their honeymoon. It was only when they boarded the plane that Ava realized she had forgotten her trousseau case. Shrugging, she said, "Let's fly to Miami without it."

They arrived at dawn and were driven to the Green Heron Hotel. By morning, the trousseau bag sent on by the Levys had still not arrived, leaving them with nothing to wear except their going-away clothes and some odds and ends from an overnight bag.

It was a brief honeymoon—one more day in Florida, four days in Cuba, and then back to New York, where Sinatra had his ritual exchange with reporters at the airport:

"Where are you going to stay, Mr. Sinatra?"

"None of your damn business."

"Where are your boxing gloves, Mr. Sinatra?"

"That's a funny line. Very funny."

"Are you in trim?" (This from an elderly photographer.)

"If you were my age and weight I could take you."

"What do you weigh?"

"I think I could show you."

Ava put a restraining hand on his shoulder. Sinatra got into the car and slammed the door.

Days later, on the plane from New York to Los Angeles, they read that Artie Shaw had announced, "For the first time in my life, I'm engaged." Shaw's fiancée was the Hollywood actress Doris Dowling. For the benefit of those who had lost count, or never knew, the paper recalled that Shaw had been married six times but had never before made public the intervening stage of becoming engaged. He sounded somewhat defensive: "Just because I'm about to marry for the seventh time, you'd think I was guilty of something."

Perhaps because the newspaper story had jogged her memory, it was to Artie that Ava turned in her first domestic crisis. Less than a fortnight after the wedding, when Ava and Frank were at Sinatra's house in Palm Springs, a trivial late-night argument grew into a full-scale battle that neither seemed able to win or break off. Ava stormed out and drove off into the desert.

It was eight in the morning in Manhattan when her call woke Artie Shaw.

"I'm leaving," she said. "I'm going back to L.A."

"Cutting out for good?"

"Well, no. But I can't handle it—it's fucking impossible."

"We all know that. Give it two months and it'll get worse."

"No, it can't get worse."

"What are you going to do? Get a divorce?"

"How can I? How would it look?" Translation: What would people think of me if I deserted him after causing the breakup of his marriage? Also, how could I cope with the knowledge of having three failed marriages behind me before reaching thirty?

The truth, as always, was more complex. Frank's combination of abrasiveness and personal crisis, which alienated others, appealed to Ava. Her attraction to men with problems and her masochistic streak found full expression in the relationship.

She went back to him, and they continued to delight and torment each other. Ava set about trying to help Sinatra rebuild his career. It was uphill work.

In December, they boarded a TWA Constellation jet bound for London, where Frank was to appear in a big charity show in the presence of the British royal family. At a reception afterward, Ava exchanged jokes with the Duke of

Edinburgh, with whom she also did the samba. Her husband traded angry words with the press, squabbled with the orchestra during rehearsals, and received only a lukewarm reception for his singing.

After his London success of 1950, this was a bitter disappointment. His "jinx," he complained, had followed him across the Atlantic.

It certainly had. Returning to their rented apartment after the charity show, they discovered that they had been burgled. Frank's Christmas present to Ava, a diamond-and-emerald necklace, was gone from its box on the dressing table, along with Frank's cameo cufflinks and a platinum-and-sapphire ring. Ava was shocked to tears over the loss of the necklace. She knew it was a gift Sinatra could ill afford.

# 13
# Hemingway Heroine

A few weeks after her marriage, Metro loaned out Ava to 20th Century–Fox to star in what Ernest Hemingway used to refer to as *The Snows of Zanuck*, producer Darryl F. Zanuck's movie version of *The Snows of Kilimanjaro*. Fox announced that Hemingway himself, remembering Ava from *The Killers*, had urged Zanuck to cast her as Cynthia, the 1920s girl whom the big-game hunter (Gregory Peck) loves, loses and then finds again as she lies dying in a Spanish Civil War battle.

It made a good publicity story, but Fox's original choice for Cynthia had been Anne Francis. The clothes were designed with her in mind and made to her measurements. Then the studio cast Susan Hayward as Helen, the hunter's rich wife, raising serious questions about the plausibility of the crucial scene in which the delirious Peck mistakes his wife for his lost

Cynthia. The blond Anne Francis did not look sufficiently like Susan Hayward to make the mistake believable, even in delirium. Clearly one of them had to go, and Susan Hayward was the bigger star.

Frank was not thrilled to see his wife return to work. His Italian heritage demanded a family-oriented spouse. If his courtship of Ava had taught him anything about her at all, it was that she was not domesticated. Frank was fastidiously clean, washed his hands with great frequency, took two or three showers a day and often got uncontrollable impulses to empty ashtrays. He dressed with meticulous care, always wearing a hat or hairpiece to cover his receding hairline. Ava continued to leave her clothes lying in heaps where she stepped out of them, rose after noon, and cooked only when she felt the urge to do so, usually in the middle of the night. When his friends came to visit, Frank sensed the unspoken comparison with Nancy's well-ordered household. And now Ava was going back to work, just when he needed her to dispense reassurance and encouragement in his current mood of doubt and self-pity. For all her professed indifference to her career, Ava was not about to give up filmmaking. She was at the peak of her earning power and the principal breadwinner in the family, while Frank had to plead with old friends to get a concert date or a club engagement.

Besides, Ava liked and understood the character of Cynthia from her first reading of the script. Cynthia was a reflection of her own personality—bruised, cautious, generous, coarse-grained, unlucky, and tragic. Cynthia reawakened in Ava memories of Spain, Mario Cabre, guitar music and the candid stares of lusty men. Not that any portion of the picture would actually be shot *in* Spain; every one of the novel's many settings was reproduced on the Fox lot in Century City, including tracts of the African bush country and huge chunks of Kilimanjaro.

For Frank, the film could not have come at a worse time. He had persuaded an old friend to get him a show at the New York Paramount, and Ava's shooting schedule coincided almost to the day with the length of this gig. He made it clear what he expected her choice to be. Film or no film, he needed her at his side in New York. He insisted.

"But it's the perfect part for me," Ava protested.

"The perfect part for you is being my wife," Frank shot back.

When Ava took the problem to director Henry King, he squeezed and trimmed the schedule to cram her shooting into ten days. Sinatra still had to leave for New York without her for rehearsals, but at least she'd be there before opening night. On that condition, Sinatra gave his grudging consent.

On day one Henry King filmed Cynthia's first meeting with Harry, the big-game hunter, in a Paris bistro, a key scene in establishing Cynthia's character. "Are you Charles's lady?" Gregory Peck says, referring to Cynthia's date. "No, I'm my own lady," Ava replies.

But was she? Frank's incessant calls to the set were making her tense and miserable as he delivered threats if shooting overran the agreed date. And, of course, it did.

King had left the big, complicated Civil War battle scene for Ava's last day. Against a background of exploding charges and milling extras playing Franquistas and Loyalists, Harry rediscovers his Cynthia, now a volunteer ambulance driver, minutes after she has been fatally wounded in the fighting. Peck cradles the dying girl in his arms and calls in vain for stretcher bearers to come to her aid. At midday King broke the news to Ava that the shooting would spill over into the following day. She was furious. "That motherfucker is going to give me hell when I tell him," she said. "And I'm just going to sit there and take it." She was right: Frank's reaction left nothing to the imagination.

The misery of that last day's filming put a damper on what had been an exciting experience for Ava. *Kilimanjaro* was one of the few films she enjoyed making. She liked the cast and the crew, and she felt that she was giving a good performance.

Most of the critics agreed, and made a point of exempting her from the generally uncomplimentary comments about the film. Their main complaint was that Hollywood had once again failed to capture the essence of Hemingway's narrative. His simple, graphic, episodic style was half cinema already, but screenwriters have never succeeded in bringing his work the rest of the way to the screen. Ben Hecht, a master of screenwriting technique, once said of Hemingway, "The son of a bitch writes in *water*." Aldous Huxley, asked to adapt a Hemingway novel, turned down the assignment. Too tall an order, he said. "What Hemingway has to say is in the white spaces between the lines."

Ava's life continued to be torn between Frank's needs and Metro's demands. On April 22, 1952, F. L. Hendrickson, MGM's talent manager, sent a memo to Louis B. Mayer:

EJM [Eddie Mannix] advised me that Miss Gardner was in to see him yesterday, at which time she told him she would not be in *Sombrero*. She also indicated her intention of leaving for Honolulu. EJM told her that she could not go to Honolulu without permission from the company. Miss Gardner was to call EJM this morning. EJM said that she did not call him and that he had been advised that she left for Honolulu today.

EJM said that we should take whatever steps that are available to us re. suspending her contract.

\*    \*    \*

The Honolulu trip was Frank's doing; they both needed a vacation, he said. She returned to the bleak sentence of indefinite suspension, a disciplinary measure combining ostracism and financial pressure. For the first time in her career, she was literally locked out of the studio. No roles were offered her; no more money came in.

MGM was no longer trying to force her into *Sombrero;* after Ava's refusal of it the part had gone to Yvonne De Carlo, and the picture was now in production. But the studio was determined to teach its increasingly rebellious star a lesson.

Agent Charles Feldman now came to her rescue. Her seven-year contract with MGM was due for renewal and Feldman refused to enter into negotiations while his client was under suspension. Metro had to back down, revoke suspension and pay compensation for her layoff before negotiations could get under way.

In the 1940s, stars meekly accepted Metro's standard contract without a murmur, and the question of raises was left to Mayer's personal benevolence, which could be considerable. But as their power increased in the '50s so did their demands. Contract negotiations became one of Hollywood's growth industries, involving batteries of studio executives, agents and lawyers.

Ava's contract for another seven years with MGM set a new record for legal wrangling. The meetings went on through spring and summer, with Ben Thau leading the MGM team and Feldman on the other side of the table, usually accompanied by two other agents from his office, Ava's personal manager Ben Cole, and her attorney.

In its sixty-six pages of legalese Ava's new contract decreed that she would make twelve movies over the seven-year period at a rate of not more than three a year, starting at $130,000 per picture for the first three films, but going down to $90,000 for each of the remaining nine. For tax purposes, no more than $180,000 was to be paid in the calendar year, the balance deferred to the following year. The first three films were to be made outside the United States to take advantage of the generous tax breaks bestowed at the time by Uncle Sam on Americans living and working abroad.

By contemporary standards, Ava's new pay scale was respectable but hardly overwhelming. The exotic foliage of Ava's perquisites and special conditions was another matter, leading to heated debate.

The biggest battle was getting the studio to buy the movie rights to *St. Louis Woman* as a starring vehicle for Ava and Frank. MGM was horrified at the notion of pairing its top woman star with the half-forgotten crooner, but Ava stood her ground. A starring role for her husband was part of an all-out drive to salvage his movie career. A new manager and a new publicity agent, Mack Miller, were engaged for him. Ava even badgered Sinatra into being civil to the press, whose main interest in him now was as her quarrelsome husband.

The second contractual battle involved Ava's insistence on a clause to protect her from penalties should she be unable to work due to pregnancy. What came to be known as "the pregnancy clause" met with strong resistance; MGM expected its stars to avoid pregnancy if it interfered with film commitments. Ava was aware that the combination of her unpredictable relationship with Frank and her own irregular physical system made such meticulous planning impractical. Her recurring anemia made her prone to miscarriages; therefore there could be no question of working during pregnancy. She keenly wanted a child, believing that it would cement her already shaky marriage. She threatened to break off negotiations and to quit MGM altogether to win her point.

She also held out for six weeks' paid vacation after every

film, a highly exceptional concession giving her a year and a half off—with pay—out of the seven-year run of the contract. She was to receive living expenses up to a maximum of $20,000 when filming outside the United States and the services on foreign locations of a companion paid for by the studio. Bappie was not mentioned by name in this context, but the assumption was that Ava was creating a job for her sister, now divorced from the New York photographer.

Ava managed to have the number of personal appearances limited to eight per year, reflecting her horror of such publicity rituals. She was also totally exempted from the practice of endorsing products in advertisements. This unusual dispensation was the result of a compromise between star and studio. Ava was determined not to endorse deodorants. She considered them undignified and rarely used them herself. Although the studio agreed, MGM was not prepared to write a specific exception into the contract for fear of creating a precedent. So a blanket exception was inserted instead.

By October 1952 an agreement had been hammered out to everyone's satisfaction and was ready for signing. Everyone, that is, except Ava; suspicious as always about MGM's motives, she pored over the document looking for loopholes that could ensnare her in the future.

She confided in Lana Turner, who suggested she ought to consult with an attorney friend named Neil McCarthy, then considered the leading specialist in film negotiations. McCarthy found it watertight, but, at his suggestion, MGM was asked to remove a clause stating that payment to Ava did not imply an obligation to star her in movies. McCarthy argued that a situation was possible in which "Gardner could be put on the shelf, even though she receives compensation," and this would destroy her career. He proposed a clause guaranteeing one picture a year. Discussions had to be reopened to resolve this new hitch. Metro stonewalled Ava this time, although the clause was a fairly common one at MGM.

Her marriage was equally hectic. There were times when Frank and Ava seemed to be living in a state of mutual siege, both hardheaded, proud and incapable of conceding even the smallest point during quarrels. Columnists had dubbed them "the Battling Sinatras." Ava was determined not to be bossed or taken for granted. For the first few weeks of married life with Frank she sat decoratively beside him as he drank and gossiped with his cronies, but meekness did not come easily to Ava Gardner. One evening, they dined at an Italian restaurant and the owner joined them at their table for a conversation with Frank. For two hours Ava bore in silence their talk of baseball, the fights and mutual friends. Suddenly she stood up, excused herself and left the dining room. It was not until he decided to leave that Sinatra realized that Ava had not returned and was nowhere to be found.

Two days later, Frank received a phone call from his still missing wife—from Italy. She had gone directly from the restaurant to Los Angeles International Airport and boarded the first plane to Rome.

The fact that MGM offered her the remake of *Red Dust*—requiring location shooting in Africa—added to the tension between them. There were also bitter arguments about Frank's children and his frequent visits to Nancy's house to be with them. The children rarely saw Ava, and then only on fleeting visits; she could not shake off the fear that Frank might return to Nancy to ensure the kids the security of a normal upbringing. Despite these problems, Frank seemed to improve technically in his singing and to have more self-assurance during those late-summer and early-fall months of 1952 than he had had in years. For all their bickering, the intensity of the relationship gave new meaning and depth to his lyrics.

In September, however, another breach threatened the marriage. After Ava attended the New York premiere of *Kilimanjaro* Frank picked her up and drove her to the Riviera nightclub at Fort Lee, New Jersey, for his second performance. Ava was happy and animated, enjoying the stares of the crowd. Then she saw Marilyn Maxwell sitting out front and froze. When Frank sang "All of Me" in Maxwell's direction—or so it seemed to Ava—she flew into a rage, left the club after a violent series of expletives, and took the next plane to Hollywood. There she packed her wedding ring in a parcel and mailed it to Sinatra at the Riviera.

Frank played out a couple of depressed weeks at the Chase Hotel in St. Louis before returning to Hollywood and reassuring Ava that Marilyn Maxwell was only a figure from the past. He drove Ava to Tijuana to the bullfights as a peace offering. The dust had hardly settled when another bust-up erupted in Palm Springs. This one involved Lana Turner, and as news of it echoed across the desert it became the subject of much speculative gossip.

Lana's boy friend was a movie matinee idol prone to eruptions of jealousy. According to her own published account, one violent row after she danced with Lex Barker left her too bruised to report to work the following morning. She turned to Frank Sinatra for help. Sympathetically, he suggested she lie low for a while in his house in Palm Springs out of reach of both her menacing friend and her irate studio. Lana fled gratefully into the desert, accompanied by her manager, Ben Cole.

The following morning—a Sunday—Lana was lying in bed in the Sinatra master bedroom lazily watching the sun streaming through the window and contemplating the chicken lunch she had brought with her when a car drew up outside and presently Ava appeared. She was astonished to see Lana.

"What the hell are you doing here?" she asked.

"Frank lent me the place," Lana said.

Soon a second car was heard arriving, and Frank himself strode in. He was visibly enraged, clearly in hot pursuit of his wife. Without a word to either woman, he pushed Ava into the adjoining room and shut the door. Then Lana began to hear the sounds of a fight.

She and Ben Cole retreated to a hotel. It was several hours later when Lana returned for her belongings and the chicken lunch. In the driveway outside the house, she witnessed a chilling scene. Police cars with flashing lights stood outside the house and the couple were fighting in the driveway, oblivious to the restraining efforts of the policemen called by the neighbors.

"Cut that out, Frank," screeched Lana, rushing to Ava's aid.

When the policemen, Lana, Ben Cole and others finally separated the couple, Ava sped away in her car and Frank could not find her until friends arranged for them to meet at a campaign rally for Adlai Stevenson ("Madly for Adlai") a week later. Onstage in Las Vegas, Ava introduced Frank with some show-business schmaltz about "a wonderful, wonderful man." They left directly afterward for North Carolina, where Frank met Ava's sisters and family. They had survived another ruckus, but the rows were getting worse.

# 14

# Lions in the Night

The studio made no bones about it. *Mogambo* was a remake of the romantic smash hit *Red Dust*. It was an attempt to put the clock back to the King's heyday. To recapture the lost Gable magic and, incidentally, Metro's. Gable was repeating his original role, and Ava Jean Harlow's.

The idea did not originate with either MGM or Gable. Stewart Granger had thought it up. Eager to repeat his recent personal success in *King Solomon's Mines,* Granger had gone to Dore Schary with the suggestion that MGM update *Red Dust,* transpose the setting from Indochina to East Africa, and star him in the Gable part. Granger also proposed Ava for the Harlow character, Honey Bear, a chorus girl who was no better than she had to be; whores were as taboo on the screen in 1952 as they had been in 1934.

Schary was enthusiastic, and pre-production routines sprang to life. To complete the triangle, Grace Kelly was cast as the haughty English lady originally played by Mary Astor.

John Lee Mahin, a veteran craftsman, was put to work preparing a new script. In Mahin's version, the hero was a big-game hunter, and the main action centered on a gorilla-trapping safari. Gardner, Kelly, Granger and gorillas—unbeatable.

Sensing a potential box-office hit, Metro decided to go the whole hog and shoot the picture on location in Africa. The original had been shot in the San Fernando Valley and on the studio back lot.

With only a few weeks to go before filming began, Schary summoned Stewart Granger to his office and told him bluntly, "Jim, Gable wants to do your African picture." Granger's real name was Jimmy Stewart, but there was already one of those in the movies.

Granger had a sinking feeling he knew what was coming, and he was right. Gable needed a good picture to revive his fading career, Schary said. "We've got to keep the King happy, no?"

Granger protested.

Schary said, "Now, Jim, you've been to Africa. You don't want to go there again, do you? [*King Solomon's Mines* was filmed in Kenya.] You don't want to be separated from that lovely wife of yours, do you? *So* we've decided to take you out and put Gable in. Okay?"

Of course it wasn't, and Granger continued to protest, but the decision was final. He derived what comfort he could from the fact that—as Schary had pointed out—he would not be separated from his wife, Jean Simmons.

Ava was disappointed at the switch because she found Granger attractive. Sinatra had hated the thought of an anticipated four months' separation while she was away on location from the start, but the additional prospect of his wife roaming the jungle with a gun-toting, safari-suited Clark Gable—recently divorced, to boot—certainly did not help matters.

There was only one solution: Frank would accompany her to Africa. The painful truth was that he had no professional commitments to detain him in Los Angeles. Depressed, he was talking grimly to friends about the "nothingness" ahead of him and the futility of going on at all. He owed $100,000 in back taxes, and, though record royalties and sporadic club engagements still brought in a respectable income, his generous commitment to Nancy and the children siphoned off most of his earnings.

He was then making an all-out effort to convince Columbia chief Harry Cohn to give him the Private Angelo Maggio role in James Jones's *From Here to Eternity*, the distinguished World War II blockbuster set in Pearl Harbor. The starring role, Private Robert E. Lee Prewitt, a career soldier who is destroyed by the Army he loves, had gone to the gifted new star Montgomery Clift.

Maggio, a quick-talking Italian barrack-room rebel, was only a supporting character with fifth billing in the credits, but it was a plum of a role. Thanks to James Jones's tragic vision of American society and his genius at characterization, Maggio's and Prewitt's ordeals embodied the universal conflict between the system—symbolized by the Army—and the unconquerable human spirit. Declining fortunes had not dimmed Sinatra's uncanny professional instincts. Maggio was a part he could play to the hilt. "I knew Maggio," he said. "I went to high school with him in Hoboken. I was beaten up with him. I might have been Maggio."

Salivating over what he could achieve with the role and how it could save his career proved a lot easier than actually landing the part. It wasn't for lack of trying: Frank pulled every string. Ava did her bit, too, urging her friend Joan Cohn, the studio boss's wife, to intercede with her husband.

But Cohn, known variously as Harry the Horror and White Fang—he was not only foulmouthed but lethal to deal with— was not interested. To him, Sinatra was a washed-up crooner. He saw no reason for going out on a limb and casting him in a dramatic part.

Frank's stubborn streak would not let him give up. The more remote his chances appeared to be, the more obsessive he became about playing Maggio. He may even have turned for help to Frank Costello. At least, the New York mobster later claimed he had tried to use the syndicate's influence with movie unions to secure the role for his old crony. Nothing came of it. Maggio remained out of Sinatra's reach.

At the Hampshire House with Ava on the first stage of his trip to Africa, he discovered that Harry Cohn was also registered there and decided to beard him in his suite. Cohn was anything but encouraging. "You're nuts," he said. "You're a song-and-dance man. Maggio is stage-actor kind of stuff."

As a parting shot, Sinatra appealed to Cohn's parsimonious reputation. "I'll play Maggio for a thousand a week," he said. Cohn agreed to think it over.

When Sinatra left, Cohn told his studio sidekick Jonie Taps, who had been present at the meeting, "They'd laugh at that skinny little runt."

All the same, Sinatra's cut-price offer apparently had some effect, because Cohn eventually agreed to allow Sinatra to be tested for the role.

The test had still not been made, however, when Frank and Ava flew out to Nairobi via London and Zurich. He was a camp follower on *Mogambo,* his $1,467 round trip paid for by Ava, who also footed the $278 bill for excess luggage. Ava never traveled light.

Humiliation was digging deep now: his wife starring in one of the year's big-budget movies; he having to beg for a screen test for a supporting role. Ava was not in the best of

spirits, either, as the plane skimmed over the flat bush country around Nairobi at the start of her African adventure. To
be sure, the journey had been slow and tiring. She and Frank
had taken one of the new BOAC Comets, but it still took over
twenty-four hours from London to East Africa, with refuel-
ing stops in Rome, Cairo and Khartoum. And the last few
days before her departure were a blur in her memory. There
had been the fight with Frank in Palm Springs; the haggling
over her new contract, which was still going on when she left;
and the aftereffects of her numerous shots—typhoid, para-
typhoid, tetanus, cholera, smallpox and, worst of all, yellow
fever. On top of everything, there had been the secret suspicion that she was pregnant. Though she dearly wanted a
child, the timing of her pregnancy made it very much a
mixed blessing.

Whatever its merits as a movie, *Mogambo* was a logistical
nightmare. The production involved 175 American and
British actors and film crew members, over a hundred vehi-
cles and an assorted number of planes, including some old
wartime DC-3s.

All told, a thousand black Africans from a variety of tribes
were recruited as extras; Metro made a special effort not to
employ sworn enemies in the same sequences. The studio
was anxious to avoid a repetition of its tribal problems on
*King Solomon's Mines* when the Kikuyu and the Masai appearing in the film had clashed violently and four tribesmen had
died. In the not too distant past, the Masai had raided the
Kikuyu on a regular basis, killing all the men and carrying
off the women as concubines, and the old tribal enmity had
not taken long to resurface. This time, in some scenes Metro
used the tall, majestic Masai, who seemed inseparable from
their shields and broad-bladed spears, and in other scenes
several hundred Sumburi tribesmen imported from the
Congo who subsisted on milk and blood from live cattle.

Nine professional hunters led by Frank "Bunny" Allen, a noted American white hunter, provided technical expertise and protection from the wild animals. In fact the animals behaved beautifully. The real danger was from accidents caused by driving on rough terrain in the bush. By the end of the four months' shooting, two young blacks had been run over and killed, and a British assistant director had died when his jeep crashed and overturned.

On November 1, Bunny Allen led a safari consisting of most of the film crew out of Nairobi to prepare the location sites before the arrival of the stars. In eight days of forced march on foot and in trucks, they covered a thousand miles to the Kagera River, on the border with Tanganyika and Uganda. There, amid majestic scenery, they set up a base camp, some hundred miles or so from Lake Victoria.

The *Mogambo* settlement amounted to a luxury hotel under canvas. It had lavishly upholstered sleeping tents, thirteen dining tents, a portable movie theater, an entertainment tent with pool tables, and a hospital tent complete with an X-ray unit. The women's tents included bathrooms with hot and cold running water. At the back of each tent were two large oil drums, one containing cold water and the other, propped up over a wood fire, delivering the hot.

Beyond the tents an 1,800-yard landing strip had been hacked out of the jungle, and the stars now flew in on DC-3 planes. Five smaller location camps were also set up in the surrounding jungle, each with its own airstrip, and the director, John Ford, sometimes shuttled between the various sites in the course of a day's shooting.

Ava's spirits rose when she arrived at the river location. She gazed about her like an excited tourist. In a nearby clearing impalas were doing their incredible leaps, and the trees were full of chattering baboons. A herd of elephants passing over the distant horizon trumpeted a welcome. To her consternation, tall tribesmen, their faces daubed with ocher, began to trail after her, flashing incredibly white teeth in broad lascivious smiles. Behind them followed the women, barebreasted and with very close-cropped heads.

A troop of black servants had been assigned to Ava and waited outside her tent. There was one young boy in attendance whose sole duty was to see that the water drums behind the tent were topped up at all times, and that there was always a fire going.

The Ugandan game wardens warned the film unit not to stray too far without an escort. They were in the middle of a highly populated game reserve containing many elephants and rhinos, besides the crocodiles and the hippos infesting the river and its banks.

To say nothing of the lions. On Ava's first evening in the African wilderness, a brilliant moon illuminated the broad sweep of the river. But as she stood at the entrance to her tent letting her mysterious surroundings saturate her thoughts and feelings, a lion loped casually by. Another stood roaring in the clearing. Ava fled in terror. "Jesus Christ, a fucking *lion* just walked right past me," she shouted to Bunny Allen.

The lions were lured away by dragging an animal carcass on the ground and hanging it from a tree outside the camp. Even so, there was no question of sleep for Ava as she listened to the night sounds of the jungle and the breathing of the scavenging hyenas sniffling around the tents for food scraps. By morning, the hanging carcass had disappeared, and after that it became a practice to leave the lions a nightly offering.

The going was rough from the start. Though the rainy season was officially over, the rains had come back with a vengeance. Whole days of filming were washed out by the torrential weather. The river flooded its banks, and water oozed into part of the encampment.

Whenever there was a break in the clouds, John Ford drove his troupe hard to make up for lost time. A humid heat rose from the rain-soaked jungle; the atmosphere was like a steam bath. But gruff John Ford called for one camera setup after another and plunged on. Accustomed to the all-male casts of his famous John Wayne Westerns, he made few concessions to his two women stars. To their credit, Ava and Grace Kelly gritted their teeth and endured his brusque manner.

Ava, who had told no one about her pregnancy, was suffering side effects, and Ford mistook this for nervousness. "You're damned good," he growled reassuringly one day. "Just take it easy."

In one difficult scene, a car in which Ava and Gable were traveling was attacked by a rhinoceros. The sequence became altogether too realistic for comfort when two other rhinos decided to get in on the act and charged the camera truck directly ahead of the car. The truck was thrown out of control and driven off the narrow dirt track, and the two rhinos were about to turn their attention to Ava and Gable when Bunny Allen, who was riding shotgun in the camera truck, took aim and felled both animals in rapid succession.

Some days later Ava, Grace and Gable were charged by a mother hippopotamus as they drifted down the Kagera River in a convoy of canoes. The hippo was nursing her young calf on the bank when she spotted the string of boats in midstream with the camera boat in the lead. Alarmed by the intrusion, the hippo charged bellowing into the water and headed straight for Ava's flimsy craft. Fortunately for Ava, she was in the hands of expert rowers who managed to dodge the attacker in time. A minute later and Ava would have been in the water.

Such narrow escapes left her edgy and abrasive. Frank, meanwhile, fidgeted on the sidelines, waiting for the summons from Columbia which never came. The high point of his day was the early-morning arrival of the mail-and-supplies plane from Nairobi, bringing letters and telegrams from Hollywood. After that, there was little for him to do except watch his wife work. His enforced idleness was not calculated to make him a model of empathy and understanding.

Out of pity, the crew involved him in the construction of an outdoor shower stockade supplied by water pumped from the river and used in one of Ava's scenes with Gable. In the same scene in *Red Dust,* Jean Harlow used an old rain barrel; Ava's bath was more refined.

To mark their first wedding anniversary, Frank rounded up fifty African singers and dancers and rehearsed them in a surprise show with himself as the star. It was an especially significant landmark for Ava; she had been married twice before—but never for a whole year.

One thing was certain: Frank's jealous nature had nothing to fear from Clark Gable. The King was fond of Ava, but he had eyes only for Grace Kelly. Not merely beautiful but a fine sportswoman and a crack shot, she stirred strong memories of his beloved Carole Lombard, and a close relationship blossomed during hunting expeditions. She called him "Ba," the Swahili for father, which wasn't too far off from Lombard's "Pa."

The Gable-Kelly association was to carry over for some time, on and off, after *Mogambo* was completed. Gable seriously considered marriage to Grace Kelly, but eventually came to the conclusion that the twenty-eight-year difference in their ages was too great. She was put off by his false teeth, the most famous set of dentures in the movies and, after George Washington's, perhaps in history.

Gable was as much in his element in the African bush as Frank Sinatra was out of it. He had made his mark early on location, spotting a large crocodile moving in on the camera crew working on a riverbank some distance away from where he stood. The four men around the camera were so intent on what they were doing that they had not noticed the approaching danger. Gable leveled his Holland & Holland .375 magnum. One shot. One. The reptile was dead in its tracks.

To the tribesmen on the set Gable was the big white chief after that, and even Bunny Allen's hunters accepted him as an equal. In their free time, he and Grace accompanied them on shoots, and on one famous afternoon he bagged four animals with four bullets: a zebra, an impala, a reed buck and a topi. This was, of course, before ecological consciousness-raising made mass murder in the bush unfashionable, not to mention illegal.

Ava refused to kill any wild animals, but Grace could match him shot for shot. She had a good eye and a remarkably cool nerve, and her trigger finger itched whenever they came across a rhino or spotted a herd of buffalo. The studio had, however, expressly barred them from going after anything that could effectively strike back, specifically rhinos and lions, and they were forced to concentrate on lesser game. Ava frequently tagged along on these safaris.

At last, the mail plane brought the news that Frank was expected in Los Angeles for his screen test for *From Here to Eternity*. The invitation did not even mention expenses, and again it was Ava who paid the return fare for Frank's date with the movie camera—his first in nearly three years.

As Frank told it later, "I left Africa one Friday night. I had a copy of the scene and I sat up all night on the plane. Didn't sleep the whole trip. Monday morning, I made the test. I finished at three in the afternoon and that night I flew back to Africa. My adrenaline was bubbling."

Frank returned to Ava no less edgy than when he'd left. A different anxiety now assailed him—was his test a winner? He did two scenes: the drunk scene, when Maggio is found AWOL in the hotel garden, and the poker scene in the saloon. But when Frank returned to Africa he still had no word from Harry Cohn on whether he had the part.

Back in Africa, he heard that Eli Wallach, the Broadway actor, had also been tested for Maggio. Sinatra had seen him in *The Rose Tattoo* and knew him to be a fine actor. His hopes plunged. "I'm dead," he kept saying. "I'm dead."

"They haven't cast the picture yet," Ava said. "All you get is a stinking message and you let it get you down."

Gable told him, "Skipper, relax. Drink a little booze. Everything will be all right."

Now a new disaster hit the Sinatras like a thunderclap: One morning on location Ava collapsed.

Publicly she blamed it on the intense jungle humidity, which was certainly one reason, as were Ford's driving pace and the pressure of Frank's mounting anxiety over the outcome of his screen test. Secretly, however, she feared that she had lost the baby, and she begged Ford to give her time off to fly to London for a medical checkup.

Ford agreed without hesitation. But when the news of Ava's intentions was relayed to Culver City, Sam Zimbalist, the producer of *Mogambo*, concerned about the shooting schedule, which had already fallen badly behind because of the bad weather, quickly wired Ford: "FEEL GARDNER'S TRIP UNWISE FOR MANY OBVIOUS REASONS . . . SUGGEST YOU USE YOUR PERSUASIVENESS AND HAVE LADY STAY PUT."

Ford sensed, rather than knew, the seriousness of Ava's situation. She had revealed little. But he wired back:

"GARDNER GIVING SUPERB PERFORMANCE VERY CHARMING
COOPERATIVE STOP HOWEVER REALLY QUITE ILL SINCE AR-
RIVAL AFRICA AND DEEM IT IMPERATIVE LONDON CON-
SULTATION OTHERWISE TRAGIC RESULTS STOP NOT AFFECT
SCHEDULE WEATHER HERE MISERABLE BUT WE TRYING
STOP REPEAT BELIEVE TRIP IMPERATIVE STOP AFFECTION
JACK."

On November 22, without waiting for a reply from Metro,
Ava quietly boarded the London flight at Nairobi Airport,
accompanied by Morgan Hudgins, a studio executive. Frank
traveled separately to avoid attracting attention. In London
Ava was met by Bappie, urgently summoned from Los Angeles. Ava was hospitalized at the Chelsea Hospital for
Women for four days, and the press was told that she was
suffering from "a severe case of anaemia."

In reality, Ava had miscarried. "All my life I had wanted a
baby, and the news that I had lost him (I was sure it was a
boy) was the cruelest blow I had ever received," Ava said
later. "Even though my marriage to Frank was getting
shakier every day, I didn't care. I wanted a baby by him."

But there was a movie to finish, and within twelve days Ava
was back on the *Mogambo* location, tired, miserable, guilty,
and resentful at having to return to work. Cast and crew
were full of sympathy for her but showed little concern for
Frank, who still paced the set, like some caged beast, awaiting
word from Columbia. The loss did not, as such things sometimes can, create any bond between Ava and Frank. On the
contrary, they seemed to others to drift further apart.

Besides Grace and Ava there were only two white women
in the troupe. But there were over 130 men, most of whom
had now been living abstemiously in the jungle for nearly six
weeks without a break, and Frank was beginning to get resentful looks.

Christmas crept up on them almost unnoticed in the heat.

On Christmas night, cast and crew gathered around a large campfire to listen to Frank singing carols. Then Ford gave a surprisingly arresting rendition of " 'Twas the night before Christmas . . ." The black extras, draped in blankets, sang French songs. After that the celebration moved into high gear, with a liberal consignment of whiskey flown in from Nairobi.

The principal stars went to a party hosted by Clark Gable in honor of Ava's birthday. The shock of losing her baby overpowered any trauma occasioned by reaching thirty. Both she and Frank had little to be cheerful about, but they put on a brave show. Frank was entertaining and charming, as he could be when he had an audience. Ava was her usual irreverent, ebullient self.

Ford introduced her to the district commissioner, the senior British officer in the area, and his wife. The director joked, "Ava, why don't you tell the commissioner what you see in that hundred-and-twenty-pound runt you're married to."

Ava opened her eyes innocently and replied, "Well, there's only ten pounds of Frank, but there's a hundred and ten pounds of cock."

Ford went green. He had visions of the British authorities canceling their cooperation, which was indispensable to finishing the picture. He need not have worried. The commissioner and his wife burst into delighted laughter.

When gifts were exchanged, Gable was shocked to witness Ava tossing aside the mink coat Frank gave her. No woman is ever going to treat a gift of mine like that and get away with it, Gable thought. But Frank appeared not to notice the slight.

Sinatra was alone in the camp one day when the long-awaited wire arrived. A deal had been signed for him to play Maggio at the agreed $8,000 fee. Had money been the decisive factor? Eli Wallach asked for more than twice that sum. Sinatra didn't know—or care. He was exultant. "I'll show those mothers," he shouted. "I'll show those wise guys."

Although filming was not scheduled to start for several weeks, he had to leave for the United States because of night-club commitments. Ava was stuck in Africa until the end of January, but the separation was made bearable by her relief that Frank had achieved his objective and a light now glowed dimly at the end of the tunnel of his career.

He continued to make his presence felt on location. He air-freighted to Ava a record player and a stack of his own recordings but no one else's. After that, his voice crooned out from her tent anytime she was not filming. His other contribution to brightening up her life was to send her trunkloads of food, including frozen steaks, to break the monotony of movie location menus.

Ava was not present during the filming in Hawaii of *From Here to Eternity,* and there was little communication between her and Frank. All she knew was that the Frank who joined her in London in the spring of 1953 was far from the fright-ened, lost soul she'd said goodbye to in Africa. The returning Frank was assertive, full of confidence, and went out of his way to show that he was no longer tied to her apron strings.

Her first thought was, Is there another woman? But it soon became apparent that the key to this abrupt change lay in the movie, and especially in Frank's performance as the tough little Italian with the talc bottle and the cherished picture of his kid sister. It was a classic portrait of the sly, grinning enlisted man surviving the Army routine from one furlough to the next.

For weeks, Sinatra had lived and breathed the role of Pri-vate Angelo Maggio. He had meticulously worked out and practiced each scene until it became second nature. And as he sensed the impact on those around him of his electrifying performance, his self-confidence came back, first a trickle, and then a surge. What's more, his instincts about the role had not been wrong. Already Columbia was talking headily of a possible Academy Award nomination.

It did not take long for that confidence to thicken into arrogance as the old cronies and sycophants, who had fled when his career began to sag, reappeared to pander to his nastier side.

There were still singing tours to make under old agreements, and Sinatra was on the point of setting off for Italy for four weeks of stage and nightclub appearances. The old Sinatra would have insisted that Ava accompany him. The new Sinatra gave every indication of not really caring whether she did or not.

It was typical of his nature that he went from the extreme of finding her indispensable to utter indifference. It was equally typical of Ava's that she deplored his arrogance as much as she had his earlier dependence on her, and was somehow unable to comprehend why he could not find a happy medium.

His attitude increased her determination to go along, even though she was on the point of starting work on a costume saga in England, *Knights of the Round Table*. Once again, she was caught between the conflicting pressures of marriage and work.

The film was a perfect illustration of the Hollywood dictum that if a movie hit it big you should make ten more just like it. With *Knights of the Round Table* Metro was hoping to repeat the success of *Ivanhoe*.

Robert Taylor, who played Ivanhoe, was cast as Lancelot, and Ava was King Arthur's wayward Queen Guinevere. Even the castle built for the earlier epic at Metro's British studios at Boreham Wood, north of London, was recycled as King Arthur's Camelot. After the engaging sensuality of Honey Bear, Ava found her role empty and vapid. The elaborate costumes were heavy and uncomfortable, and though she had been allowed a three-week vacation in Spain at the end of *Mogambo* she still felt drained from her African experience and angry over the pointlessness of her new film assignment.

"Do you want me to come?" Ava wanted to know.

"Sure, but you do what you want," was Frank's maddening answer.

The studio was a great deal more emphatic. "Ava, we have a tentative starting date of May eighteenth, but we need you now for wardrobe and makeup tests, and to teach you to ride sidesaddle," said the head of Metro's British operation. It was the afternoon of May 7, and he had come to her rented London apartment to try to persuade her not to leave the country.

Confrontations with studio executives brought out the worst in Ava. All too often, she felt, Metro still treated her like a contract starlet instead of one of their principal stars. "I don't need riding lessons," she told the executive. "I rode a horse with Clark Gable in *Lone Star,* and with Bob Taylor in *Ride Vaquero.*"

He pointed out that under her new contract she was not entitled to six weeks' vacation until after her fourth picture, yet the studio had already agreed to a three-week rest.

"I know, but I'm going anyway," Ava retorted. "If those guys [at Metro] don't like it, they can try suspending me. But I've got a picture deal for $130,000, and they can't suspend me. If they want to take the fucking picture away, that's fine with me, but I've made up my mind to go with my husband on this trip regardless."

"Well, you're going without the studio's permission," said the executive. Ava told him what he could do with the studio's permission. Frank, who was present, said nothing. The executive had the distinct impression that Ava had been trying to impress her husband.

Off they went, to Milan, Rome and Naples.

# 15

# Breakup

The Italians went crazy over Ava. Four of her movies happened to be playing in Rome at the time, and wherever she went people collected to gaze at her in fervent admiration. In the difficult years of postwar reconstruction, Hollywood movies brought escape, and a distant, fabled glamor. The arrival of an American star in the flesh was like the descent of a creature from heaven.

Frank was not amused to find himself basking in Ava's reflected glory. In Rome, there were clashes with the *paparazzi* who swarmed around her hysterically. In Naples, an uproar in the theater where Frank was appearing led to more domestic strife. The trouble started midway through his concert: the audience suddenly began to hoot and jeer and call for Ava. Frank walked out in a huff. When he learned the reason for the barracking, he became even more enraged. It turned out that Ava had been billed in the advertising as his co-star, and the audience was clamoring for her to appear.

Police were called in to calm the crowd. The city's police chief arrived and persuaded Frank that it was in everybody's best interest for Ava to show herself. She stepped gingerly onstage to a thundering welcome of cheers and wolf whistles, waved to the audience and walked off again. They were anything but appeased. They had expected the star of *Show Boat* to sing. It did not seem a good time to explain that Ava was not an experienced singer or that someone else had dubbed her songs in *Show Boat*. While the Neapolitan police forcibly cleared the theater, Ava fled out of town and caught the train to Milan. As for Frank, he continued to fight all and sundry, but by now it was obvious that his public aggressiveness was the result of personal uphappiness. The fights in their hotel rooms echoed through the corridors—to the delight of an audience of chambermaids and other guests.

But the trip forged another link in the chain of Ava's growing attachment to Europe and things European. She became a client of the Sorelle Fontana, two Italian sisters with a talent for designing the glamorous, high-fashion style Ava liked to wear on major occasions. Ava's approach to clothes tended to go from one extreme to the other, either casual in jeans or a skirt, worn with a shirt or sweater, loafers on her feet and a large silk scarf covering her hair, or dressed to kill.

On her first visit to the glass-fronted couture house in the Piazza di Spagna, Ava tried on every evening gown in the place while Fontanas fussed around her, and Sinatra, who had accompanied her on her shopping expedition, watched patiently. After that, Fontana created as many as thirty gowns and formal outfits a year for Ava. As often as she could, she insisted that they design her movie clothes as well, and the name Fontana appeared in the credits of several of her subsequent films. Black was her favorite color on and off the screen, though she had a weakness for powder blue. She

AVA •

had no false coyness about her physical attributes and insisted they be shown off to full advantage: "More cleavage,"
she would say when they were fitting an evening gown. She
also had a weakness for small hats, for evening as well as
daytime.

Back in London, the Sinatras rented a flat in St. John's
Wood while Ava turned her attention to the chore of playing
Queen Guinevere in *Knights of the Round Table*. Stewart
Granger and Jean Simmons arrived one evening in the wake
of a fierce squabble between Ava and Frank. All four were
going to the Ambassadors nightclub, where Frank was singing. As the British couple entered the apartment, they could
sense the tense atmosphere; the Sinatras were hardly speaking to each other. It was decided that Frank would go ahead
and Stewart and Jean would bring Ava, and throughout the
drive Ava complained about how impossible Frank was to
live with.

When they were seated at their table, and Frank came on,
everything changed. He sang love songs as only Sinatra can,
and he sang them straight at Ava. She started to cry. "Look at
the goddamn son-of-a-bitch. How can you resist him?" Frank
joined them later, and everything seemed to be all right.
Until the next altercation, which was not long in coming.

Filming went quickly for Ava, if uncomfortably in her tight
bodices and long, heavy skirts. Her role was "in the can"
when Frank was asked by Columbia to return to New York
for the premiere of *From Here to Eternity*, which bore all the
advance signs of being a great hit.

He didn't need to be told twice. "I think I'd better be
going," he told Ava. "You're going to have to stay here
awhile until they finish the picture, so I'll go alone and you
can follow."

Well, said Ava, maybe I could get away, too. MGM agreed,
stipulating she would need to return if retakes were re-

194 •

quired. Elated by this news, she rushed back to the apartment. Frank's bags were already packed and he was on the verge of leaving without even waiting to see whether she could accompany him. The ensuing quarrel was so heated that neighbors complained and the landlord threatened eviction.

This was one occasion when Ava resisted the impulse to chase after her husband. Later, when he telephoned from New York on arrival, she missed him terribly. One sweet word of reconciliation and her resistance would have crumbled. But the voice at the other end of the line remained cold and distant, the conversation formal and barren. Ava started to cry. "I don't like crying women," Frank said, and hung up.

Hurt and angry, Ava decided to return to New York the long way—via Madrid. Though she may not have been conscious of it, she was beginning to look upon Spain as a salve for her emotional wounds. She had a standing invitation to visit an American couple, Betty and Ricardo Sicre, whom she had met on a previous Spanish trip, and it was in their country home outside the Spanish capital that she holed up for a week—without bothering to let her husband know where she was.

Ricardo Sicre was a Catalan who had fought in the Spanish Civil War on the Loyalist side, that is, against Franco. In 1939, he fled to the United States and joined the OSS, the precursor of the Central Intelligence Agency, and became an American citizen. His experiences as a secret agent had provided him with material for a novel, *The Tap on the Left Shoulder*. Sicre had married Betty Lussier, another OSS operative. They first met when she was dropped in German-occupied Andorra. She was also American.

When the war ended, Sicre returned to Barcelona—as an American, he was of course out of reach of Franco's vengeance against an old enemy—and made several fortunes buying and selling in partnership with another American, Frank Ryan, and eventually had Spain's first Pepsi-Cola concession. The Sicres were to become Ava's closest friends.

When she finally flew back to New York, Ava said nothing to Frank of a chance meeting which was to make the breakup of her marriage less painful for her.

Luis Miguel Dominguin, the bullfighter Ava met through the Sicres, was nothing short of a Spanish institution. In fact, two institutions. There was Dominguin the country's number-one matador, with a spectacular record of kills, and scion of a famous bullfighting dynasty. Even his sister Carmen had performed in the ring with style and verve as a teenager. Now she was married to Antonio Ordóñez, a young bullfighter who was Dominguin's up-and-coming rival. And then there was Dominguin the prominent Madrid socialite, a lean, handsome, joking playboy with an equally spectacular record of feminine conquests.

"At his peak," his friend Ernest Hemingway said, "he's a combination of Don Juan and Hamlet." Facing death in the ring had accentuated in Dominguin a Spanish tendency toward broodiness, and when Ava met him he had something to brood about. A *cornada*, or bad goring, in the stomach had put him out of the ring for a year, but he had recently received a lucrative offer for a South American tour which was forcing him to face up seriously to the prospect of a comeback.

Ava brought out the Don Juan side of his nature, and he lavished charm and attention on her. After Frank's rough treatment, being with Dominguin was like changing from sackcloth into pure silk. But Frank still loomed large in her thinking, and she decided to tear herself away from the handsome, considerate Spaniard before it was too late, and rejoin her husband.

When she landed at La Guardia there was no Frank waiting to greet her. And in her present mood of resentment, the fact that she had omitted to tell him that she was arriving seemed a lame excuse for his not being there. The following morning, over breakfast in his Waldorf suite, Frank learned from the papers that his wife was in town and staying at the Hampshire House.

It was not the most intimate form of communication between a married couple, and Frank continued to ignore her arrival. For all the notice they took of each other, they could have still been on different continents. Neither seemed capable of making the first move. When Frank opened at the Riviera in New Jersey, Ava was conspicuously absent from the opening performance.

The marriage would have been all over but for the timely intervention of Frank's mother, Dolly. Worried that her son was drifting into a second broken marriage, she went to the Hampshire House to talk with Ava. She had grown genuinely fond of her daughter-in-law, admiring both her beauty and her direct, plain-spoken manner. Then, in Ava's presence, she telephoned Frank. She told him he had a wonderful wife and to stop being a fool. She said Ava would go to the Riviera for his show if he would ask her. Sinatra agreed. His mother's word was—more or less—still law. Ava drove to the Riviera that evening and sat at a ringside table while Sinatra crooned ballads to her.

Ava melted. They had supper with Dolly in Weehawken, where she lived. Frank moved out of the Waldorf and into the Hampshire House to join his wife. Making up was everything either of them could have hoped it would be, but Dolly had achieved only a temporary truce. They were soon quarreling again over Frank's poker nights, stag parties, prizefights and cronies.

Frank was not very often seen without a few, and sometimes as many as ten, of "the boys." The entourage included his manager Hank Sanicola, his songwriter Dan McGuire, his makeup man (to fix his hairpiece), and assorted beards and hunkers. A beard was Hollywood parlance for someone engaged to make a threesome out of what was really a twosome. A beard accompanied a star when he or she appeared in public with someone else's spouse. The practice was usually successful in avoiding domestic trouble or gossip columnists. A hunker was kept on the payroll to know baseball scores, send out for coffee, and strike matches on. "Just think of having a sportswriter for a rival," Ava commented.

As the couple whizzed around the country on separate junkets, Metro took a hand by announcing on October 27 that Frank and Ava were separated, pending a divorce. Metro was acting on information from Ava herself, but she had not intended to go public. Following Sinatra's recent success, MGM was beginning to revise its thinking on *St. Louis Woman*. There was talk of making the picture. Now it was Ava who did not relish the prospect of working with Sinatra. She wanted to put as much distance between herself and Frank as possible and not co-star with him in a movie. She begged the studio to find her a film in Europe and away from a situation which was rapidly becoming intolerable.

She was offered a picture called *Paris Story* which had the attraction of being filmed on location in Paris, but it had nothing else going for it. Far more compelling was the script United Artists had sent her, *The Barefoot Contessa*.

It was perfect casting. Rarely has a screen role become so firmly welded in the public perception to the identity of the star—Garbo as Camille, Leigh as Scarlett, Davis as Margo Channing, and Gardner as the Barefoot Contessa. Yet the part only *seems* tailor-made for Ava. It was originally intended for Rita Hayworth, whose own life inspired the character of Maria Vargas.

Like Rita, Maria Vargas began her screen career dancing

in small nightclubs and rose to dizzy heights in the movies and in society. Rita was part Mexican; Maria Vargas was Spanish. Rita married Aly Khan; Maria's husband in the movie was rich (like Aly), impotent (unlike Aly) and extremely jealous—an Italian count who takes the beautiful Maria's life in the end.

In *Barefoot Contessa,* however, art paralleled life in a broader sense. The film focused attention on European high society, which Rita Hayworth had brought to the notice of Americans by marrying Aly Khan. Rita had, in effect, added a new and exotic dimension to a Europe which was still thought of largely in terms of the Marshall Plan, CARE packages and postwar reconstruction, and the movie elaborated on this new dimension.

Mass tourism was about to change all that. Nearly half a million Americans left the United States on vacation in 1952. But when the magazines showed Rita at the wheel of the car Aly had given her as an engagement present, many Americans were probably gazing at the sleek lines of a British-made Jaguar for the first time. The pictures did more than a full-blown advertising campaign to start a vogue for foreign cars in the United States, and when Frank gave Ava an automobile as one of their many reconciliation gifts it was not a Cadillac but a Facel Vega.

Rita Hayworth refused to play *The Barefoot Contessa*—it was probably too close for comfort—and her loss was Ava's gain. Ava was captivated by the role, with its Spanish setting and frenetic flamenco dancing sequences, and its glamorous, if ultimately tragic, associations. The part did not exactly fall into Ava's lap. On the contrary, when she first asked Dore Schary to approve the loan-out, the studio boss turned her down.

"What about *Paris Story*?" Schary said.

"I've been telling you for months I don't want to do *Paris*

*Story,*" Ava replied. "I'm surprised the studio would want to put me in that kind of material."

Schary did not press the point, but went on to discuss other pictures the studio had in mind for her.

Ava said it was a relief to know the studio did have plans for her. "I was beginning to have the feeling you weren't interested in using me."

When Schary firmly refused to discuss the loan-out, she went over his head to Nicholas Schenck, president of Loew's, Inc., in New York. In a long plaintive wire (drafted for her by her agent) she said:

I AM DESPERATELY ANXIOUS TO DO THIS PICTURE NOT ONLY BECAUSE IT IS GREAT BUT BECAUSE MY PERSONAL PROBLEMS WOULD BE ALLEVIATED BY MY LEAVING TOWN AND GOING ABROAD FOR SEVERAL MONTHS AND WORKING.

YOU MUST KNOW MY TERRIBLE DISAPPOINTMENT AT NOT BEING ABLE TO ACCUMULATE SOME MONEY AND SECURITY WHICH I HAD CONTEMPLATED WHEN I MADE MY NEW CONTRACT WITH METRO AND I THINK THE LEAST THAT THE COMPANY CAN DO IS TO GIVE ME SOME MEASURE OF HAPPINESS IN DOING THE KIND OF PART I WANT TO DO AT THIS TIME AS I COULD LEAVE FOR EUROPE IMMEDIATELY.

The mention of money was a reference to a sizable tax assessment with which she had been hit on her return from Africa and which had gouged a large hole in her income. This, coupled with some ill-advised investments, had left her in poor shape financially. But Schenck, known throughout Metro as "the General," would not countermand Dore Schary's decision. If she wanted to get away so badly, there was *Paris Story*.

Ava was not the only star clamoring for the part of the barefoot contessa. Its undisputed allure was considerably enhanced by the reputation of Joseph Mankiewicz, who had written the script and would direct the film. Mankiewicz had just won an Academy Award for *All About Eve*, and women stars of all ages were badgering their agents and studios to secure them the part of Maria Vargas.

All the way from the Dorchester Hotel in London, Elizabeth Taylor pleaded with Ben Thau to loan her to United Artists. She wired:

> DEAREST DARLING BENNY SAW JOE MANKOWITZ [*sic*]
> IN ROME AND ASKED HIM TO LET ME READ BAREFOOT
> CONTESSA STOP I WANT TO DO IT MORE THAN ANY
> SCRIPT I HAVE EVER READ STOP I KNOW WHAT HAP-
> PENED BETWEEN AVA AND SCHENCK BUT IF METRO HAS
> NOTHING IMPORTANT FOR ME PLEASE HELP ME WITH
> THIS BECAUSE AS YOU KNOW IT WOULD DO MORE GOOD
> PERHAPS THAN ANYTHING I HAVE EVER DONE STOP
> PLEASE BENNY LET ME KNOW AS SOON AS POSSIBLE DOR-
> CHESTER FONDEST LOVE ELIZABETH TAYLOR

In the end, the decisive factor was money.

With Rita out of the running, Ava was Mankiewicz's next choice. United Artists made Metro an offer it couldn't refuse: $200,000 for six weeks of Ava's services.

As the date of her departure drew near, word reached Ava that Sinatra had been taken to Mount Sinai Hospital in New York suffering, according to the hospital records, from "complete physical exhaustion, severe loss of weight and a tremendous amount of emotional strain." The loss of weight was indeed severe. Brooding over Ava, Frank had dropped fourteen pounds—from 132 to 118.

They had tried calling each other throughout the summer,

but one or the other always hung up. Their second wedding anniversary had gone unobserved with Ava in Palm Springs, hiding from the press, and Frank in New York, taping radio shows for NBC and recording a string of melancholy hits that captured the sad disarray of his personal life—especially "A Foggy Day in London Town," recalling their trips to London, and "I Get a Kick Out of You."

When Ava failed to come to his bedside, ostensibly because of pre-production work on *Barefoot Contessa,* Frank discharged himself prematurely from the hospital, boarded a plane—in a hangar at La Guardia at midnight to avoid reporters—and took off for Hollywood to see her. He carried three radio scripts and a couple of sleeping pills, and he had a sleeper reservation. He was going to be fresh for what he hoped would be, if not a reconciliation, at least a peace conference.

The meeting was strained and faltering. Frank chose his words with the care of a man picking his way through poison ivy. Ava, on the other hand, was committed to leaving immediately for Rome, where the Fontana sisters had thirty outfits she was to wear in her new picture ready for fitting. She did not raise the possibility of Frank going with her. There was no reconciliation; but there was to be no divorce either. The couple agreed to look upon Ava's two-month absence in Europe as a cooling-off period.

When Ava got to Cinecittà Studios, her elation over landing the coveted role quickly soured. Filming *The Barefoot Contessa* was a thoroughly unpleasant experience. Mankiewicz was a martinet whose personality generated a constant tension on the set. He worked at grueling speed and was so obsessive about not wasting time that he instituted a series of fines for anyone reporting late for work. And that meant anyone, from the top stars to the lowliest grip. His behavior played havoc with all those around him, keeping them constantly off balance, and especially Ava because it compounded her usual insecurity.

To make things worse, not much camaraderie existed among the cast. Rossano Brazzi, the impotent Italian husband in the picture, complained about everything. He was so wrapped up in his own problems that he hardly seemed to notice that Ava was there at all. Humphrey Bogart, who played the recovered alcoholic movie director who discovers Ava, needled her about her friendship with Luis Miguel, who had accompanied her to Rome. Bogart was a charter member of the Holmby Hills Rat Pack, a "club" with no premises, no membership dues, no rules to speak of and no particular activities except drinking and running down the establishment. Other members included Robert Benchley, the humorist, Sammy Davis, Jr. and Dean Martin. Rosalind Russell was den mother. Sinatra was president. As a true Rat Packer, Bogart disapproved of Ava's treatment of her husband.

"I'll never figure you broads out," he told her on their first meeting on the set. "Half the world's female population would throw themselves at Frank's feet, and here you are flouncing around with guys who wear capes and little ballerina slippers."

Ava did not point out that the guys in the ballerina slippers exposed themselves to more physical danger in an afternoon than Sinatra saw in a lifetime. Instead, she said, "Aren't you being just a bit nosy?"

Ava had a brought a sizable following consisting of Bappie, one of the Fontana Sisters, a seamstress, a couple of makeup people, and—shades of Joan Crawford—a young man laden with stacks of flamenco and Sinatra records and Ava's record player. This small army gave Bogart an opportunity for more needling.

"Let me get a running start toward the set," he said. "I

don't want to get trampled by your entourage. And if I waited until it passed, I wouldn't get there until Thursday."

"I'll give you a ten-second head start," Ava said. "Then you're on your own."

Between takes Bogart called her the Boon Hill gypsy and said she was afraid to drink too much because her Southern accent surfaced when she was drunk and the bullfighters would realize that she was just a "li'l hillbilly girl."

But Ava never rose to the bait. "That's what attracts them, honey chil'."

Despite the problems, Ava gave a creditable performance in a long and complex part. For the dancing sequences, she had to master the basics of flamenco. She threw herself into the lessons and became proficient. She had always been drawn to flamenco, the ancient dance that lays bare the Spanish soul, but now that she appreciated the eloquence of the gestures and sensed the depth of feeling in the singing, it became a real passion, drawing her even closer to Spain itself.

As soon as the Christmas holiday began, Ava flew to Madrid with the handsome matador. Complications set in when Frank announced that he was joining his wife. By day, Ava had to recruit friends to distract Frank and keep him busy while she went out with Dominguin. "Tell him I'm at the hairdresser's, tell him anything, keep him amused, as long as he doesn't find out about Luis," she told Betty Wallers, an English writer friend who was her guest at the house she had rented in La Moraleja, Madrid's posh garden suburb. Frank paced gloomily around the house, playing record after record, while he waited for Ava to return. The house was called La Bruja—The Witch.

On one occasion, Ava stayed out well into the evening. When she telephoned to scout out the situation, Frank had already gone to bed complaining of an earache. "Tuck him in and give him a nightcap," Ava told Betty Wallers. When Betty went upstairs with the drink she said, "Don't worry, Frank. Things will work out." He let out a stream of choice curses, and Betty ran from the room.

If Sinatra had any doubt that there was another man it could hardly have lasted after Christmas night, when Ava gave a party at La Bruja. Among the guests was Dominguin. The matador looked haughtily right through Sinatra. He kept drawing himself in, and up, as if he were about to dominate a raging bull. Sinatra, his pain-clouded eyes masking his annoyance and irritation, fiddled with his highball glass. Ava herself was in tremendous form. She ladled out drinks of the special powerful punch she had concocted, and showed off her newly acquired skill as a flamenco dancer. The other guests, who knew about her affair with Dominguin (and who in Madrid did not?), waited expectantly for the explosion, which never came. All the fight seemed to have gone out of Frank Sinatra. As for Dominguin, his natural pride wouldn't even allow him to acknowledge the existence of a rival.

Mercifully for everyone concerned—with the obvious exception of Ava and Dominguin—the Christmas interlude was short-lived. Ava had to go back to being the barefoot contessa. Dominguin went back to practicing with the bulls for his South American comeback, and dreamed of his auburn-haired movie queen. Frank went home.

The minute the film "wrapped"—finished—Ava was back in Spain negotiating to buy La Bruja for $66,000. But in February she was hospitalized with a painful gallstone. Dominguin was given a bed in Ava's room—a practice usually limited to spouses and close relatives. Among her visitors was Ernest Hemingway, brought over by the matador so that Ava could have someone to talk to. Dominguin's English was rudimentary, and Ava's Spanish still in its infancy, and there was not much conversation between the two of them. The scene of Ava's first meeting with Hemingway was amusingly recorded by A. E. Hotchner in *Papa Hemingway*.

Ava was surrounded by hospital nuns. They were fixing her bed, taking her pulse, marking her chart and cleaning her room. Ava, meanwhile, was on the long-distance telephone to Ben Thau at Metro. As usual, it was not a friendly conversation.

"I don't give a goddamn how many scripts you send. I am not, repeat not, *not*, NOT, going to play Ruth Etting."

Five-second listening pause.

"And you can take that contract and shove it up your heinie."

A sister smoothed the sheets and pulled them up higher to cover Ava's shoulders.

"Don't give me that crap about commitment or you'll get . . . and don't interrupt me; it's my call. What in Christ's name are you trying to do to me? Great part! I stand there mouthing words like a goddamn goldfish while you're piping in some goddamn dubbed voice."

Another pause.

"I said a *dramatic* part, for Christ's sake, and you send me Ruth Etting. It's no wonder I've got this attack. I ought to send you the bill. . . . Oh, shut up."

Ava hung up, swept her hand out to Ernest, smiled beautifully, and said, in a soft lyric voice, "Hello, Ernest."

"I take it the sisters are not bilingual," Ernest said, taking her hand.

"The sisters are darling," Ava said, "and I love this hospital so much I almost don't want to pass this goddamned stone. Sit here on the floor, Papa, and talk to me. I'm absolutely floored you could come."

"Are you going to live in Spain?" Hemingway asked.

"Yes, I sure am. I'm just a country girl at heart. I don't like New York or Paris. I'd love to live here permanently. What have I got to go back to? I have no car, no house, nothing. Sinatra's got nothing either. All I ever got out of any of my marriages was the two years Artie Shaw financed on an analyst's couch." (This was, of course, movie star's license. Ava owned a house in Los Angeles in which her sister Bappie lived, plus a car. Sinatra owned a home in Beverly Hills, and another in Palm Springs, and had just signed a new recording contract with Columbia.)

"Tell you the truth, Daughter, analysts spook me, because I've yet to meet one who had a sense of humor."

"You mean," Ava asked incredulously, "you've never been in analysis?"

"Sure I have. Portable Corona Number Three. That's been my analyst. I'll tell you, even though I am not a believer in analysis, I spend a hell of a lot of time killing animals and fish so I won't kill myself. When a man is in rebellion against death, as I am in rebellion against death, he gets pleasure out of taking to himself one of the godlike attributes, that of giving it."

Ava said gently, "That's too deep for me, Papa."

She was too forthright a woman to pretend that she understood that kind of waffle.

When she left the hospital she was suspended by MGM for turning down *Love Me or Leave Me*, a decision she would later regret because the movie, starring Doris Day, was a huge success. "We made a big mistake," she once told the director George Cukor, who had also refused the assignment. Cukor shrugged, saying, "Dear, if you and I had done it, it wouldn't have been so good."

Under suspension, she could dally in Spain with Dominguin. One sunny afternoon he took her to a famous bull-breeding ranch owned by the brothers Angel and Manuel Peralta, the leading breeders in Spain, where he had arranged a *tienta,* testing of calves for bravery. Only this *tienta* was also intended to test the matador's form and nerve.

Hemingway and his wife Mary went along as well, and as they watched the matador's remarkably graceful perfor-mance in the ring Ava said, "He's a lovely man, isn't he?"

"Are you serious about him?" Ernest asked.

"How do I know?" said Ava, hedging. "We've been to-gether for two months now, but I speak no Spanish and he speaks no English, so we haven't been able to communicate yet."

"Don't worry—you've communicated what counts," Ernest said.

Ava and Hemingway remained good friends after that. Their paths continued to cross either by design, as when she visited La Finca, Hemingway's estate in Havana, in pre-Cas-tro days, or by chance in some European city—Madrid, Bar-celona, Paris. Always, these intermittent reunions were full of warmth. Each was flattered by the other's attention. But they never went beyond friendship. True, Hemingway once wrote to his friend Harvey Britt that Ava had the body and he (Hemingway) certainly had the morale. Yet his physical attraction for the beautiful young star was simply not re-ciprocated. Ava was no more interested in collecting sexual trophies than she had been in amassing big-game trophies in Africa.

Now, in the first months of 1954, she certainly gave no thought to complicating her life even more than it already was by taking on Hemingway as a lover. Frank Sinatra and Dominguin were enough to occupy any woman's attention.

Emotionally, Ava felt rather adrift, with her marriage in a shambles and her liaison with Dominguin not yet in clear focus. Language was part of the problem. Hemingway had said they communicated what counts; if so, why didn't she know where she stood with Dominguin?

He had asked her to accompany him on his South American tour. As what? Presumably as lovers. But the sexual aspect of the affair was still very tentative and was destined to remain so.

Ava's first step was to resolve some unfinished legal business at home. Together with her beloved corgi Rags, her beloved matador Luis Miguel and her sister Bappie, she moved into a rented cottage in the Sierras, on the shores of Lake Tahoe, and filed divorce papers in the Nevada court. She asked Howard Hughes, of all people, to help her find a good lawyer, and he supplied one of his own. The crack on the head was apparently forgiven. She paid a price for accepting Hughes's help: the two fishermen stationed close to her cottage all day and most of the night were in reality—a typical Hughes touch—detectives reporting her every move.

By now there was, of course, no hiding the rift with Frank Sinatra. It came as no surprise when Ava stayed away from that year's Academy Awards presentations even though Sinatra was the odds-on favorite nominee to win the Oscar for the best supporting actor with his performance as Angelo Maggio. Frank caused a mild stir by appearing at the Pantages Theatre in Hollywood with his teenage daughter Nancy and son Frank Junior. The previous evening he had had dinner with Nancy Senior and his children, who presented to him a Saint Genesius medal inscribed "Dad, we will love you from here to eternity," and Little Nancy had added a St. Anthony medal of her own.

Sinatra's rivals in the supporting-actor category were Brandon de Wilde, the child actor who played Joey Starret in *Shane;* Jack Palance, the soft-spoken sinister gunfighter from the same movie; Eddie Albert in the role of Gregory Peck's photographer sidekick in *Roman Holiday;* and Robert Strauss, who played Stosh in *Stalag 17.* It was a formidable lineup, but Sinatra had one natural advantage over the competition:

Hollywood's fascination with its own mythology. The movie community was riveted by the saga of his comeback. The image of the actor struggling back from oblivion struck a strong responsive chord.

As Sinatra recalled it later, "The minute my name was called I turned around to look at the kids. Little Nancy had tears in her eyes. For a second I didn't know whether to go up on the stage to get [the Oscar] or stay there and comfort her. But I gave her a peck on the cheek and reached for young Frankie's hand."

After receiving the gold-plated statuette from the actress Mercedes McCambridge, he made the ritualistic acknowledgment speech, paying tribute to the director, the producer and others connected with the picture. There was not a word about Ava. Perhaps he felt that it was too late for public appeals.

Later, he gave her a miniature Oscar which she added to the crowded charm necklace.

# 16

# The Long Goodbye

Professionally, Frank was reaping a rich harvest of screen roles from his success in *From Here to Eternity*. In thirteen months he made five films, his pent-up energy erupting like oil from a gusher as he snared starring roles in *Young at Heart, Suddenly, The Tender Trap, Not as a Stranger* and *Guys and Dolls*. In record sales it was the same story. Whereas three years earlier his best record, "Goodnight, Irene," sold 150,000 pressings, the theme song of *Young at Heart* went over the million mark. His albums "Songs for Young Lovers" and "In the Wee Small Hours of the Morning" sold 250,000 at $4.98 apiece. He expected to have to pay close to a million dollars in taxes on the year's earnings.

The public Sinatra was as hard-edged and cocksure as ever; only his intimate friends knew of his moments of inner torment. There was the evening when he tore up *her* picture and then began searching desperately for the pieces to put the face together again. One piece—her nose—could not be found. Then a delivery boy arrived with a case of liquor, and Frank spotted a small scrap of paper lying by the open door. Reverently, like an archaeologist handling an Egyptian papyrus fragment, he laid it in the one empty space in the reconstructed photograph. It fit. Sighing with relief, he wrenched his gold watch off his wrist and handed it to the astonished delivery boy.

Once again, Ava stopped short of finally ending her marriage to Frank. A couple of weeks before her Nevada decree became final, she left Lake Tahoe for South America on a four-country publicity tour for *The Barefoot Contessa*. If anyone had suggested that she was running away to avoid closing this chapter in her life, her response would probably have been loud, clear and colorful. The publicity tour also supplied a convenient excuse for being with Dominguin, who was also touring in South America.

The tour was a boisterous triumph until she reached Rio de Janeiro. Seen from the approaching plane, the half-mile-high Christ statue on the mountain, arms spread out, clouds gathered around the head to form a natural halo, lent an air of serenity to the vast city. On the ground, all hell broke loose when Ava stepped from the plane, barefoot, into a howling mob. Men's hands roamed boldly over her body, buttons were wrenched off her suit, and her hat toppled from her head as she was engulfed by savage fans.

At the Hotel Gloria, Ava invited some Brazilians for drinks. The party picked up steam, and other hotel guests were soon complaining about the noise from her suite.

The following morning, Ava moved out of the Gloria and into the Copacabana and from her more luxurious quarters fought a running battle against the manager of the Gloria. He told Brazilian reporters that he had presented her a bill for a smashed glass-topped table, several broken glasses, and liquor stains on the carpet and the furniture upholstery. She called a press conference at which she claimed the Gloria Hotel had faked the damage in order to discredit her because she preferred the Copacabana and had asked to be moved there.

By now she was getting a bad press in Brazil. Her *Barefoot Contessa* "goodwill" tour was benefiting neither star nor picture. The junket was cut short and she retreated to New York, vowing never to set foot in Rio again.

Ava had the last word. "I think the Communists are behind it," she observed. "They have sneaked into all the Latin American countries. Sneaked? I guess I don't mean that. They just moved in boldly. There was nothing sneaky about it." The year was 1955.

Shortly after this "Communist plot" to discredit her, Ava left for Pakistan to make *Bhowani Junction,* based on the novel by John Masters. This meant separation from Dominguin, but there were compensations.

Her part, Victoria, the Eurasian girl caught between two societies, the British Raj and the Indians, was a prestigious plum. *Bhowani Junction* had George Cukor as its director. In Hollywood, where labels are easily acquired and stick fast, Cukor was known as a woman's director. This reputation was truer than most because Cukor handled women stars with unusual skill and insight. Ava welcomed the opportunity to work with the man who had directed Garbo in *Camille,* Katharine Hepburn in *The Philadelphia Story* and Judy Holliday in *Born Yesterday* and had just scored another personal success with the remake of *A Star Is Born,* starring Judy Garland.

Some of the more virile Hollywood types found his manner stagy; on the set of *Gone With the Wind,* which he directed for ten days before being removed, Gable used to cringe when Cukor addressed him as "dear." But he was witty, widely read, amusing and gave the most interesting parties in

Hollywood. His house was not the most opulent in Beverly Hills but was certainly one of the most beautifully furnished, and there were personally signed photographs from everybody who had ever been anybody on stage and screen in every room. In short, a Cukor movie was a class-act even when it involved hot months on location in remote Pakistan.

Ava's co-star was her old friend Stewart Granger. He was cast as Colonel Savage, the British officer in the Indian Army and the most important of Ava's three loves in the picture. (Cukor wanted Trevor Howard, but he was not a big enough star.) Until the moment when Ava joined Granger in Copenhagen for the flight to Karachi, he waited with bated breath for a call from Dore Schary announcing that a bigger star had snatched the role away. But fortunately there was no repetition of the *Mogambo* situation.

The very bumpy flight did not discourage Ava from putting away a substantial meal of pork chops. Granger, on the other hand, was hard put not to disgrace himself. On arrival in Karachi, he staggered off the plane partly propped up by Ava, and faced a battery of cameras. One of the curses of stardom in the aviation age was that, after being tossed all over the sky, there were always cameras to face on landing.

Karachi was actually a stopover en route to Lahore, where *Bhowani Junction* was to be shot on location. Cukor had been refused permission by the New Delhi government to use the novel's actual setting on the ground that the story's backdrop of Anglo-Indian politics, plus the heroine Victoria's interracial love affairs, could result in public protest. One of her lovers is white, another is Eurasian, the third Indian. Metro turned to Pakistan, which was only too happy to take advantage of India's refusal and offered its full cooperation.

While they waited in Karachi for a connecting flight, Ava and Granger received an invitation to spend an evening with King Hussein of Jordan. What Hussein was doing in

Pakistan was never made clear to either of them. But there was no mistaking the commanding tone of the two burly royal guards who delivered the king's invitation.

"Who in God's name is King Hussein?" Ava asked.

Granger told her.

"Where the hell is Jordan?" Ava wanted to know.

Granger explained. He also advised her to curtsy when presented to the king and his young queen.

Her reply was typical. "I'm an American. I don't curtsy to anybody. If I didn't curtsy to Frank Sinatra I'm sure as hell not going to curtsy to some goddamn Arab. You curtsy."

When they arrived at the palace, which was guarded by fierce-looking tribesmen, the diminutive king revealed himself to be an avid film fan, producing an autograph book for them to sign. Then they were offered Coca-Cola, to Ava's disgust, and ushered into a room with rows of chairs and a screen and shown a movie. "Oh, shit," Ava muttered audibly as the titles appeared. The movie was *From Here to Eternity*.

Lahore was hot, dirty, smelly and infested with flies. Yet even the Felatti Hotel, the best in town, where Ava had what passed for the best suite, had no air-conditioning. Her rooms were an oven throughout most of the day and half the night. As for the shooting, location scenes were filmed in the garbage-strewn streets amid wandering cattle and large, milling crowds of Pakistani extras playing Indians. It was very authentic atmosphere but hell to work in.

Yet there was none of the misery she had experienced on *Barefoot Contessa*. Cukor took the curse off with his sympathetic direction. For all her declared dislike for filming, Ava was always more agreeable when she was working than between pictures. When she had confidence in her performance—as, thanks to Cukor, she did now—she was happy, punctual and cooperative, with no sign of the temperament for which she was gaining notoriety.

There was real warmth between her and her co-workers. As on *Mogambo,* this was a predominantly male troupe, the key difference being that this time there was no Frank Sinatra to complicate things. Her usual after-work companions were Bill Travers, the British actor who played her Eurasian lover in the film, and some of the crew members.

Stewart Granger prudently steered clear of his friend Ava's boozy nightly sessions in the local restaurants or in her hotel suite, because he knew where they could lead. Instead, he kept himself busy writing letters to Jean Simmons, at home in Los Angeles making *Guys and Dolls.* By one of those curious Hollywood coincidences, *her* co-star was Frank Sinatra.

Ava, by now less inhibited by the matrimonial ground rules, couldn't understand his self-restraint. It became a kind of challenge to draw him into her circle, and eventually into her bed.

As the days trundled on, tedium and loneliness began to corrode Granger's resolve. But according to his own account years later, he managed to resist temptation by "constantly running the cold shower to quieten things down." Not that there weren't a few close shaves. One night, around two o'clock, Ava burst into his bedroom and demanded to know why the hell he avoided her and refused to go anywhere with her. Granger was in bed. Ava was in her cups. She was wearing a sari, having fallen in love with her movie costume because it was cool and because she looked good in it—and knew it.

"I always have go with Bill [Travers] and that boring publicity man. Why won't you take me? Don't you find me attractive?"

"Ava, you're probably the most attractive woman in the world, but I'm married. Remember? I'm married to Jean," Granger said.

"Oh, fuck Jean," exploded Ava.

"I'd love to, darling, but she's not here."

Ava began to giggle. "All right, you faithful husband, I'll see you tomorrow." She was off on the prowl again, leaving Granger sweating.

There was hardly anyone in the *Bhowani Junction* cast and crew who did not succumb to some illness. Ava had sunstroke and food poisoning, at the same time, and had to be given morphine shots. A few fared worse than others. One morning, Stewart Granger's stand-in, Bob Porter, a burly Londoner with a cockney sense of humor and one of Ava's cronies, disappeared. When Ava learned that he had been taken to the local Pakistani hospital, she and Granger immediately set off to find him.

They traced him to an overcrowded ward where he was tucked away in a corner, and the busy Pakistani doctor told them that he had meningitis and could not be moved. Without a word, Granger picked up his stand-in and, aided by another member of the film crew, carried him to their car and took him to the hotel. Ava cradled Porter's head. He was burning with fever. The best doctor in Lahore was quickly summoned. He looked grave as he examined Porter and after giving him several shots said that he would send over a nurse.

"We don't need one," Ava said. "I'll nurse him."

Porter's face had swollen to twice its normal size. The doctor said he was not suffering from meningitis after all but from an infection of the membrane covering the brain. For two days and nights, his condition was touch and go. The filming forgotten, Ava sat with Porter making compresses from towels and ice to cool his head, sponging him down, murmuring and cooing to him in a soft voice. Porter heard nothing. He was completely delirious.

Then, on the third day, the doctor's antibiotics began to

take effect and the infection began to drain away. With the worst over, she left Porter's bedside for the first time, went to her own room and sank into an exhausted sleep.

When *Bhowani Junction* was previewed in Los Angeles, the audience's reaction to Victoria was unsympathetic. Cards had been distributed at the door, and the comments on many of them showed that her three affairs flew in the face of the conventions of the time and seemed like too much promiscuity. Alarmed Metro executives ordered the film recut to tone down the heroine's amorous activities.

The story was reconstructed as a flashback, with narration by Stewart Granger "excusing" Victoria's behavior: as an Anglo-Indian she faced the dilemma of living between two worlds, and everything she did reflected this. Ava's scenes were also sanitized to make the character more respectable. Sex scenes were taboo, of course, but Cukor had included small touches to convey the impression that she was not as respectable as she could be. One of the scenes cut was on a train—Ava takes Granger's toothbrush and cleans her teeth with it in front of him, first dipping it in a glass of scotch.

Ava's own personal situation, estranged but not divorced from her husband and carrying on in public with a Spanish matador, may well have contributed to the public's evident disapproval. But she was not about to censor her private life for the benefit of movie audiences. After *Bhowani Junction*, she and Dominguin picked up where they had left off. In a repetition of her friendship with Mario Cabre years earlier, there was talk of their making a film together, and two scripts were being prepared. One was unimaginatively called *Matador*, and the other was a Spanish Civil War romance provisionally entitled *Ziano*.

Ava was not so far gone that she did not have residual doubts about the wisdom of plunging into either project with a novice like Dominguin, and she expressed them to her agent Bert Allenberg, the highly capable head of the William Morris Agency. "I must say I think *Ziano* is very interesting," she wrote from Europe, "but I'd be a little afraid of doing it with Luis in the lead because, as you know, he's had no experience and, not being able to speak English too well, it might be very difficult. Please don't tell Luis this because I wouldn't want to hurt him. But I do think we should be sure he can do it before I get involved. Don't you agree?"

Dominguin's potential skill as a screen actor was never put to the test. The relationship with Ava began to cool before his prospects of partnering her in a movie could be realized. It was the familiar story of Ava's personality simply proving incompatible with Latin expectations. Dominguin was less bent on "domesticating" Ava than Frank had been. But in the long run any Spaniard, even a highly sophisticated one like Dominguin, was going to find it hard to accept her brand of independence. There was no stormy breakup. Just a gentle drifting apart, like the tide ebbing away from a sandy shore, and in Madrid they would remain friendly members of the same social set.

The four months' separation while she was in Lahore had not helped matters, but the exigencies of moviemaking were only part of it. When she returned to Spain, Dominguin began to detect telltale signs that there was someone else. Small clues. A sudden rash of phone calls came from Italy, always taken in private.

Dominguin was right. The new man in Ava's life was a popular Italian comedian named Walter Chiari. They met when Ava stopped over in Rome on her return journey from Pakistan. Ava's command of Italian was no better than her Spanish, and Chiari's English would have fitted comfortably onto a postage stamp. But, in Papa Hemingway's phrase, they communicated what counted. What counted may have included the obvious fact that Chiari bore a marked physical resemblance to "my man Francis," as she occasionally called the still brooding crooner back in Hollywood.

Chiari had the same narrow, mournful features, the same angular leanness, but none of Sinatra's hard-edged brashness. He had made several highly successful Italian movies and every year starred in his own stage musical comedy, but he was virtually unknown outside Italy. His personality in real life was not far removed from the screen persona he had created—a gentle, slightly bewildered Milanese to whom strange and sometimes wonderful things happened.

Nothing could have been stranger and more wonderful than meeting Ava Gardner. That he should fall head over heels in love with her was inevitable, for the Hollywood screen goddess was the apotheosis of every Italian male's dream of an affair with La Bella Straniera, the beautiful foreign girl. That Ava should show any interest in *him*, even to the extent of going to bed with him, was for Chiari nothing short of miraculous. From their first meeting, he was enslaved. In a matter of hours he had dumped his steady girl friend, a striking young actress named Lucia Bose.

The romance brought Chiari what his forty films had not—international recognition. Before he knew it, Hedda and Louella were on the line from Los Angeles, and (through an interpreter) he was declaring his undying love for Ava Gardner, four years his senior, and even—with suitable prompting—his hopes of marriage. Ava was more circumspect, both in private as well as in public, reminding questioners that she was still technically Mrs. Frank Sinatra.

Her new Italian find aroused Ava's maternal instincts. In the winter months of 1955 she spent hours waiting in a small bar, or in his dressing room, every night, the picture of true devotion, while he appeared in his new musical, *Buonanotte, Bettina*.

It was partly to launch her new protégé boy friend as an international star that Ava agreed to make *The Little Hut,* an attempt at light sexual comedy that was doomed from the start because Metro carefully took the sex out of the original Broadway play and the comedy was too trivial to carry the full load alone. Ava played a showgirl—shades of Honey Bear in *Mogambo*—shipwrecked on a desert island with three handsome men when the yacht on which they are cruising is caught in a violent storm, and part of the film's failure was due to the highly improbable premise that she does not sleep with any of them.

Chiari's Hollywood movie debut was singularly unspectacular. He was cast as the yacht's Italian cook. In one scene he appears in a loincloth and comic-opera feather headdress, wooing Ava wordlessly because he spoke no English—an ironic parallel with their real-life relationship. Half naked and completely speechless, poor Chiari never stood much chance of making an impact, especially with such formidable co-stars as David Niven and, once again, Stewart Granger. Ava had no illusions about the quality of the picture, but she was delighted to be working with Chiari.

Before filming began at Cinecittà studios in Rome, the couple had a brief interlude in Paris, where Chiari got his first glimpse of Ava's wilder side. By day, Ava was on hand for costume fittings at Christian Dior—the official excuse for the trip. At night, they toured the bistros. Early one morning they dropped by a well-known transvestite club and Ava roared with delight at an imitation of Gloria Swanson. Then they moved to a Spanish club, Puerto del Sol, where Ava cut loose with a frenetic flamenco and danced until dawn.

Their expenses for that little jaunt came to $3,500. Since Ava was technically in Paris on pre-production business, Metro footed the bill. It was a tidy sum for the fifties, and it added to her growing reputation as an extravagant, difficult star. Her salary was fixed by contract, but when she was filming she now demanded every perquisite she could think of, and usually got it. It wasn't greed. In her more reflective moments she was beginning to worry about money. She had been in the movies for nearly sixteen years, yet she had virtually nothing to show for it. There was the newly acquired house in La Moraleja, and the earlier home in Los Angeles now principally used by Bappie, but little else to fall back on as the years advanced. She had never been frugal with her earnings, and it was too late to start now. But if she could not reverse the tendency of money to flow through her fingers like water, she was determined that, whenever possible in the future, it should be someone else's.

The studio waged a running battle against what it saw as her extravagance. On her return from Paris, the producer of *The Little Hut,* a tough-minded Scotsman named Henry Henigson who had looked after the pennies on such costly epics as *Quo Vadis,* gave vent to his exasperation in a long telegram to Culver City:

AT AVA'S REQUEST ENGAGED AND SENT TO PARIS SPE-
CIFIC HAIR STYLIST FROM ROME TO SET HER HAIR
EVERY MORNING AND SEPARATE PERSON TO MAINTAIN
IT DURING THE DAY STOP WITH KNOWLEDGE OF THIS
AVA MADE REQUEST FOR ADDITIONAL BRITISH HAIR-
DRESSER . . . WE HAVE DONE MUCH TO MATCH HER RE-
QUIREMENTS AS TO WARDROBE HOTEL HAIR
CHAUFFEUR AND AUTOMOBILE STOP . . . WE HAVE
DONE EVERYTHING REASONABLE AND EFFECTED RE-
QUESTED ARRANGEMENTS . . . BUT THIS MAY BE POINT
WHERE YOU MUST DECIDE WHETHER AVA RUNS THIS
PICTURE OR COMPANY DOES AS I HAVE TOO MUCH OF
ME IN THIS TO STAND BY WHILE SHE TAKES OVER AND

DO NOT INTEND TO COUNTENANCE DISRESPECTFUL
ACTION. . . .

In a later complaint about the size of Ava's food and drink
bill in the Grand Hotel in Rome during the making of the
picture, Henigson made the point to Metro that "this is a city
where one would really have difficulty in spending five dollars in the best place for the best dinner with wine, and I
assure you that if they constantly so partook they would re-
quire medical treatment." Ava contrived to average $100 per
day, more or less evenly divided between food and alcohol.

# 17

# The Expatriate

In press interviews Ava had but one word to describe *The Little Hut:* "lousy." In private, her language was visceral. The picture was poorly received—and fittingly so—and, as usual, she blamed Metro for putting her into another disaster.

She withdrew to her red-brick house La Bruja, which got its name from the iron weathervane of a witch riding a broom, and, with the help of Harris Williams, an American businessman in Spain who became a close and trusted friend, she threw herself into decorating it with the same aggressive, all-out attack with which she approached any undertaking that captured her interest and fired her enthusiasm. Whether she was playing tennis or pitching coins, her concentration was total. If she was decorating a house, nothing else mattered in life except buying furniture, hunting for interesting paintings at an affordable price, choosing patterns for drapes and upholstery, and looking at rugs. She bought a large Spanish fourposter bed for her second-floor bedroom and, with the help of two Spanish workmen, spent an entire day heaving and shoving it all over the room because she couldn't decide where it would fit best.

But no one could maintain interest at that high pitch for very long, and Ava's petered out before the house was finished. For Ava, yesterday's *cause célèbre* was today's forgotten task.

Or forgotten man. Walter Chiari first sensed that Ava's passion was waning shortly after the fiasco of *The Little Hut,* for which in her eyes he probably bore some of the responsibility, since she had agreed to star in it partly for his benefit. Clearly, too, distance was not helping their relationship. Chiari dropped everything and flew to Madrid to be with her.

But Chiari in Madrid was not the same as Chiari in Italy. In Rome or Milan he was on home ground, his name was a household word, and his face in the street brought smiles and friendly greetings from passersby. He could offer Ava protection as well as love. But in Madrid she saw him in a different context—a handsome unknown, unsure of his surroundings, and even of her undivided attention, for in Madrid Ava's life was a crowded canvas. She never seemed to go anywhere without her coterie of handsome, brooding young Spaniards who eyed her with smoldering intensity. Several were matadors. Ava's growing passion for bullfighting intensified her already keen personal interest in the practitioners of the *corrida.*

This partiality was so well known they even made jokes about it in far-off Hollywood. When 20th Century–Fox again sought to "borrow" Ava for a movie, executives from Fox and Metro met to negotiate the loan-out agreement. The Metro executive said Fox would be expected to pay transportation and living expenses on location for "Ava Gardner and her companion or companions, if any." To which his Fox counterpart replied dryly, "And does that include the bullfighter?"

But not all Ava's friends were bullfighters. The Sicres sent her to meet the poet Robert Graves, an old and dear friend. Ava flew to Mallorca, hiding in the toilet of the plane on the way down to escape the unwanted advances of a Spanish wolf. She wanted to know about poetry and how she should start reading it. Graves answered that most of it was a waste of time. He gave her an autographed copy of his poem *The Portrait*. She asked him to write a movie script for her, and he immediately suggested that she should play Calpurnia in his adaptation of his own novel *I, Claudius*. The production was supposed to star Alec Guinness as Claudius and the formidable Italian actress Anna Magnani as Messalina. But no studio was willing to finance it and it fell by the wayside. Graves was instantly taken with Ava, even though her language and plain speaking occasionally grated. "It isn't what she does that creates her solitary reputation, but what she says," he wrote to a friend. "She can't control her tongue at times."

This was Ava in Spain in the 1950s, vivacious, outspoken, independent. Shortly after Bappie moved to Madrid, both sisters were invited to a cocktail party in honor of the visiting American writer John Steinbeck. On entering the room, Ava recognized many prominent Spaniards and Americans. Here was an opportunity to get Bappie off to a good social start. So she positioned herself at her sister's elbow and systematically began introducing her to the other guests, while at the same time issuing instructions in a stage whisper— "Bappie, this is count so-and-so (you address him as 'your excellency')."

Shaded by a cocktail hat of immese proportions, Bappie greeted Spanish dons and ambassadors with genteel cordiality. As the evening wore on, however, and waiters continued to serve drinks in a persistent carousel, her grand style began to fray around the edges, and by the end of the party the more familiar Bappie had broken through.

As they said goodbye to Steinbeck, Bappie launched into a rambling description of a visit to a practice bullring where the frightened bulls had been chased by small dogs. Bulls frightened by dogs? Steinbeck asked, puzzled. "Well listen," Bappie said conversationally, "those fucking dogs were leaping at the fucking bulls' balls and literally hanging on by their teeth, and the bulls were roaring their fucking heads off."

Steinbeck grinned, and Ava said, "Darling, don't you know that a real lady never repeats herself?" Steinbeck roared with laughter. Ava looked indignantly at him. "What's so fucking funny about that?" she said.

Chiari's prospects suddenly brightened as a result of another decisive step in the dissolution of Ava's marriage to Frank Sinatra. Frank's film career was moving along at a confident canter. He was nominated for an Oscar for best actor for his performance in *The Man with the Golden Arm,* but lost to his mortal enemy in *From Here to Eternity,* Ernest Borgnine, for *Marty.* He romped through the delightful *High Society* with Bing Crosby and Grace Kelly. He tried his hand less successfully at playing cowboys and Indians in *Johnny Concho* and made a brief cameo appearance as the piano player in *Around the World in Eighty Days.* Then director Stanley Kramer cast him as the Spanish guerrilla leader in the Peninsular War in *The Pride and the Passion,* with Sophia Loren and Cary Grant.

When Ava learned that the film was to be shot on location in Spain she took it for granted that she and Sinatra would be seeing each other. She even prepared a guest room for him at La Bruja. It was almost two years since she had set foot in the United States, and their only contact had been by telephone, sometimes amicable, sometimes stormy, but never indifferent.

Every time she read of another "Sinatra romance" she raged about "that bastard," never mind that these tirades were sometimes addressed to her own lover. Yet the sound of Sinatra's records filled her house, and after seeing *The Man with the Golden Arm,* one of the few movies she watched in all her years of living in Madrid, she is said to have sent him a telegram of congratulation. For his part, Sinatra alternated between snarling at her and sending her large, generous gifts. There was the Facel Vega, which she would drive at great speed and overturned at least twice, and on one occasion, after a riotous night at Biarritz, the French luxury resort just over the border from Spain, she drove across a sandy beach right into the sea at San Sebastián. There was also a piano, shipped from New York after she had said she needed one for her house.

Frank arrived in April 1956 complete with starlet of the moment, Peggy Connolly, and checked into the Castellana Hilton. Days passed, and to Ava's mounting fury he made no attempt to contact her. One night, he arrived for dinner at a restaurant where Ava was already dining with one of her young Spaniards, and pointedly behaved as though they had never met.

Filming *The Pride and the Passion* in the intense summer heat was a nightmare. Kramer's film unit soon discovered that the rugged foothills around Madrid which had proved hard going for Napoleon's army hadn't changed much. To cut down on the wear and tear of traveling to and from the locations, Sophia Loren and Cary Grant often roughed it in local digs. But Frank insisted on sleeping in his hotel in Madrid every night, even when the shooting was a hundred miles away and required several hours' drive in the early morning and late at night. Eventually, relations with Sinatra were so tense that Kramer shifted his schedule to finish Sinatra's part weeks earlier than originally planned.

When Ava realized that Frank was not about to make the first move, she flew to Rome with Chiari and publicly hinted that she was going to marry him. Then on July 31, the same day Sinatra flew home to Los Angeles, she announced that divorce papers had been signed. But it was not until almost a year later in Mexico that they were picked up.

She spent Christmas with Walter's parents in Milan, amid middle-class aunts and cousins, gorging herself on pasta and enjoying the warmth of an Italian family welcome. Walter's combined Christmas and thirty-fifth-birthday gift to her was not so middle-class: a twenty-four-carat diamond solitaire, which she wore on her engagement finger.

Typically, she tried to persuade 20th Century–Fox to cast him as the bullfighter Pedro Romero in a screen version of Hemingway's classic *The Sun Also Rises,* for which she was loaned out by Metro to play Lady Brett Ashley. But Fox refused, having already signed a handsome newcomer named Robert Evans—later a leading Hollywood producer—to play the role.

Evans was an "immigrant" from the Seventh Avenue rag trade; with his elder brother he owned a highly successful pants-manufacturing company. When filming began on location in the southern-Mexican town of Morelia—the weather in Pamplona, Spain, where the novel is set, was too cold—his co-stars Tyrone Power, Mel Ferrer, Errol Flynn and Ava treated him as an outsider. Ava moved into a fifteen-room villa with Bappie, her maid and the Fontana sisters, and immediately gave a series of housewarming parties around the blue-tiled swimming pool. Everyone was invited except Evans.

In their love scenes together, Ava was offhand and completely mechanical, as if she was sure that she was going to have to reshoot them later with someone else. Finally director Henry King sent a wire to Darryl Zanuck, who was in

Europe, telling him that the cast was upset, Evans was wrong for the part, and Zanuck had better come over and settle it.

Zanuck flew to Mexico and told Evans to put on his suit of lights and go into the bullring. Then Zanuck summoned the cast, looked at the director and said loudly, "Henry, this kid is gonna play the role. And if anyone doesn't like it, *they* can leave. He's playing the part." With that, he flew back to Europe.

We are now accustomed to Hemingway's monosyllabic, bare, lean, clipped style of writing that sometimes seems like a parody of itself. Brett, for example, seldom uses a pronoun. "Must bathe," she announces. "Come and have a drink, then, before you bathe," says Bill. And she replies, "Might do that." So they do. In fact, they have several. "Have another," says Jake. Brett answers, "Might." For some time after making the film of *The Sun Also Rises*, Ava, never very voluble, discarded pronouns almost altogether. When she got back to Spain she would say things like "Need a drink."

When the book was published, its characters reflected a whole generation of post–World War I American expatriates and international middle-class Bohemians disoriented by the war, rootless, restless and rebellious—among them Hemingway himself. As she approached forty, Ava reflected some of that feeling. Like Brett, she could not seem to come to terms with herself. She had beauty, fame, tremendous flair, spirit, enough money—everything except that impenetrable inner security without which the rest is dust in the mouth. She said she wanted to settle down and lead the simple life. Ava was a movie star with no more idea of the simple life than Brett had. Escape, the expatriate life, seemed like the next-best thing. Ava continued to be Brett, on and off, for years.

Yet this role which was to become an extension of her own self became hers by default. It was originally meant for Jennifer Jones. At the last minute, her husband, David Selznick, decided that the script was not up to par, a sentiment shared by Ernest Hemingway himself when Ava showed him her copy.

On the set, Ava created a traffic problem. There was, inevitably, a matador. His name was Alfredo Leal. He was Mexico's handsome number-one bullfighter, hired by Fox to teach Robert Evans the ropes. There were also one or two other young Mexicans who partied with her at her rented villa when Leal was otherwise engaged. When Walter Chiari showed up from Rome and joined the male quadrille around her, the tension on the set was unbelievable.

Chiari, soft-spoken and charming, stood at her side constantly. Consequently her squad of escorts gave Ava a wide berth. Infuriated by Walter's possessiveness, she behaved like a child separated from her favorite toys, sulking and pacing. A magazine writer observed at the time, "Her green eyes glowed like phosphorous on a dark sea."

She began to flirt openly with other men in Chiari's presence, but nothing seemed to shake his saintly tolerance and good humor. When the filming moved to a movie studio in Mexico City, she disappeared for twenty-four hours without explanation, leaving him to fret alone in her suite in the Bamer Hotel.

One night she went to the Plaza Garibaldi, in the city's old quarter, picked up a troupe of itinerant musicians and singers—mariachis—and took them to the Bamer. She rang Sinatra in Hollywood and held the phone while the mariachis serenaded him with boleros—depressing Spanish love songs. Even that failed to dislodge the devoted Chiari, and they were still together when filming ended and they left for Los Angeles and Madrid.

Before her departure, she performed an important and long-overdue task, picking up her divorce at the Central

Courthouse in Mexico City. Her stormy marriage had whimpered to an end at last.

The divorce did little to calm the turbulence of her nature. If anything, she became more erratic. She was still quarreling and making up with Walter, and her behavior in public was less restrained, her drinking more pronounced. Mistrust was endemic in her nature. No one was immune, not even Bappie. After five straight nights of partying at La Bruja her maid broke down and lunged at her hysterically with a kitchen knife and had to be disarmed by a visitor. The maid went.

Early in 1957, she received a visit from Vittorio De Sica. The grand old man of Italian films had been asked by MGM to direct a film version of the life of Goya called *The Naked Maja*. By long-standing agreement with Metro, Ava was to play the willful Duchess of Alba who was supposed to have posed for Goya's reclining nude, and De Sica felt it was essential that he should meet the star before accepting the assignment.

An important and skillful realist as a filmmaker, De Sica had serious reservations about working with Hollywood stars, whom he considered not only difficult but an insurmountable obstacle in achieving the natural quality he sought to capture. Nevertheless, he was persuaded to journey to Madrid to see Ava, and he duly arrived at her house with his wife, Maria Mercader, a Spanish actress, and his teenage son Christian.

Ava received them barefoot, martini in hand. Latin music throbbed through the house from a record player. For a while, she sat on the couch and listened to De Sica's ideas about the picture as he sought to make himself heard above the blaring samba. Suddenly she sprang up, yanked Christian to his feet and said, "Hey, c'mon, honey, let's dance."

De Sica continued to talk about the movie from the couch

while Ava danced with his son, putting on record after record, and occasionally throwing out a "Yeah" or "Uh-huh" over her shoulder in response to the legendary director's comments.

When it was time to go, they parted cordially enough. But the visit confirmed De Sica's worst fears. "Not for all the money in America," he vowed to his wife in the taxi. Back in Rome, he politely turned down the project.

While she waited for MGM to find another director for *The Naked Maja*, Ava tried to interest the studio in producing a film based on the career of Concita Citrón, the famous lady bullfighter. It was almost inevitable that Ava's passion for the ring would eventually lead to a desire to try her hand as a female *torero*. The idea, somewhat dismaying to her friends, grew to an obsession, and in October she paid a visit to the Peralta ranch, where an incident occurred which was to profoundly influence the whole tenor of Ava Gardner's life.

Peralta agreed to arrange a special demonstration of a *rejoñada*, a technique of fighting bulls on horseback. He offered her a good horse—one of his finest, in fact—and a special lance to taunt the bull. Ava immediately accepted the challenge. A young bull, no more than eighteen months old, charged violently at her, and she struck it with the rubber-tipped lance. As she did so, her horse reared, and she was badly thrown. When she tried to rise to her feet the bull charged directly at her. She was able to throw up one arm to protect her face, but the bull struck one cheek and threw her into the air. She screamed and broke into tears as Peralta's men chased the bull away.

Crying hysterically, Ava was carried into the ranch house. Peralta stuffed ice into her swollen cheeks, but when she looked into a mirror she saw with horror that the left side of her face was a mess.

Her face swathed in a scarf, she drove back to Madrid,

where friends arranged for her to see a well-known British plastic surgeon in London, Sir Archibald McIndoe. The following day she was on the plane to London, her head again encased in a large silk scarf covering half the face, and dark glasses hiding most of the rest. McIndoe told her that he could do nothing; that in time the swelling—medically known as hematoma—would subside and that she must simply sit out the ordeal.

Walter Chiari, whom she had summoned to Madrid, tried to reassure her. "I've had worse wounds myself, give it time and it will disappear," he said. "Play around with surgery and it will be worse." But Ava was hysterical; she vomited and had to lie down for long periods. For weeks she was almost a recluse at her home, seeing only a few close friends such as Betty Sicre.

In time, she tired of her own company. She still hibernated in La Bruja, but several times a week she was on the phone inviting people over for a party. The mark on her cheek was soon almost invisible, even when she was not wearing makeup. Only on the minutest examination did a shadow show on a slight rising of the skin. But the mirror told her otherwise—in her eyes the mark was large, hideous and disfiguring, and she would curse her image as it stared back at her.

When, with great reluctance, she went to Rome to film *The Naked Maja,* she was quarrelsome, complaining about the costumes and insisting on filming only at night. Shooting did not start until six in the evening. Hypersensitive about her face, she scrutinized the daily footage for telltale shadows and blemishes on her injured cheek. At her request, a ban was imposed on visitors to the set. It was so total that even Shelley Winters, wife of Ava's co-star Tony Franciosa, found herself barred from the elaborate sound stage at Rome's Cinecittà Studios.

Shelley Winters was not the type to accept such strictures

without protest, and doubly so when rumors were flying of an affair between Ava and Shelley's husband. In reality, relations between the tense young actor who played Goya and his difficult co-star were coldly correct, but Shelley continued to suspect otherwise.

One day, she appeared at the studio gates looking very pregnant and insisted on being allowed to see Franciosa. No Italian doorman was going to stand in the way of an expectant mother, and before anybody knew it Shelley was on the *Naked Maja* set. Her intention was to defy Ava's "No Visitors" rule. But Ava saw her coming. "Get out, this is a closed set," Ava yelled. Shelley asked colorfully what right Ava had to prevent a pregnant wife from seeing her husband. Ava, resplendent in a period gown, bore down on the intruder.

In the ensuing scuffle a strange thing happened. Shelley's pregnant stomach seemed suddenly to go down like a deflated balloon. As everyone, Ava included, stood back in shock, a cushion plopped silently at Shelley's feet, falling from under her dress.

During the filming, Ava met Frank Sinatra and promptly had a row with him over his reported romance in London with American-born socialite Lady Beatty. Producing her old wedding ring from her purse she threw it at him in fury. A year later, however, they would patch up their quarrel in Melbourne when he was on a concert tour and she was making *On the Beach*.

For Ava, *The Naked Maja*—an otherwise costly failure—was distinguished in one important respect. It marked the end of her MGM contract. A few months after the movie's completion, the seven-year agreement with the studio that had launched her career expired and, for the first time in her professional life, she was a free agent. Neither Ava nor MGM sought a renewal. Another link with the past had been severed.

At every available opportunity, she consulted specialists in plastic surgery about her scar. Early in 1957 she went back to Sir Archibald McIndoe, who performed a small operation to remove what traces of the hematoma were still visible. But to Ava, the haunting shadow would remain emblazoned on her cheek forever.

In the spring of that year, a bout of flu developed into a touch of bronchitis. By now she had been in Spain long enough to give Spanish doctors a wide berth, so she found out the name of a medical officer from the United States Air Force base at Torrejón, close to the Spanish capital, and appeared one afternoon without warning at the door of his Madrid apartment: "Hi, I'm Ava Gardner."

The doctor was a tall, blond, solid-looking Iowa boy serving a five-year stint in the Air Force and nursing an ambition to become a surgeon. He didn't need to be told the identity of the pale, disheveled but still arresting creature in dark glasses and slacks and a sweater standing at his door. Nor did he wonder what she was doing in Madrid. A lurid mythology had grown up around her. Gossip had it that her sexual appetite bordered on nymphomania, and there were colorful tales of wild nights in bed.

Normally, the Air Force did not encourage its doctors to treat civilian private patients, but he decided that the situation called for an exception. He prescribed medication, sent Ava to bed, and the following day made the first of many house calls which, when she recovered, led to dates and to a close friendship lasting several months.

The young bachelor Air Force officer represented the "normal" life Ava occasionally yearned for. He was twenty-eight, Ava thirty-six, but it was obvious who was the more mature. She was drawn to his no-nonsense directness and his refusal to subordinate himself to her whimsical nature. Despite the undeniable thrill of winning Ava Gardner, he treated her as he would any other woman. "I'm not going to be your slave, Ava," he said flatly when she failed to keep a date with him without warning and without subsequent apology.

He refused to wait for hours while she dressed to go out, or to sit quietly by while she held court at restaurants to half a dozen friends. There were compensations, of course. She and the young American were robust but tender with each other. All that talk about Latins being wonderful lovers was bullshit, she told him. American men knew more about taking care of a woman's needs. When she was sober and relaxed, her old humor and vitality reasserted themselves. Her beauty and sense of fun still served to captivate men—including Papa Hemingway, whenever their paths crossed. And she could be lavishly generous with gifts and praise of her friends.

The trouble was that "normal" life was a thin diet after a while for a woman of Ava's appetites. She began to go on what the doctor called "binges" to escape from his solidity—a quick trip to Rome to see Walter Chiari, a drive to Paris to tour the bistros, a brief interlude with a new *torero*, a burst of partying with a fresh crop of young Spaniards.

After her binges she returned to his apartment, which he shared with two other Air Force officers. She would arrive unannounced at one in the morning, looking wilted, nervous and contrite, like a puppy dog coming in out of the rain. Never once were her absences explained. Never for a moment did she seem to consider the possibility that the occupants of the apartment would not be there, awaiting her arrival. Chain-smoking and drinking endless cups of black coffee, she poured out her problems, her uncertainties about her career, her money worries, and her latest exchange with her ex-husband. One night it was "God, how I hate the son-of-a-bitch," and the next it was "I can't get him out of my system." One minute she would be making conversation, and suddenly a light would go on somewhere inside her. She would get up and clap her hands and start dancing a flamenco. She was escaping from herself, from reality, and from everything else. At five in the morning, the doctor would drive her home, where she collapsed.

When he began to see her in nightclubs with other men he soberly realized that he had no monopoly over her. The final break came one evening when he was dining with a friend in the Bodegón, a popular Spanish restaurant close to the Castellana Hilton, and Ava swept in with three young Spaniards in tow. Hurt and uncomfortable, he decided that the best course was to ignore her. But Ava came to his table, pecked him on the cheek and said sweetly, "Aw, c'mon, honey, don't be jealous. You know they're just friends of mine."

In due course she found a substitute—an Air Force major from Puerto Rico stationed at the Torrejón base—thirty-five, married, a pipe smoker with a calm and soothing manner. For a while, they were inseparable. They rode together, went to bullfights in Madrid and Seville, and appeared in each other's company at parties. Fluent in Spanish, Muniz had acquired a wide circle of Spanish friends and moved easily in both Madrid and American military circles. But in due course he quietly faded out of the picture.

Free of her contractual obligations, Ava was torn between the necessity to earn an income and the tempting prospect of an idle life in Spain. There is a quotation from *The Sun Also Rises* which is perhaps pertinent. Bill Gorton says to Jake, "You're an expatriate. You've lost touch with the soil. You get precious. You drink yourself to death. You become obsessed by sex. You spend all your time talking and not working. You hang around cafés." And Jake replies, "It sounds like a swell life." Ava would have preferred to hang around Madrid's cafés, but January 1959 found her flying to Melbourne to film Neville Shute's novel *On the Beach*. The fact that she knew Frank Sinatra would be touring Australia at the same time may or may not have influenced her decision to accept the role of the heavy-drinking party girl who is one of the last survivors of an atomic war.

The assignment brought out the best and the worst in her. She worked with diligence and concentration and gave a well-rounded, exceptionally warm performance. At the same time, her brushes with the Australian press were among the least edifying in her long and tortured history of troubled relations with the media.

Sinatra's own chronic dislike for the press, often expressed in the crudest terms, had clearly rubbed off on Ava. But that intensified rather than initiated her own lifelong suspicion of reporters' aims and intentions. Her phobia for the still camera, especially in the hands of a news photographer, was rooted in a feeling that many people were not necessarily anxious to photograph her in a favorable light. She was perhaps less capable of coping with a press conference than any other star. Stand her up in front of journalists with pads and pencils and she began to tremble. It never turned out well. She thought the dice were loaded against her.

In the press conference she gave on January 5, the Melbourne press bombarded her with personal questions. They asked about her taxes (she owed the United States government a bundle), whether Frank Sinatra was coming to Melbourne to see her, how often she phoned him, and he her, whether her face was injured at a wild party. Her replies were curt, cryptic and controlled, but afterward she flew into a rage, vowing not to speak to the press again.

She was still simmering several weeks later in Sydney when

a reporter who approached her table at a restaurant had a champagne glass hurled at him. (She attracted more attention in Melbourne when she gave a party during which two horses were brought up to her suite and fed champagne.) Although reporters would have been as susceptible to her charm as anyone else, they were never exposed to it. Her suspicious nature made her stiff and nervous in their presence.

This deep mistrust was also an increasing problem for her close friends and colleagues. On the set of *On the Beach* Stanley Kramer, the director, said to her, "Ava, why bother fooling with your hair now? It's better the way it is." She let it go by, but for the next four days she was so hostile toward him that he finally confronted her.

"Well, you were so cruel about my fixing my hair, as though you thought that was all I cared about," she told him. Kramer had to rack his memory to remember the incident and had to work hard to convince her that her interpretation of it was wrong. It took a week. Later, she delayed and vacillated about making return reservations from Australia for herself, Bappie, her maid and her manager. By the time she had settled on a departure date, bookings were hard to come by and they could not all travel back on the same plane. When Kramer called to ask when she was leaving she became very angry about her flight problems, and the director couldn't get a word in edgewise. They never said goodbye.

She didn't say goodbye to Walter Chiari either. He had arrived in the middle of the shooting, to a truculent welcome. On edge because of the heat, the hard working pace set by Kramer, and the boredom of Melbourne, a handsome but prim city with virtually no night life, she made him, as always, the scapegoat, picking quarrels with him until he pointedly began to be seen around publicly with an attractive Australian dancer named Dawn Kellar. Ava's reaction was to bar him from the set.

# 18

# A Year in the Life

By 1963, Ava had moved out of the country setting of La Moraleja and into an apartment house in Madrid. As a free lance she could now work when she felt like it, free to pick and choose her films from the scripts offered her.

Producers were hardly beating a path to her elegantly furnished duplex at 8 Calle Dr. Arce. She had just turned forty, an age when a leading lady who hopes to pass muster before the camera must practice discipline and self-denial. Ava, on the contrary, bore the wear and tear of a hectic life like a badge of honor. Of her performance in *On the Beach*, *Newsweek* magazine said: "Miss Gardner has never looked worse, or been more effective."

Her reputation as a creator of general havoc on the set, tolerated in her heyday when she was good box office, had come home to roost. This was the era of independent producers on tight budgets who thought twice before engaging a star widely known for her expensive habits and her potentially costly tantrums and foibles.

She had been scarred by the failure of her last two pictures—unfairly so, since Ava was no better or worse than usual in either. *The Angel Wore Red* turned out to be such a bomb that it was barely released in the United States and had only sporadic showings in Europe, and *55 Days at Peking* greased the skids under the movie industry's nine-day wonder Sam Bronston. His career never recovered from the financial losses.

Few scripts came in now, mostly duds; Ava rejected them, usually without a cause for regret. One exception: she would later say she was sorry she had refused the Geraldine Page role in *Sweet Bird of Youth*. After years of manifesting her lack of commitment to stardom, she accepted the twilight of her career with an indifferent shrug and another drink—in fact, several other drinks.

By the early 1960s, Spain had all but supplanted Italy as the European Hollywood, Cinecittà having virtually priced itself out of the market. Madrid was full of figures out of Ava's studio past. Actors, actresses, producers and technicians converged on the Spanish capital and immediately got busy re-creating Beverly Hills. Ava remained aloof from the growing movie colony. She had to be the only film star in Spain who did not subscribe to *Variety* and the *Hollywood Reporter*. The news and gossip in the "trades" simply did not interest her. She rarely went to the movies. In her deliberate self-extrication from her professional past, her circle of friends, which included the Sicres, Frank Ryan and his wife Marsha, and Harris Williams, consisted of Americans and Spaniards most of whom were not connected with the movies.

One evening she was dining out with friends when—in an echo of the escapades of her youth—a woman approached her table. "Are you Ava Gardner?" the woman asked.

"No, but a lot of people tell me I look like her," Ava replied.

"You really do," said the woman, walking away.

Ava adopted this line of defense several times after that, and part of her believed it. She was no longer Ava Gardner, movie star. She had divorced herself from her widely acclaimed star persona. If her name had been invented by the studio, she would probably have renounced it now, returning to her real one the way a divorced woman often returns to her maiden name.

The prospect of living without working makes a lot of people uneasy, but Ava wasn't one of them. She had always had a talent for filling her days with pleasurably aimless activity, and in Madrid *dolce far niente* became her daily routine—or rather nightly, because she led a nocturnal existence.

The advent of morning signaled the end of her topsy-turvy day, and she went to sleep in her big movie star's bed raised on a platform. Sometime past noon, she resurfaced and put away a sizable rural breakfast. For all her acquired polish, Ava never lost her farm girl's appetite.

Her bedroom was surrounded by walk-in closets, one for gowns and others respectively for shoes, hats and day clothes. She now dressed casually and wore no makeup except lipstick.

She woke up sparkling with good humor. No matter how much drinking had gone on the previous night she was rested, refreshed, and never seemed to know the torment of a hangover. "Why can't she always be as she is in this first hour?" one of her succession of male secretaries, Ben Tatar, an out-of-work New York actor, used to ask himself as Ava sat in bed gossiping about friends or rummaging among the memories of her colorful past.

Her long, comfortable living room had Louis XV chairs at
one end and leather club couches at the other. On the walls
hung Dong Kingman watercolors and paintings by the Spanish artist Fortuny and the American Orry-Kelly. The décor
was created by George Heuningen Heune, a gifted designer-
photographer and close friend of George Cukor.

Her first act of the day after bathing and dressing was to
go to the armoire where the drinks were kept and pour
herself a gin and tonic. Lunch was late and long in the Spanish tradition—and boozy in Ava's tradition. Usually, she went
to Madrid's fine German eating house personally supervised
by its august owner, where she would kick off her shoes
under the table and the waiter would thoughtfully bring a
velvet cushion for her feet. Sometimes she went to the elegant Jockey, where she, an unrepentant Stevenson Democrat, dined among the prosperous establishment of Franco's
Spain.

Never very fond of her own company, she tended to pre-
side over large tables consisting of friends, visitors from the
United States, hangers-on, plus the man of the moment—not
necessarily always a lover, but definitely straight, in contrast
to her increasing tendency to attract a gay coterie.

Early in 1963, the man of the moment was another handsome major in the American Air Force from Torrejón Air
Base. Aside from his good looks, his qualifications included a
cheerful nature, a liking for gin rummy, and a more than
average skill as a golfer. Gin rummy occupied a large pro-
portion of Ava's waking hours. Golf in the afternoon was her
favorite form of exercise.

Ava was always prone to crazes. When President John F.
Kennedy launched his national fitness campaign, she did her
bit by exercising daily on the bedroom rug to the accompani-
ment of Ray Charles records. When she felt she had to do

more, she began to talk of organizing a hike to Toledo, a distance of thirty miles, but she never got around to it.

For a time, one of her after-lunch activities was to drive to Torrejón and attack the slot machines on the base. She would keep her coins in a paper cup like the old ladies in Las Vegas, shriek with laughter when she hit the jackpot, and curse when she was losing. She was equally capable of slipping back into the Lady Brett role, the rootless beautiful expatriate, and whiling away the afternoons knocking back vodka and boilermakers at Pepe's, Madrid's answer to Harry's Bar.

Torrejón, conveniently located on the southern edge of Madrid, continued to be a handy source of occasional escorts whenever she felt homesick for American company, but the major lasted longer than most of them before eventually fading from the scene, leaving behind a parcel of uncollected laundry, delivered after his departure, and a mechanical talking parrot which Ava bought for him at F. A. O. Schwarz on a trip to New York.

Even at the height of its movie boom, Madrid was never so blasé that it could take Ava's exploits in stride. Ava stories, true and apocryphal, circulated regularly among American expatriates and Spaniards alike. One perfectly factual story that made the rounds detailed how Ava became persona non grata at the German restaurant. It involves an American writer, an old friend who was her house guest, and it starts on a spring afternoon with Ava surfacing at her usual waking hour in an unusually snappish mood. Ava and the writer spent the rest of the day bickering over trivialities. But in the evening a truce was declared and the writer invited Ava to a reconciliation dinner at the restaurant. Ava accepted.

She was bowed to the table by the owner himself, his heels clicking like castanets, monocle rammed into his eye, hair bristling in a fresh crew cut. Central Casting could not have produced a more archetypal Prussian *Junker*. She ordered a dry martini. When it arrived, she held up her glass, shouted *"Falsificado!"* and slowly poured the drink onto the floor. The buzz of conversation in the crowded restaurant snapped to a halt as if it had been switched off. *"Falsificado* means fake, ladies and gentlemen," she announced to the room in general. "That's Spanish gin, and they're passing it off as genuine English."

In a flash, the German was back at her side. "Please, Miss Gardner. You know ve don't serve fake gin." It was not unknown in Spain for the contents of a seemingly authentic English gin bottle to have been distilled no farther away than the outskirts of Madrid, but Ava had been downing the restaurant's martinis without cause for complaint for years. To humor his famous client, however, the German called for an unopened bottle of gin, broke the seal in her presence, and personally mixed her a fresh drink. Once again, Ava tossed the contents of the glass on the floor.

As the owner stood speechless in a puddle of martinis all eyes were on Ava's table. In an attempt to salvage the situation the dismayed writer said, "Why don't we switch to vodka? That's something the Spaniards have not started to make." To his relief, Ava agreed. But whether he fully realized it, he was the principal target of this performance. The demons of mischief were by now in full cry, and worse was to come.

A vodka martini was brought. The restaurant owner served it. "Is this all right, Miss Gardner?" he asked. Without a word, Miss Gardner hooked her index finger inside his belt and tugged. Then she tossed the drink inside his immaculately pressed striped pants.

For an instant he was beyond speech. Then he began to scream with rage. Ava's companion, aghast at the havoc she was creating, pleaded with her to leave. Ava rounded on him. "What's the matter? Are you scared?" But waiters were gathering menacingly around their employer, who continued to babble furiously at her in three languages, and even Ava could see that forcible ejection was not far away. As she made for the exit, he pronounced the sentence of expulsion: "You vill never be allowed in here again. Never. Never."

Outside, Ava refused to allow her companion to ride home in the same taxi. Not content with leaving him standing on the sidewalk, she leaned out of the cab window yelling insults like "Yellow" and "Chicken." The writer had to walk to Calle Dr. Arce because he couldn't find another cab. He entered the apartment building just in time to see his suitcase—packed by Ava—hurtling down the stairwell toward him, closely followed by his Olympia portable. Her revenge for the afternoon's disagreements was complete.

Between Palm Sunday and June 30, Sunday and Thursday afternoons were sacrosanct: they were bullfighting days, and only illness could keep her away from Madrid's vast Las Ventas bullring. From her customary vantage in the front row above the *barrera,* Ava would run an expert eye over the matadors as they made their stately entrance into the ring in the opening parade, commenting appreciatively on the ones who caught her fancy.

She was well known at Las Ventas, and hardly an afternoon went by without one of the matadors dedicating a bull to her. She was constantly carting home blood-soaked bull's ears, her trophy from the kill. Often a matador's silk cape would be spread out on the railing in front of her while the owner confronted the bull in the ring. The young bullfighter's reward for such signal honor was an invitation to dinner at Ava's home to sample her expertly cooked pasta and fried chicken.

For the young matadors there was more to Ava than beauty and sexual promise. She had the added attraction of being an aficionada of the first order. She knew a savage bull when she saw one, and she appreciated a daring veronica. She never cringed from the necessary business of the picadors as they struck their lances into the bull's shoulders. When it came to the kill, she was not one of those fainthearted women who hid their faces at the sight of blood on the sand. She sat on the edge of her seat, and a clean, firm thrust of the muleta brought her to her feet in a frenzy of cheering and applause, especially if the matador was dedicating the bull to her.

Hoarse and excited, she would toast the bull with a couple of nips from her double flask, containing brandy in one section and vodka in the other, usually carried by her secretary or escort.

In the evening, the pace quickened. First there was dinner at the Commodore Hotel, focal point of social life for expatriate Americans in Madrid, or perhaps at the Castellana Hilton, which had a good dance band. Then came a stop at a nightclub, but this was merely a way of marking time until two in the morning, when she headed for one of the flamenco dancing clubs. No flamenco club worthy of the name opened for business before midnight, and in Madrid no self-respecting nightbird would be seen in one before two in the morning.

Flamenco had remained one of Ava's enduring passions, and she knew every club within a fifty-mile radius of the city. Her favorites were Las Brujas, which was downtown and classy, and Manzanillas, which was neither. To get to Manzanillas you had to drive almost all the way out to Torrejón, and it was a place with a shady reputation where debutantes rubbed shoulders with some of Madrid's disreputable characters. The police occasionally raided it looking for mobsters. The dancers, real Andalusian gypsies, were magnificent.

Spaniards have the same historical commitment to flamenco as they do to bullfighting, and they went to the clubs—and still do—to drink great quantities of whiskey and to be stirred to the depths of their Latin souls by the raw passion of the songs of jealousy, seduction and infidelity, and by the extraordinary combination of sensuality and discipline of the gypsy dancers. Young Spanish men of good family were there to look over the latest crop of gorgeous female dancers just up from the villages around Granada and Córdoba. An affair with a flamenco dancer did wonders for a man's macho image.

Ava drank the whiskey, too, but unlike the Spaniards she got no charge out of being a mere spectator. She wanted to dance herself. For a price, she was allowed to choose the partners she wanted from among the slim-waisted male dancers, plus her favorite singers and guitarists, sometimes leaving the club bereft of its best performers. Whisking them and her party into a private room she would begin to dance, which she did with tempestuous energy, skirts swirling, hair tossing, and not without skill. All the hard work of preparation for the flamenco sequences in *Barefoot Contessa* was not forgotten, and expressive hand language complemented her natural sense of rhythm.

At closing time, she piled the whole troupe into her dark-blue Lincoln Continental—which had replaced the Facel Vega—and transported them home to pick up where she had left off, thereby, incidentally, breaking a Spanish social taboo. Not that there was anything unusual about taking flamenco dancers home at dawn to continue the party; what flew in the face of convention was that a single woman was doing it. If Ava was even aware of this breach of Spanish manners it certainly did not bother her.

The almost nightly strumming, stamping and clapping was the scourge of her neighbors, especially the gigantic elderly Argentinian who lived directly below her and who frequently called in the police. The arrival of the Guardia Civil quieted things down and signaled the start of Ava's cooking phase, when she produced dinner for the whole party. By the time goodbyes were said, and the gypsies were paid for their night's work, the early-morning traffic was already rattling down the Calle Dr. Arce.

Eventually, Ava's downstairs neighbor, convinced that it was a matter of time before the bedroom chandelier came crashing down on his bed, or that the nightly reverberations would bounce off its plinth on the mantelpiece the urn containing his first wife's ashes, quietly moved out of the apartment and put it up for sale. Ava's irate neighbor was Juan Perón, the exiled Argentinian dictator. The ashes were Evita's.

As the city came noisily to grips with another working day, Ava went to bed. After such a night's drinking and physical exertion, sexual activity, however devoutly wished, was usually out of the question. There were nights when she even had to be helped out of her clothes by her maid.

Yet often sleep would not come. A taste for late nights had become tinged with insomnia. One night, Ava summoned Ben Tatar and complained, "I can't sleep. Sing me a lullaby." Tatar took her hand in his own and sang her a Yiddish lullaby with which his mother used to sing him to sleep as a child, and, presently, Ava slid into a surface slumber. After that, singing his employer to sleep was added to his list of occasional tasks.

Ava always maintained, "I can't be an alcoholic. Anybody who eats as much as I do can't possibly be one." And it is true that the enormous amount Ava ate clearly blunted the effects of her equally considerable alcoholic intake. Regular visits to Main Chance, the famous fat farm in Phoenix, Arizona, on what she still quaintly referred to as "health kicks," also helped. But the impact of the drinking on her personality was another matter. As the day wore on, well might her staff long for the affable creature sitting up in bed eating her habitual hearty breakfast. Her tongue could be as sharp as a knife, and her temper erupted without warning like a flash storm at sea, drenching friends and strangers alike with abuse and profanity. Friendship with Ava often required both patience and toleration, and working for her could be a physical and emotional endurance test. One evening, Hugh O'Brian, the movie star, dropped by unannounced. They had met the previous evening when he had been designated her escort to a movie function, and they had got on so famously that he was hoping to invite her to a restaurant. But Ava was on the point of sitting down to dinner with a group of her friends. She sent her maid out to tell him that he was not welcome.

Highs of warmth and generosity plunged to lows of suspicion and antagonism. As was the case with Renée before her, Petra the maid was treated more like a companion than a servant. Occasionally, she accompanied Ava to restaurants, resplendent in Ava's elegant almost new cast-off suits and coats designed by Edith Head and the Fontana sisters. They looked more like girl friends meeting for a good gossip. Yet Ava also complained to friends that the maid was "robbing me blind," and that Pepe the chauffeur, with whom she believed Petra was having an affair, was her accomplice.

Ben Tatar found himself summarily dismissed after six months' employment as a result of a flaming row over two missing golf balls. It was a bizarre conclusion to an equally bizarre association. When Tatar was hired in New York on

New Year's Eve 1962, he was first screened by Ava's sister Bappie, then by Renée, who was visiting her ex-employer, then by Ava's onetime brother-in-law Larry Tarr, who tended to resurface whenever Ava and Bappie were in New York, and then for some unaccountable reason by Frank Sinatra's private secretary, who happened to be visiting Ava. Without exception, all of them had the same question: "Do you know what you're letting yourself in for?" Of course he didn't. However, this lantern-jawed but otherwise good-looking actor of twenty-nine was attracted by the glamor of working for a star of such beauty and wide renown. Besides, he saw the job as a way of establishing himself in Spain, where the movie action was.

When he finally met Ava, she tested his typing skill by having him answer two letters. One was to Henry Luce, owner of *Time* magazine, declining an invitation to attend the publication's fiftieth-anniversary dinner in April of the following year honoring *Time*'s cover subjects, and the other to the Governor of North Carolina accepting the freedom of her home state.

Those were the first and last letters Tatar was ever called upon to type for Ava. Typing turned out not to be one of his many duties. In a remarkably short time, he was woven into the fabric of her life. He filled a need which the studio system had rendered essential to her, even in her premature "retirement": paid companion, assistant and general factotum; an extension of the woman herself.

He went to bed after she did, and was up before her. He was her escort during the romantically fallow periods but faded discreetly into the background with the blossoming of a new involvement. Whether out shopping or to dinner, Tatar paid the bill, because Ava, like royalty, carried no money.

One spring afternoon, following a round of golf with

Tatar, Ava counted the balls. She was two short. Their disappearance became a matter of major concern to her. When a search of the house failed to produce them, she accused her secretary of having taken them.

The ensuing argument quickly escalated into a bitter row. Ava vented her pent-up resentment, ranting about Tatar's past disloyalties and misdeeds. Tatar hit scathingly back at her chaotic life style. She fired him on the spot. The maid blocked his exit through the apartment's main door, and he was forced to leave through the service entrance. When he asked for time to collect his belongings, Ava refused. They were delivered by her chauffeur a few days later, and Tatar never set foot inside her home again. If the golf balls were ever found, he certainly didn't hear about it.

The incident was the climax of Ava's slow accumulation of complaints, real or imagined, against her young secretary. She had earlier told at least one friend that he had become overbearing; that on more than one occasion, he had burst into her room without knocking and made a scene. The fact was that the delicate balance of such relationships was never destined to last very long. Ava and Tatar had simply reached the point of no return.

Over the weeks and months, visitors trickled in and out of the apartment at 8 Calle Dr. Arce. Hemingway's wife Mary, on a rare return visit to Ernest's Spanish haunts, spent a weekend. Bappie, no longer a divorcée but the wife of a cheerful American prop specialist working in Europe, lived close by and was a frequent caller.

Then, in the fall of 1963, John Huston flew into Madrid expressly to see her.

They had been friends, Ava and the gangly, battered filmmaker, since the early days of both their careers. *The Killers* had first brought them together. In Hollywood, they moved in the same social orbit, frolicking in the same swimming

pools, drinking at the same watering holes, flirting at many
of the same dinner parties.

They were in many ways kindred spirits. Each recognized
and appreciated the other's charm, honesty, humor and
force of character. Later, their paths crossed sufficiently frequently in their travels to keep their friendship alive.

Meanwhile, the complex twists of Hollywood marital traffic had contrived to link them together. Artie Shaw was married to Evelyn Keyes, who had, in more or less chronological
order, played Scarlett O'Hara's younger sister Suellen in
*Gone With the Wind,* been married to Huston and been (by her
own account) one of the busiest lays in Tinseltown.

Shaw and Evelyn Keyes were now living on the Spanish
Costa Brava, then still relatively unspoiled. Evelyn Keyes was
wife number six, but then, as the writer Malcolm Mug-
geridge once punned, "None but the Brava deserve the
Costa." Ava would run into them about once every six
months. Like Ava, Shaw had gone into voluntary early retirement. His clarinet was gathering dust in its black case in a
corner of his study while he sat at a typewriter, still trying to
recycle himself as a writer.

This domestic juxtaposition caused Ava and Huston much
amusement, but Huston was a man with a mission. Draping
his seemingly endless body across one of her leather couches,
he offered her the role of Maxine the hotelkeeper in his film
version of Tennessee Williams' *Night of the Iguana.*

If Huston had been any other director to come to her with
such a proposition, Ava would probably have refused out-
right and shown him the door. The prospect of returning to
the screen in such a demanding part was truly daunting.
"But why me? You need a strong actress. You know I'm no
actress."

Yet she was genuinely fond of Huston, and extremely susceptible to his persuasive manner. The director spoke to her

gently, as if coaxing a frightened horse. If the truth were told, Tennessee Williams would have had difficulty recognizing the lethal Maxine of his creation in Huston's touching, vulnerable portrait, but it did the trick. Still rather dubious, Ava agreed to play the role, starting in December on location in Puerto Vallarta, Mexico.

# 19

# Portrait—with Dogs

Before the shooting started, the doubts resurfaced and Ava—already in Mexico City—told Huston she could not possibly cope with the part and was going home. Recognizing that the time had come for firmness rather than charm, Huston told her, "Come on, Ava, that's quite enough of this now, you're going to do it, and I don't want to hear *one more word* about backing out of it." She put up a mild resistance at first, but finally she shrugged and said, "Well, all right."

At first she grumbled about her costumes, by designer Dorothy Jenkins, wishing that she could have been allowed to engage the Fontana sisters. But once she had agreed to undertake it she quickly came to grips with the physical implications of playing Maxine. After experimenting with several hairstyles with Sydney Guilaroff, she settled for a severe ponytail, with her hair pulled back tightly from her face. Then she penciled in lines under her eyes, and used makeup to accentuate the bluish bags of flesh under her lower eyelids. When she looked in the mirror, she burst into tears. What woman wants to be confronted by her future looks? But she did not flinch from the makeup, accepting it as an essential element of the character.

Ava installed herself in a small rented house in Puerto Vallarta with her two dogs Rags and Cara, and Renée Johnson, her black maid. Reconciled with Ava after many ups and downs, Renée was making one of her periodic appearances as Ava's confidante and traveling companion. She gave Ava massages after work, ran interference with reporters and studio officials, and harangued airline employees and porters at airports.

Magazine and newspaper writers swarmed into Puerto Vallarta to cover the shooting. And no wonder; the assembled cast was a gossip writer's dream. Richard Burton was cast as the unfrocked priest. Elizabeth Taylor, fresh from *Cleopatra,* had followed him to Mexico at the head of an entourage consisting of two black maids, a laundress, a green parrot and a former slot-machine repairman engaged as masseur for Burton, plus assorted children. Deborah Kerr, the second female lead, was accompanied by writer Peter Viertel, who for a brief while had been one of Ava's occasional beaux. There was also Sue Lyon to provide the ingenue touch, and Tennessee Williams himself to spice up the mixture.

The press was quick to report Burton's great fondness for tequila and beer chasers, adding that Elizabeth did not lag far behind. But the press learned only the half of it. Burton and Taylor quarreled often. They seemed to other members of the cast and crew to be forever either fighting or making up, and both with equal ferocity.

The main filming took place in Mismaloya, an island village reachable only by water. Everyone had to be ferried across from Puerto Vallarta, and since the studio controlled the jetties at either end, everyone, including the press, was at the studio's mercy—except Ava, who usually waterskied to and from work behind her own speedboat. Mismaloya had been built by the Mexican government expressly to serve as a setting for *Night of the Iguana*, after which the houses were to be sold to the public.

Given the temperaments involved, tension between Ava and Liz Taylor was inevitable. Burton hardly fitted into the mold of Ava's past men, but she found him attractive and didn't hide it. The Welsh actor found her equally fascinating, but when he began flirting with her on the set Liz was not amused. Burton got the hot blast of her jealous rage. There were screaming rows, and Liz would storm off the island set vowing to leave Mexico altogether. Burton, on the other hand, would camp in one of the bungalows on Mismaloya, nursing his pride like an angry bull. Then notes would fly back and forth and Liz and Burton would make up, but Ava had only to appear on the set in a flirtatious mood for the drama to erupt again.

On the tense *Iguana* set director John Huston called the stars together and solemnly presented to each of them a gold-plated derringer pistol with gold-plated bullets inscribed with their names. "If the competition gets too fierce," he said, "you can always use the guns."

Filming conditions were hazardous in other respects as well. Mismaloya was riddled with large insects, was intensely hot and humid, and was isolated from the outside world, with erratic electricity and poor communications. For Ava, it was *Mogambo* all over again—ancient DC-6s flying into Puerto Vallarta with food, drink and other essentials.

Heavy rains often interrupted the filming, leaving the troupe with little to do but play gin rummy and drink tequila. Actually Ava's preference had a wider scope: she drank everything she could find or was offered. For amusement, she frolicked with young Puerto Vallarta beach boys, some of whom ended up as extras in the picture.

Yet, ironically, she had trouble in the scene where Maxine makes love to two boys on the beach. Her performance in front of the cameras was stiff and awkward. Then Huston made her join him in several stiff drinks and showed her graphically what he wanted in the sequence. After that she had no problem. Huston had an instinct for finding the right approach to Ava's anxiety, but he had the advantage of an intimate friendship. On late nights, the cast bedded down in bungalows around the set, and it was common knowledge that Ava and Huston occasionally shared the same quarters.

On the whole, Ava handled the role with considerable skill. Once she got into the character, her extraordinary intuition took over. Even so, she was on edge and explosive, especially with the visiting press. When the Rumanian photographer Gjon Mili, an immensely painstaking and persistent craftsman, took too many stills of her for a *Life* cover, she lost her temper and kicked him in the stomach. "Christ," she shouted, "haven't you taken enough pictures?" Then she chased him off the set.

Part of the problem was that she still had not recovered from the shock of learning, before she left Madrid, that Ernest Hemingway had committed suicide. Only a few months earlier she had seen him on both sides of the Atlantic—first in Madrid and later at his home in Ketchum, Idaho, where on July 2 he shot himself through the head. Perhaps, too, the sad, wounded woman at the end of the world whom she was portraying in the movie, the rootless, lonely Maxine, was in some ways too close to home.

Then, on November 22, the cast heard the news on the radio that John F. Kennedy had been assassinated. Ava was sitting in the only bar in Mismaloya drinking at four-thirty in the afternoon when a silently weeping Deborah Kerr joined her. The shooting continued but when, in the early evening, the unit observed a minute's silence, Ava and Deborah clung together and cried unashamedly.

For all her gamboling with beach boys, and her friendship with Huston, Ava was essentially lonely and aloof. Her circle of friends, never very large, had dwindled over the years, to a hard core who were willing to make the effort to break through her barrier of suspicion and reserve and to tolerate her whimsical nature. Those whom she genuinely admired were fewer still. With the death of the adored Papa Hemingway, perhaps only Robert Graves held a truly high place in her esteem.

The poet and the "filmstar with a heart," as he once called her, continued to correspond, and Ava's letters to Graves were touchingly revealing. "So often when I'm sad I write to you—I almost never send them to you—but I feel better," Ava wrote on one occasion around this time. "Robert, I tried to explain to someone today that getting your letters makes up for all the motion picture crap. Instead of feeling dirty and useless I felt very strong and worthwhile—it's nice to know someone I love and admire so much takes the time out of a busy life to say good things to me."

Few men in Ava's life heard themselves praised in such heartfelt terms, and certainly not her three husbands. Yet she remained steadfastly loyal to each one of them. Once, a friend sank into a deep armchair and made a joke about seeing the world from Mickey Rooney's eye level. Ava turned on him angrily and snapped, *"He* was a giant!" Frank Sinatra was always described as "wonderful," and his singing voice from a radio or record player could stop her in her tracks. Distance even lent enchantment to the two years she spent with Artie Shaw, whom she remembered as a brilliant musician and a distinguished intellectual.

The last weeks of shooting weighed her down, and she did

not even attend the cast and crew Thanksgiving Day party, clearly thinking that there was little to give thanks for, though she did go to the "wrap"—or end-of-shooting—bash. Moody and depressed, she flew back to Mexico City, and thence to Madrid, just in time for Christmas and her forty-first birthday.

Ava was pleased with her performance in *Night of the Iguana*, not least because Huston had "deglamorized" her. At home she kept a stack of stills of herself in the film and—unusual for her—showed them off to all her friends. For once, she had been allowed to be herself on the screen. Moreover, there was general agreement among the critics that Ava had excelled. *Newsweek* noted that Ava had returned to her North Carolina drawl and "she is all high blood and blowsiness . . . a great woman to play a great woman."

She seemed poised for a promising second career as a character actress. That the transition did not materialize was largely her own doing. Lacking the self-confidence to build on her successful performance, she turned down one good offer after another, preferring to lie fallow again in Madrid, where she had returned to her Lady Brett routine. Some years later, she would say of *Night of the Iguana* in an interview, "I was determined to do my best in the film. I even made myself look awful. And what happened? When the film came out, instead of giving me credit for trying, the critics just said, 'Ava has lost her good looks.'"

The truth is that the critics said nothing of the kind. Ava rationalized her fears by falsely accusing the reviewers. It was only when John Huston approached her again that she consented to return to work. Huston offered her the role of Sarah, the barren wife of Abraham, in *The Bible*, his elaborate film re-creation of several books of the Old Testament.

Again, it was up to Huston to coax Ava bit by bit into playing the part, showing her the beauty, suffering and patience in the character of Sarah, the quiet acceptance with which she endured her barrenness, and which led her to induce Abraham to take another woman in order to sire a son. For Ava, who had never borne a child, the role evidently had a deep meaning, and her recurring regret that she had never raised a family surged to the fore. Once, while visiting an American family in Madrid, she was shown their three-year-old daughter. As she watched the little blond freckled creature playing on the rug at her feet, she said longingly, "If I had had a child by Frank she would have looked exactly like her." With her complexion and Frank's, a blond child was unlikely, but her romanticized regret envisioned her unborn daughters as Shirley Temples. She also used to enjoy telling how she was once walking in Manhattan with Frank's teenage daughter Tina and a man yelled out, "Hey, lady, that's a mighty pretty daughter you've got there." Tina said, "Ava, are you *sure* you're not my mother?"

Thanks largely to Huston's consideration, Ava enjoyed playing Sarah. Huston even gave in to her insistence that the Fontanas design her Biblical costumes. Although the movie, made in mid-1964, also included extensive location work in Egypt and North Africa, Ava's scenes required her to go no farther than the Dino De Laurentiis studios in Rome. In published interviews on arrival in Italy, Ava said there was "nobody special" in her life. And knowing her of old, the *paparazzi* staked out her rented villa on the Via Appia Antica and waited.

Sure enough, shortly after filming began, George C. Scott, who played Abraham, became a regular caller. It had not taken long for the film and real life to converge, and the two of them became inseparable. Nothing quite like Scott had ever happened to Ava. He was a brilliant actor, a hell raiser, a robust and demanding lover. For a woman more accustomed to taking the initiative in such matters it was a new experience. She felt as though she had been hit by a bus. He read her poetry and drank her under the table. He talked about acting as if it were religion, and threw her into her own swimming pool fully clothed when she became too argumentative. Unlike Sinatra, he did not hire strong-arm bullies to fight the *paparazzi*. A former U.S. Marine, he fought his own battles, chasing photographers down Roman alleys and breaking their cameras. One day, he opened his trousers and relieved himself on them from his hotel balcony as they waited for him in the street below.

Ava should have realized that trouble lay ahead, of course, but when you're forty-two and a man of thirty-eight is sweeping you off your feet even the most efficient early-warning system is liable to fail. She remembered Puerto Vallarta and Elizabeth Taylor. Here at last was *her* Richard Burton.

Scott's wife, actress Colleen Dewhurst, who was appearing in a Broadway production of *Desire Under the Elms,* read the gossip items about her husband and Ava with rising anxiety. In fact, however, Ava's interest waned fast and the affair quickly became one-sided. Ava would complain to John Huston that Scott's appetite and intensity frightened her. On more than one occasion, she refused to come to work because she and Scott had quarreled and she was afraid there would be a confrontation on the set. Another time, it was Scott who refused to come to the studio in the morning because he did not want to work with Ava. She sought relief from the drama briefly by joining her friends the Sicres in Naples on their ninety-six-foot yacht *Rampager*, with their friend Adlai Stevenson. She arrived by helicopter with a mountain of luggage: Stevenson had expressly asked them not to invite her along fearing that the press would make something of it, but he took her arrival with good grace.

"Dinner was a splendid pasta with sausages and meat balls and glorious sauce—very piquante—cooked by Ava," Stevenson wrote in his diary for May 4, 1964. "Then [she] went to bed afraid to face it and anxious about our reaction. Strange, lovely, lush girl." The following day was spent sailing around the Aeolian Islands. Ava swam in Lipari harbor. Sailing conditions were ideal, but Ava remained as turbulent afloat as she had been ashore. Stevenson tried gamely to calm her down. Her long-standing admiration for him was evident. She cooked the party another magnificent pasta dinner—and once again went to bed refusing to eat it.

The yacht made its way southward to Sicily, docking at Messina. Stevenson and Ava took a cab along the coast road and up and up to Taormina, around horseshoe turns to the Greek Theater—"certainly as beautiful and spectacular setting as there is in the world," Stevenson wrote. At the San Domenico Hotel they settled down for a quiet drink. But as they were leaving Ava suddenly announced that she was flying to Naples at 7 A.M. the following day.

So she went back to Rome to face George C. Scott and an extraordinary scene of passionate rage. Ava said he had no proprietary rights and for good measure threw him a body punch which left him unharmed but fractured her collarbone. As a result, she had to wear a neck brace.

When her role in *The Bible* was in the can, she flew quickly to London and checked into the Savoy Hotel. Scott, who still had scenes to film, promptly followed her and also took a suite at the Savoy. Then, though it was late at night, he stormed into her suite while she was talking to her London agent, threw him out and seized her violently.

Ava fled, calling for help, and Scott was eventually bounced from the hotel by uniformed porters. Outside, police were waiting and arrested him. After a night in a police cell, he appeared at Bow Street Magistrate's Court, where he pleaded guilty to being "drunk and disorderly" and was fined ten shillings. Then he returned to Rome to finish the picture. He deluged her with telephone calls which she refused to take, and her rejection plunged him into such a deep depression that he had to be put into a Connecticut nursing home by Colleen Dewhurst.

Ava's affair with George C. Scott would have a brief aftershock in November 1971 in Tucson, Arizona. Ava agreed to make a fleeting cameo appearance as the nineteenth-century theatrical star Lillie Langtry in *The Life and Times of Judge Roy Bean*. This was the story of a hanging judge in the West, played by Paul Newman, who is obsessed with Lillie Langtry and names his town after her. Ava appeared briefly in the last scene as the star whose train makes an unscheduled stop in the town. By coincidence, Scott was also working in Tucson on location on a different picture. The director of *Judge Roy Bean*, aware of the antecedents of the situation, gave orders that Scott was to be kept at bay at all costs, but several secret meetings were arranged all the same. "George and I kept ducking under the guards," Ava told a friend. When the director found out, he was furious. The director was John Huston.

Ava's affair with George C. Scott during the making of *The Bible* was the last time her love life captured the headlines. Not coincidentally, the drama was played out against the background of her last movie role of any substance. Ava did not announce her retirement. Her public life merely went into a slow fade and the contemporary Ava emerged, an intensely private, handsome woman of middle age who walks her corgi (not Rags or Cara, both now dead, but Morgan) in the park and relishes obscurity.

Her looks and appearance echo with uncanny accuracy the severe makeup she devised for *Night of the Iguana*—the hair pulled back into a ponytail, the once glamorous features a mite jowly and well scrubbed. The clothes fit the part—sweaters, jeans and sneakers by day, conservative dresses by night. The famous eyes—large, green, deep wary pools—are less easy to disguise, and a passerby will sometimes do a double take and time freezes in an instant of recognition.

Her move to London in 1968 constituted a definite break with her movie past, though she probably didn't look upon it in such clear-cut terms herself. She had never liked movie-making. She liked the life the movies made possible, and her occasional insistence that she would make a better secretary than she did an actress was a tacit admission that there was no satisfactory alternative to Hollywood for her. Few secretaries are given a Facel Vega for Christmas. But, though she was on the whole a conscientious worker who had given some convincingly human performances as a vulnerable woman protecting herself behind a veneer of cynicism, she got no charge out of screen fame. "Sanity is more important than stardom any day," she once said to explain why she no longer made films.

One wishes that she had starred in more than her two dozen or so films, because there would have been more to remember her by. Yet it was as much her off-screen persona that made her seem the most accessible and appealing of the great Love Goddesses. Lana Turner, Rita Hayworth and Kim Novak always seemed to have a core of coolness beyond the reach of any man. Ava had the insecurity, familiar to everyone, that comes from having been through too many of life's red lights.

Turning her back on Hollywood—except for the occasional cameo role to raise quick cash, or to help a friend, or to keep her professional resources tuned—was not enough of a break with her past life; gradually, the idea formed that she should move to England. On her frequent London trips in the late 1960s, she was impressed by the calm orderliness of her surroundings. The contrasting hurly-burly of other European cities with their strikes and student unrest made them less appealing. Even Madrid, though more controlled in many respects than Paris or Rome, was losing its old allure.

"I can't tell you what a thrill I used to get coming back to this city," she once told a friend who came to greet her at Madrid Airport and drive her home. "Now I can't wait to leave again." Things that had once amused her began merely to annoy her—the telephone not working, not being able to get things except in season, the meat shortage. She bought steaks by the caseful in America and kept them in the freezer for rare treats. Young men still hovered around her, now not so young but still trying to squeeze into the illusion of youthful machismo.

In London, she was just "some old broad," she told the formidable Italian writer Oriana Fallaci. "They take three or four photographs when you arrive and then they forget you exist. I love London, the climate, the people."

"But there is no sun in London; it rains all the time," Fallaci pointed out.

"What does the sun mean to me?" Ava replied. "I never see the sun. I sleep during the daylight. The night is company. It clarifies the mind. When I was a child, I was terrified of the dark. I cried all the time. Not now. I love the rain in London. The thin, fine rain, it gives me tranquility."

Before leaving Madrid, in a burst of newfound thrift, she had a house sale and got rid of kitchen appliances and other items she did not intend to cart to England. But her elegantly furnished flat in a quiet Victorian square in Knightsbridge, fitted with barred windows as befits a woman living alone, contains many of the antiques she bought in Madrid for La Bruja.

The brass fourposter is there, sheathed in delicate white lace, and in it most midnights Ava lies reading and perhaps wishing that she had other company besides her corgi and a

highball glass. Not that there haven't been occasional partners over the years. For a while, the entertainer Bobby Short
was her steady companion. Later there was the black singer
Freddie Davis, aged thirty. The year was 1974 and Ava was
fifty-two. For Freddie's sake she even went on the wagon,
more or less, checking into a well-known English health
farm, Grayshott Hall, to dry out. "I'm not drinking anymore
because I'm in love with Freddie," she told friends. "There
was a time when I drank a lot, but I've drastically reduced the
whiskey now."

Ava is a woman whose passion is spent. What she seeks is
companionship, the occasional visitors from her Hollywood
days such as George Cukor, the Gregory Pecks, Lucille Ball,
or friends from Madrid, Betty Sicre, even Luis Miguel
Dominguin. Her London friends include Paul Mills, former
head of Metro's British operation. Her neighbor Charles
Gray, a forty-nine-year-old English actor who has never married, escorts her to opera performances at Covent Garden,
usually to the dress rehearsal so that she doesn't have to dress
up. Gray lives in the next building and has a balcony adjacent
to hers from which they confer almost daily when Ava is in
residence. Ava has friends at the Laundromat, and in her
gym class, just as she is on nodding terms with dog owners in
the park. But in London she has something she has yearned
for all her life, personal privacy. Her relationship with the
now widowed Bappie, after many vicissitudes, probably benefits from the fact that they live on opposite sides of the
Atlantic, and though Renée Johnson, like Bappie, also lives
in Los Angeles, she is the more frequent visitor.

Contact with Frank Sinatra was never broken, not even
during what Ava regarded as his ill-advised marriage to Mia
Farrow. The issue of alimony was never raised in the divorce
proceedings between Ava and Frank, but he has continued
to look after her in his own way. For years following the

breakup Ava spent part of the winter in Sinatra's house in Acapulco, and when visiting New York she still uses an apartment which he owns in Manhattan. In 1976, Ava went to Rome to appear in *Cassandra Crossing*. Fearing for her safety from terrorists and kidnappers, Frank telephoned a car rental firm in the Italian capital owned by a friend and arranged for the owner's son to act as her driver and bodyguard. "Tell your son to look after her, and he'd better treat her well," were his instructions.

In a reversal of this situation, Ava helped Mickey Rooney when he was out of work, and still keeps in touch. Occasionally, Artie Shaw's phone in Pasadena will ring, and Ava's familiar drawling voice will be at the other end.

She is fundamentally alone, but perhaps she has always wanted to be. Looking back on her life, she has always dismissed her movies out of hand. It was a living. As she reaches what she calls "the big six-oh" and looks at the casualty list among her contemporaries, she is perhaps proudest of one thing—survival.

"I haven't taken an overdose of sleeping pills and called my agent, I haven't been in jail, and I don't go running to a psychiatrist every two minutes," she has said. "That's something of an accomplishment these days." And, of course, it is.